British Baseball
and the West Ham Club

British Baseball and the West Ham Club

History of a 1930s Professional Team in East London

Josh Chetwynd *and*
Brian A. Belton

McFarland & Company, Inc., Publishers
Jefferson, North Carolina, and London

LIBRARY OF CONGRESS CATALOGUING-IN-PUBLICATION DATA

Chetwynd, Josh, 1971–
    British baseball and the West Ham club : history of a
1930s professional team in East London / Josh Chetwynd
and Brian A. Belton.
        p.   cm.
    Includes bibliographical references and index.

    ISBN-13: 978-0-7864-2594-5
    ISBN-10: 0-7864-2594-6
    (softcover : 50# alkaline paper) ∞

    1. West Ham Hammers (Baseball team)—History.
2. Baseball—England—London—History.
I. Belton, Brian.   II. Title.
GV875.W45C54   2007
796.357'094212—dc22   2006033530

British Library cataloguing data are available

On the cover: from left to right: 1936 White City supporters
badge; 1936 Catford Saints team; Roland Gladu in batting
position; National Baseball Association Challenge Cup

Manufactured in the United States of America

McFarland & Company, Inc., Publishers
 Box 611, Jefferson, North Carolina 28640
   www.mcfarlandpub.com

To Jennifer, your love and support sustain me;
to Miller, may you find passion
and enjoyment in all you do.

J.C.

To Rosy and Christian—
my Big Show, my Mendoza line, my Moonshot—
what I run home for.

B.B.

Acknowledgments

We would like to acknowledge and thank the following without whom this book could not have been the historical, social, and sporting record we have been able to offer: David Allen, Gary Bedingfield, Daniel Bloyce, Patrick Carroll, Jean Crook, Doug Dickson, Ellis Harvey, Louis Jacobson, Albert King, Michael Lewin, George Livsley, David Mankelow, William Morgan, Patrick Morley (SABRUK), Herb Rogoff, Mark Ross (SABRUK), Clive Russell (Major League Baseball), Wanda Rutledge, Robert Shearer, Ian Smyth, Christian Trudeau and Dow Wilson.

Contents

Preface

For a brief time in the late 1930s, baseball seemed to gain attention in the British sporting landscape. One of the teams at the center of that spotlight was the West Ham Baseball Club, the Hammers of baseball. In 1935 professional baseball in the British context emerged in Lancashire and the following year ambitious promoters brought the game to London. Baseball quickly bloomed and some respectable clubs emerged. But it was the West Ham team which was the most professional of all. They were run by an astute businessman and for the two seasons of pro baseball in London, they were the league's most consistent winner. In addition, the team boasted the best positional player in the country, Roland Gladu, and two members of the West Ham family—owner L.D. Wood and player Eric Whitehead—penned books on the rudiments of baseball, which had some lasting impact on the sport in Britain.

Like most of London's other professional baseball organizations of the era, the Hammers shared their stadium with greyhound racing. However, at Custom House, in the heart of East London, West Ham baseball also rubbed shoulders with the famous Hammers of Speedway[1] and West Ham Stadium, the baseball's home in the Docklands of London, was also, at one time, the headquarters of the Thames Football Club. The arena was the place where the cockney classic, the greyhound Cesarevitch,[2] provoked the famous "West Ham roar" and drew as many as 80,000 spectators to watch the mighty motorized encounters of the "knights of speed." This being the case, the "Diamond Hammers" can be said to have inhabited a truly sporting environment.

This said, the history of West Ham baseball had almost disappeared and has only been resurrected in these pages thanks to an extraordinary relationship between Josh Chetwynd and Brian A. Belton. Over many years and hundreds of hours, Chetwynd has reached back over seven decades and sought out the only rare bits of information about West Ham, exploring the complex web of secondary sources through newspaper archives and ancient literature published in connection with the

West Ham's game day program certainly tried to offer added value to the team's neophyte fans. Along with a schedule, team rosters and standings, the program provides an explanation of the rules and a history of the sport.

club. He has interviewed acknowledged experts on English baseball and individuals who were part of the time, many of whom participated in the development of London and British baseball. This committed effort, together with Chetwynd's own passion for the game as a distinguished national team player, has been the bedrock on which the pages that follow are built.

However, this book has also called on community memories and interactions collected over something close to half a century. Belton's family has lived in the East London area from where the Hammers have drawn their support and players from a time well before even the coming of Thames Ironworks, the shipbuilding company that gave birth to the West Ham United soccer club. It is hard for those who are not familiar with the era from the days when the 'Ammers were hitting for the East End to understand the nature of the area in which the West Ham baseball club developed. West Ham Stadium, the home of cockney baseball, was a central focus for sport and the sportsman of the Docklands and grew into one of the most important cultural influences in the East End of London and one of the largest businesses in the district. When the speedway or the dogs were racing, the great arena directly and indirectly employed hundreds, maybe thousands of people, most on a casual, part-time basis and even though baseball attracted far fewer spectators, dozens of these same people were needed to staff and run the stadium. One was Belton's paternal grandfather, Jim Belton, who worked on the turnstiles and was also involved in maintenance of the West Ham Stadium from time to time. Jim's wife, Eleanor, sold programs. Jim's full-time job, as a stoker in Beckton Gas Works, had been inherited from his father (William). The Hills family, who had founded Thames Ironworks (see Belton, 2003), had been among the founders of gas production and supply in London.

It is their reminiscences and the memories of other family, friends and members of the East London community that clustered around West Ham Stadium, as well as responses from contacts all over the world, that form the second pillar of this book.

Context is all

The West Ham Baseball Club was never to compete with more "traditional" sports in terms of audiences, but it did make its mark. Crowds of upwards of 10,000 attended baseball games at West Ham Stadium. The team was led by the likes of Roland Gladu, the "Babe Ruth of Canada," who would play in the American Major Leagues with the Boston Braves. The West Ham side even took on some of America's best—the United

States' 1936 Olympic team—and prevailed in the contest. Who knows? Had history been a little kinder, East London might have emerged as a hotbed of baseball.

However, it would be impossible to adequately understand the strides West Ham made without an awareness of the history of baseball in England. Although the game has an ancient lineage (many suggest that the game's direct ancestry comes from British games) the chronicle of actual baseball in Britain goes back close to 150 years and more than 60 years before the Hammers existed. This is an epic tale in itself, a story of historical campaigning by a courageous and committed few against huge sporting, economic, and social resistance set within a transatlantic struggle for status, wealth, and power. And baseball made it in the end. It created a gallant heritage via the energetic endeavor of a rising entrepreneurial class, swashbuckling "privateers" who foiled the covert efforts of the British establishment and the media it controlled to "protect its interests."

What did and did not happen to West Ham and English baseball make fascinating reading and a succulent invitation to the realm of what might have been. It is a saga of brave pioneers, embryonic success and the nobility of enterprise. But perhaps more symptomatic of the Docklands district where the baseball Hammers burned briefly but brightly, the parable of cockney baseball is one founded on audacious optimism, belligerent defiance and uncompromising hope. These are the stuff of our dreams of honorable athleticism—the diamonds we seek in sport.

Introduction

British baseball sounds like a contradiction in terms to most people. Throughout the sporting world, if and when the two words are used in immediate conjunction it is almost sure to provoke a response like, "But, the British play cricket!" Taking credibility to the brink of being supposed mad, one might tell the tale of the well-supported and able West Ham baseball team. The horizon of East London sport is so totally dominated by its fickle but well-loved soccer club West Ham United and its tough professional boxers that it would be hard for anyone knowing the area to associate it with the sophistication and colorful American persona of baseball. But there was such a baseball phenomenon housed in London's Docklands "north of the River, east of the Tower, within the sound of the great bell at Bow," and the sport has had and does have a British following, players, and spectators. Devoted British fans individually, as families, and more formalized groups make a regular pilgrimage to watch their teams in the United States and there is a vibrant community of dedicated baseball players who compete in Great Britain; they have added their own unique British ethos to the way the game is played.

In the U.S., baseball players bring a particular attitude to the game. It might manifest itself in quiet confidence or overt egotism, but most ballplayers in America have a steadfast belief that they should, without fail, be part of their team's starting line-up and the man on the mound in any critical moment during a game. However, British baseball players have a rather different manner.

Britain has just a couple of fields that would pass for high school-level diamonds in America. As such, the Great Britain National Team squad often practices together on ragged makeshift fields. Without the facilities or attention that other, more popular sports get in England, baseball is certainly a different beast in England than in the United States, the emphasis is consistently on team success rather than on individual performance.

Perhaps Britain's history of dedication to the Corinthian code of amateur sport, fidelity to the team, the "all-row-together" sportsmanship which inclines players to step aside for the good of the squad, contributes to this attitude. The strict amateur ethos reigned long in the United Kingdom. Right up to the mid–20th century British tennis still carried the baggage of its non-professional past and while early in the new millennium England became the World Champions of Rugby Union, the game did not become a fully professional sport until close to the end of the 20th century.

British baseball may not be in a position to compete with the likes of the U.S. and Japan as the numbers of baseball players in the UK amount to no more than a few thousand. However, the *esprit de corps* that exists within the sport in Britain marks it out in the world game and along with the tremendous enthusiasm of the British players and fans, baseball in the context of the United Kingdom has a tremendous potential.

For all this, most of Britain's population, even that relatively small fraternity involved with baseball, has little knowledge of its history in the British milieu. Few people have any idea about the leading British baseball players of even the past decade and no more than a handful will be able to talk with any conviction about players of the era in which West Ham was among the sides that dominated the game in Britain. Once more, this might be a cultural inheritance. The fascination that exists in the United States with being able to declaim historical baseball statistics going back to antiquity is not as prevalent in Britain. There was a time when Britons would recall details of soccer and cricket matches in much the same way, but while there continues to be a core of dedicated and loyal supporters of most sports, connection with the history of popular games and affiliation with the past is becoming somewhat passé, and associated with middle-aged fans and "anoraks"—a British term for numbers-obsessed "geeks."[3]

One explanation for the lack of awareness of British baseball history is that the sport has been subject to varying levels of interest. During low points the chronicle fragmentizes as the continuity of enthusiasm becomes disrupted. But there is more than a century of British baseball history that implicates royalty, Major League Baseball players, leaders of industry, adventurous entrepreneurs, Robespierres, Shakespeares, playboys and bums, and there were times wherein some top-class baseball was seen and played. One venue of this celebration of the migration of the sport was West Ham Stadium, in the Custom House area of the Docklands. For a little while the great American game was played in cockney heartlands with gusto and the intense feeling of joy and confidence engendered by the "sport of diamonds."

In many ways baseball's informality, improvisation, and sense of theater suited the East End mentality. West Ham was a place well used to embracing difference and the fruits of immigrant culture. From the time when the docks were built, the great influx of Irish labor brought an accent that added to the Essex twang of the locals. With the completion of the "Royals"[4] the East End became the first stopping place (and often the settling place) of Chinese, Jews, Russians, and the initial waves of Asian and black immigrants from the four corners of the greatest and farthest reaching imperial domain the world had ever seen. West Ham was by the 1930s a great anvil of music, language and general culture; the *entreport* to the very center of the world that the great capital of the empire was. This was made manifest in 1936 when the Sir Oswald Mosley's Fascist Black Shirts attempted to storm the East End to "reclaim" the area for the Aryan race. Thousands of Dockers and steel-booted gas workers along with men and women from the great swath of labor, a cavalcade of nationalities, creeds and native cockneys that was the life force of East London, marched west up the Commercial Road to face the racists, chanting the defiant mantra, "They Shall not Pass!" And they didn't!

As such, West Ham was almost the perfect place for baseball to find a home as the 20th century came into its prime. The seed sprouted but the coming of war and the continuing economic depression, together with sport in Britain still being a class battleground in the 1930s, was not an environment that could support the flowering of baseball, although it oh so nearly did. If the sport had consolidated its roots at that point it is likely that today Britain would be among the great baseball nations; the United Kingdom had so many advantages that the likes of Australia, Japan and Cuba did not possess, but who, in the 21st century, can compete with the baseball monolith of the United States on the international scene.

This book is then the story of what happened but also what almost happened. It tells the tale of British and world baseball from the perspective and focus of the performance of the West Ham Baseball Club, an entity that gave so much more than what could have been expected from the brief time it blazed in the firmament of sport. We, the authors, have stood in its brief glow with respect and fascination; we hope something of the same feeling will be yours as you turn the pages that follow. But let this be a home run that you hit for the Custom House boys, become, even just for the passage of this work, one of "Gladu's Gang"— the Hammers of baseball; this is a warm invitation. However, it is only fair to warn you, as they say down where the Thames rushes out of the oxbow of "Dog Island"[5] and gathers up the waters of the River Lea, carrying the echoes of Big Ben's voice atop its city-soiled but honest waves ... once a 'Ammer always a 'Ammer!

The Big Bang
of British Baseball

When curious patrons entered West Ham Stadium in 1936 to see baseball, they must have thought they were among the first Britons to watch the game on English soil. In fact, by the time baseball came to West Ham in its professional incarnation, the sport[6] had a long British history dating back more than six decades.

For fans purchasing programs for two pence at West Ham baseball matches, the explanation of baseball's British lineage was limited. As might be expected, the program tried to put distance between the sports of baseball and the rudimentary children's game rounders and show the latter to be a very early ancestor of baseball. West Ham organizers wrote that during the mid–19th century, as North American "sinews waxed, Rounders changed from a child's frolic into a keen competition, in which skill had to be met with skill." The result was baseball. Despite this effort to distinguish the sport there is little doubt that dating back to the Victorian era (which began in 1838 and continued up to 1901), the middle and upper class British psyche that dominated sport in the United Kingdom dismissed the "American game" of baseball as something born of a child-like mind and that did not offer the spiritual and intellectual challenge posed by more established sports like rugby and cricket.

However, beginning in the late 19th century, such attitudes did not come without American efforts to disabuse their British cousins of such beliefs. Americans have always been fond of sharing good ideas as well as the entrepreneurial spirit, and in 1874 the Boston Red Stockings—winners of America's professional championship the summer before—together with the Philadelphia Athletics, arrived in Britain with the intention of introducing baseball to the United Kingdom. Inquisitive spectators attended what were seen as almost exotic spectacles between 31 July and 25 August. The tour was devised by Boston owner Harry Wright, who was born in Sheffield, England, in 1835 but had gone on to

In 1936, the marketing push for West Ham and the rest of the teams in the London Major Baseball League included newspaper advertising. This ad appeared early in the 1936 season in a local West Ham newspaper, *The Express*. Used with permission of Archant.

become one of baseball's key developers and owners during the sport's formative years. The event encompassed London, Kensington, Crystal Palace, Richmond, Sheffield, Dublin, Liverpool, and Manchester. Regrettably, the arrangement of the matches was a bit bizarre. In Richmond, Manchester, and Sheffield the exhibitions involved the Americans playing some baseball, followed by a game of cricket against local sides. However, during the tour, the baseball men also met top county and representative teams from the English summer game, including the MCC, Surrey, and an All Ireland XI, with the Americans fielding 18 players against the usual 11 playing for the British teams. This turned the exhibitions into something of a circus. Newton Crane, a British baseball organizer and former U.S. consul in Manchester, England, wrote in 1891 that the tour failed to create interest because "the game of baseball was not understood, and in the short hour or two devoted to the exhibition matches but little idea of it could be acquired by the bewildered spectators."

For all this, the tour did spark some enthusiasm.[7] An eastern Canadian, James Ross, who was seen as the man responsible for taking the game into the west of his nation, becoming a rancher and later a member of the Canadian Senate, was said to have been a member of London's champion amateur team of 1877.

Albert Goodwill Spalding, one of baseball's great early visionaries,

Professional baseball organizers made their first effort to sell the game to the British in 1874 with a tour that featured the Boston Red Stockings and the Philadelphia Athletics. Future tours would spark some enthusiasm for the sport, but this first attempt was met with a relatively lukewarm reception.

was to bring longer-lasting attention to baseball in the British Isles. In his lifetime Spalding took almost every role in the world of baseball; he had been a player, manager, owner, organizer and sports equipment manufacturer. But perhaps one of his most ambitious enterprises was the organization of a world baseball tour. Starting in October 1888, Spalding, who played in the 1874 tour, financed two teams of baseball players to spread the word of baseball across the planet. One was a mixed squad of players mainly drafted from other National League clubs dubbed the "All Americans"; the other, the Chicago White Stockings, was the team he had managed and was now president of in America.

Spalding and his merry men visited the Sandwich Islands, Australia, New Zealand, Ceylon, Egypt, Italy, France and finally Great Britain; it was 15 years after the first attempt to recruit proselytes to baseball. Patrick Carroll, a British-based baseball writer, has undertaken considerable research on Spalding, and refers to the man as, "a Gilded Age archetype." Carroll describes Spalding's adventurous mission as "a typical mixture" of the man's "passionate missionary zeal for the game, go-getting business 'push,' and his often Machiavellian politicking." Spalding had been a prodigy of Englishman Harry Wright, the organizer of the first British tour and Spalding's former baseball boss. Spalding saw his tour as a way to enhance the game he loved, a venue, as author Peter Levine has written, "to spread American manliness and virtue by introducing baseball to the world in dramatic style," and, maybe most importantly from a practical standpoint, an opportunity to augment his ever-growing sports equipment empire. If he could create fervor for the game in new countries, nascent players would need bats, balls, catching equipment, uniforms, and bases. Spalding saw the opportunity to take advantage of a monopoly of his own making in these virgin markets. With this in mind, the athletes who accompanied him were some of America's greatest and included Adrian "Cap" Anson, who became a baseball Hall of Famer following a career that is considered by some to be the best among 19th century players. Still, it should be noted that there was some criticism about the standard of the All-American team. Although that squad did include two players—Monte Ward and Eddie Crane—from the first-place New York Giants, the *Sporting News* suggested that the quality of the All-Americans squad was low because Spalding was unwilling to offer the kind of money necessary to attract top talent. Spalding's reaction was that the paper was merely attacking him because he'd withdrawn advertisements from the publication.

Spalding's knack for bringing attention to the game he loved so much was clearly evident in London on 12 March 1889. That day, the Prince of Wales settled into his seat to take in a game of baseball at the Kennington Oval, one of England's most famous and prestigious cricket grounds. Along with about 8,000 others, the man who would become King Edward VII watched every move attentively, staying to the last out as the Chicago White Stockings beat the All Americans 7–4 in a rain-soaked and muddy match.

After the contest, the royal personage was asked about the game by a newspaper reporter. The future king of England asked for the journalist's notebook, and the reporter obliged. Prince Teddy scribbled a brief note, returned the pad to the dumbstruck reporter and marched off. The next day, the prince's words were reproduced as part of the report of the match: "The Prince of Wales has witnessed the game of Base Ball with great interest and though he considers it an excellent game he considers cricket as superior."

That statement, although it seems to reflect the British attitude toward baseball historically, says more about the latent fear of the power of what has been seen as an American game. The reception soccer has had in the United States over the years is not dissimilar in kind. There have been, and are vested interests on both sides of the Atlantic—commercial and political—that influence the growth and development of mass sport. These have created and nurtured a British attitude that baseball was "a game" devised by "colonials" and therefore "beneath" the category of a "serious sport." This same attitude continued well into the modern period in the 1959 *Encyclopedia of Sport* (published less than 25 years after the rise of professional baseball in England) which included a brief section on baseball, written by Norris McWhirter, a former international athlete of the 1950s, time-keeper for the breaking of the four-minute mile by Roger Bannister and at that time, the athletics correspondent for *The Observer*. McWhirter gave the clear impression that baseball was not a game played in Great Britain. He wrote, "Baseball is a totally North American derivative of the English game of cricket (first recorded in the U.S. in 1747) and the now little played English game of rounders." Despite being for the British audience, the book made no reference to two forays into professional baseball in 1890 and in the late 1930s or any of the major league tours of England that had occurred during the previous century. To McWhirter, baseball's British history did not appear to exist.[8]

Up to the 1970s this stance was matched by a sneering contempt of cricket and soccer in the United States, and largely dismissed both games as "effete," "effeminate," and "limey" pastimes, associated with sipping tea and yellow teeth. Although in the last part of the twentieth century soccer did start to achieve the relatively high level of acceptance that it has today in the USA, there is little doubt that sport in general has suffered because of these disparaging, mirror image responses, but because baseball was deprived of the British influence, that via the empire and industrial expansion spread sports like athletics and soccer throughout the world, its growth as an international sport was stunted.

However, baseball in Britain has had its highs: dramatic moments of success, a world championship, and professional baseball. But its lows have been wholly forgettable periods. World events at times of baseball's biggest growth spurts in Britain, together with periods limited vision, regional disputes, and sporadic funding have restricted the development of baseball in the United Kingdom. This said, it seems that British stoicism, resilience, and a "stiff upper lipped," "keep-your-pecker-up" type optimism has caused baseball to endure, and at times, thrive in Britain.

For all this seemingly underlying conflict and competition, Spalding's American tourists, who arrived in Britain in 1889, played 11 exhibition games across the nation. The big London crowd was not matched in Bristol, but 4,000 spectators turned out, despite, according to British baseball organizer Newton Crane, the weather being "exceedingly unpropitious." He reported, "Most of the games [were] being played in fog, rain, and snow, and on grounds which were wet and slippery."

But from the spectator point of view there was another problem;

rather than put on the best possible exhibition of the game, the American teams took the matches they played very seriously, making every effort to win. This seemed to negatively affect the crowd's enjoyment, as the Duke of Beaufort, who helped host the baseball party, noted:

> Of course, the jealousy between All America and Chicago, while it kept all the players up to mark and made them do their best to prevent their opponents from scoring, made the game dull to on-lookers, who did not understand it. If they could have played a few games not to be counted in their wins and losses against each other, in which the pitchers would give easy balls and enable the hitters really to make fine hits and give a chance to the field to make the splendid catches they are able to make, the game would have taken the fancy of the British public much more, as it would have thoroughly astonished them.

Author Peter Levine summed up the British reaction to the American tourists as "lukewarm."

As in 1874, the tour of 1889 was teetering toward the edge of failure, when a group of young collegians "from leading universities of America" literally came to the rescue. This band had followed up the Spalding spectacular by spending their 1889 summer vacation in Britain, and took it upon themselves to teach baseball and organize games throughout the country. Unlike the professionals before them, they created combined teams of American and British players. In terms of inculcating a sport there is no substitute for playing it, and many of the Britons who were able to take an active part in baseball became committed enthusiasts.

In October 1889, a group of aficionados formed the Baseball Association of Great Britain and Ireland, with assistance from Spalding and his associates, and planned to start a professional league, the National League of Professional Base Ball Clubs of Great Britain, the following season. According to the 1890 edition of *Spalding's Official Base Ball Guide*, the organizers of the league found, "the football [soccer] clubs..., whose efforts were confined to the winter months, were disposed to encourage the movement."[9]

Three of England's top soccer clubs, Aston Villa and Stoke from the Midlands[10] and Preston North End, a club situated in the northwest part of England, decided to start franchises in the new professional baseball circuit. A team from Derby was also involved, but according to Derby sports historian Peter Seddon's 1 August 2001 *Derby Evening Telegraph* article, the club was not directly affiliated with the local soccer club Derby County (although the two teams did share a ground for some time). But the league founders understood that the major obstacle to their success was that very few people in England had played, watched, or even understood baseball. With that in mind, the organizers advertised for six to eight young Americans to serve as instructors. They received close to 1,000 applicants for the jobs. When recruited, the coaches were given a round-trip ticket from New York to London and paid 3 to 4 guineas a week (the equivalent of between £200 and £270 at the time of writing). For the average player in the league, salaries were $10 to $15 per week, according to the May 1890 edition of *Outing, an Illustrated Monthly Recreational Magazine.* This was a sizable sum considering that in 1990 a dollar would buy you loaf of bread; a dime in 1890 might buy the same loaf of bread.

When the league began in May, the performance of the players was said to be "gratifying. The novices being experienced football players,[11] finely trained in hand, limb and eye."

However, this description comes from *Spalding's Official Base Ball Guide* of 1890, which was certainly not an unbiased publication considering Spalding's involvement in the league. That said, John Henry George Devey, known as "Jack," a British native who also played for Aston Villa's soccer team, beat out all foreign imports to win the batting title with an impressive .428 average. Devey had been born not too far from the Villa Park (home of Aston Villa) in Birmingham on 26 December 1866. He played for the English national soccer team twice (scoring once).

Attendance at the games in Britain's inaugural baseball season, according to the Spalding guide was, "satisfactory, and toward the close of the season, especially at Preston, were quite as large as the average Minor League cities in the United States."

However, the media, which was owned and controlled by the same aristocratic class that dominated the staple sports of the British interest, rugby, cricket and much of soccer, was not keen to accept baseball. There was a level of anxiety that the sport might encroach on cricket's dominance in the summer months and give increased prestige to the "new money" directors of soccer. Some reporters did not believe that there was genuine interest in the game, however it is probably the case that there was little encouragement for any newspaper employee to provide the sport with good press. For example, an article in *The Birmingham Daily Post* of 16 June 1890 argued,

> The baseball business is being "boomed" with a vigour of which is a little too obviously artificial for the average Englishman.... The phlegmatic Briton does not care to have a pastime which has considerable amount of the advertising element about it foisted upon him.

On the field, the biggest controversy surrounded the Derby team. The team was run by a leading industrialist, Sir Francis Ley, and had more foreign players (three) than any other club. Within the first month of the season, Derby had gained so many victories that they could not be caught and as such won the championship long before the season's conclusion. The other clubs protested and Ley agreed to only use his ace American pitcher against only Aston Villa, the league's second-best team. When Derby reneged on that promise, the other league potentates were furious and Derby, having been guilty of dishonor, was obliged to pull out of the league. Aston Villa was then named the league's champion, while Preston North End won the separate Baseball Association of Great Britain and Ireland Cup competition. Preston is still regarded as the first English champions of baseball; thus history has been cruel to Derby County.

Away from the field of play, the circuit also suffered financial difficulties. According to William J. Harr, a former American diplomat who managed the Aston Villa team, the tremendous costs, which included advertising, recruiting players, and maintaining an office in London meant, "the campaign as a whole could not be called successful, as the gate receipts never equalled expenses."

Harr estimated that the league lost at least $25,000 during the first season. While Spalding seems to have financed much of the endeavor, one of his representatives did not completely live up to the promised financial aid, which disgruntled the league's British organizers. A newspaper article indicated that a Spalding agent, who was in England to promote baseball, left the county with more than £300 that had been set aside for the players. Presumably because of the high cost and no immediate attendance boom, Spalding never fully invested in British baseball again and the circuit folded after its first season.

For all this, the league was not a complete failure. In Derby baseball proved that it could make money. The club earned approximately £150 from the gate money while expenses did not exceed £100. Moreover, as a result of the initial attention generated by the league, the sport made considerable progress as an amateur game during the subsequent 20 years. A number of the country's top soccer clubs followed the lead of the teams from the 1890 season and developed baseball teams that played during soccer's short summer off-season. Such soccer powerhouses as London's Arsenal, Tottenham Hotspur, and another Midland team, Nottingham Forest, also took up the game. Some baseball teams, which generally included a mixture of players from the host soccer club and other athletes, featured a number of top professional association soccer players. Steve Bloomer, for example, who represented England in soccer 23 times, claiming 28 goals for his country, played baseball for Derby. Bloomer was a real soccer superstar of his era. John Henry Kirwan (known in soccer as "Jack"[12]) who was with the Tottenham Hotspur soccer club when it won the FA Cup in 1901, also competed for the Spurs Baseball Club. He also represented Ireland on 17 occasions.

In London, baseball was also developing organically through a combination of good, old-fashioned grassroots efforts and the support of wealthy American ex-pats. In the early 1890s, a handful of baseball enthusiasts went to Battersea Park in southwest London, right on the southerly bank of the Thames, to play some baseball. According to a contemporary article by Richard Morton in *The Badminton Magazine*, the local law did not take kindly to this attempt:

> [T]hey were warned off the ground by a policeman who scented danger to life and limb. Argument availed to nothing, and six Americans who desired to play their national sport had to seek another location where rules and regulations were capable of being stretched by more tolerant officers of the law.

The players resorted to a deeper part of south London, setting up on Clapham Common, but this time the locals took to the game and it quickly became a spectacle in the vicinity. At first, according to Morton, "[t]he cheering, when there was any, was sarcastic and derisive; for the Clapham folk felt that they had progressed beyond rounders, and somewhat resented a fantastic display of the schoolboy recreation by able-bodied men." Eventually, the native Londoners attempted playing and by the close of the 1892 season it was not uncommon for a thousand people to come to watch games. The following year, the Clapham team formed itself as a proper squad, calling themselves the Thespian Club. They were an immediate hit on the field, winning British baseball's national championship in both 1893, when the club remained undefeated, and in 1894.

In 1894, the London Baseball Association was formed to oversee the sport's development in the capital. Five teams competed: the J's, Remingtons, Electrics, Postmen and Thespians. Slowly but surely British players were taking part. According to an article during this period by James Wilson in *The Strand* magazine:

> Of course the greatest supporters and players of the game in London are the resident Americans, but the number of English converts are increasing every day, and are now assisting to promote the game in every way in their power. When they compare it to cricket, it is not at all to the advantage of the latter.

During this period, the bulk of London's baseball playing ultimately moved to Crystal Palace, the borderland between south London and the leafy and relatively prosperous county of Surrey, the district where the great exhibition was held in 1851 (when a massive glass palace was built and from which the area got its name[13]). From 1895 to 1914, every Football Association Cup Final was held there, along with many international matches. According to Wilson the move to the site occurred because of "the splendid inducements offered by the Crystal Palace Company to make baseball one of the main attractions of that popular pleasure resort." Wilson called the Crystal Palace stadium at Sydenham "a great natural amphitheatre" that presented games two or three times a week during the season. There was a grandstand and a refreshment bar and a musical band that played during games.

Wilson suggested that baseball was a success in London during this period because, in large part:

> Footballers have taken to it, because they find it keeps them in condition during the summer. They get splendid exercise from it, and consequently play it a good deal. Base-stealing an English audience especially likes to see, and the catcher arouses a good deal of interest.

But a key to the sport's growth in London during this period had to have been the involvement of American business firms in the area. Dewars, the great whisky producers, sponsored a team as did the Remington Typewriter Company. In addition many of the city's successful music-hall artists in London were also American and supporters of the game. Most likely, the Thespians' moniker came from this connection. In fact, Wilson, in his article in *The Strand* magazine, claimed that one music-hall regular spent close to £2,000 in support of baseball, which was an awesome amount of money for the era. Another major sponsor of baseball in London was Fuller's Cakes. The company's story is indicative of how American entrepreneurs integrated into the London business environment but at the same time added to the cultural mix that London was (and still is). At the same time, the likes of Fuller, whose London team was the national runnerup to Derby in 1895, provided a template for later British baseball organizers—including 1930s British baseball magnate John Moores and West Ham baseball club owner L.D. Wood—to build transatlantic business and sporting bridges.

Cakes and ball

Fuller's Cakes can, as a business concern, be traced back to 1889 when a group of Americans exhibited in Britain. The party included William Bruce Fuller who showed his fudge, peppermint lumps and walnut cake. He got a good reaction and opened a store in Oxford Street, one of London's high class shopping areas, selling confectioneries and cakes. In 1893 Arthur Burdett joined the firm and soon became a director. By 1895 William Fuller had established a factory in Wardour Street, not far from the up-market precincts of London's West End, and had opened shops in the capital's other high quality shopping areas: Regent Street, Bayswater and the Strand. The colors red and white were adopted at this point and became synonymous with the company. To complement his burgeoning business, Fuller backed baseball with gusto. He was a vice president of the

London Baseball Association in the late 19th century and even opened a refreshment pavilion, serving all his confections, at the London Baseball Park, which was located in the mid–1890s where Balham and Streatham Hill met. At the same time, his company continued to flourish. In 1900 cake manufacture was moved a few miles west to Great Church Lane, Hammersmith. Fuller's started to make chocolates around this time. In 1921 Rowntree, the company with a Quaker background based in York (in the northeast of England), took a controlling interest. As part of the Rowntree empire Fuller's went from strength to strength and they took over Page & Shaw Ltd., a British subsidiary of a confectionery company based in Boston. In 1947 Fuller's established production in Dublin.

In the 1950s Fuller's boasted eighty-two stores, stocking cakes, Easter eggs and specially boxed chocolates. In 1955 they opened three big restaurants in London. In 1959 Fuller's took over the Manchester-based Clifton's Chocolates. In the same year the Forte Group acquired Fuller's and in 1964 transferred the chocolate and confectionery business to York and transferred Fuller's baking interests to the Kunzle factory in Birmingham, the great industrial city of the Midlands, resulting in Fuller-Kunzle Ltd. But at the end of 1968 this company was acquired by Lyons.

By the latter part of the 20th century, the original American firm of Fuller's had encompassed a range of British confectionery institutions whose names were synonymous with everything that the United Kingdom stood for. This merging goes some way towards demonstrating that baseball, if circumstances had have been more favorable, might have been part of a similar story. Certainly it is hard to see why the admixture of American and British commerce could not have been mirrored in sport. One problem might have been the American practicality of these companies. Prominent British baseball observer William C.J. Kelly told the *Los Angeles Times* on 23 May 1906 that baseball failed to fully blossom in the last decade of the 19th century because the U.S. businesses only looked at the sport as a way to get attention and did not focus on grassroots development. "[S]everal of the big companies like the Dewar whisky people, the Remington Typewriter Company, and others, played baseball as a mere advertisement, and the general public did not take any interest in the game," Kelly said.

However, it is clear that baseball has a heritage in Britain and from the end of the 19th century there has always been "something to build on." It is perhaps perplexing that the sport has never really achieved its potential in the United Kingdom. People, from the earliest of times, wanted to play and watch it; the criteria for a sport becoming a commercial and material success—and in the late 1930s in East London the two factors so nearly came together.

There was a groundswell of playing interest in the sport within the

East End of London at the start of the 20th century. Thames Ironworks, the organization that would give birth to West Ham United Football Club, had an active amateur team from the late 1800s into the beginning of the 20th century, and, in 1910, a West Ham team is credited with playing in the British national final, losing to west Londoners Brentford 20 to 8. According to *The County of Middlesex Independent* newspaper, the finals could have been closer but the team's top pitcher, "B. Burt," did not enter the game until the halfway point and, at that stage, Brentford had amassed too great a lead. Still, the Brentford paper complimented Burt and his catcher, G. Birch, describing them as "very good."

Was this team connected to the vaunted West Ham United football team? It's hard to say, although neither Burt nor Birch are listed as first team players for the cockney soccer side. In those days soccer squads were regimental size, fielding many sides in reserve and subsidiary competitions. There were certainly many amateur teams in the East London–West Essex area during this period. According to William Morgan, British baseball historian, editor, writer and publisher of British baseball periodicals, the information about baseball from that time is "scrappy" but he knew of an "Upton Park" (the area wherein West Ham United's home ground is situated) amateur team during this period. Morgan said that baseball was also played in the Leyton area of East London (a more rural neighbor of West Ham).

On the other side of London, on the city's western borders, Brentford Baseball Club had a working agreement with its local soccer team to use its field. *The County of Middlesex Independent* gives some suggestion that the 1910 West Ham team had at the most a more tenuous relationship with the soccer team of the same name than Brentford had with their local purveyors of the "beautiful game." On 8 June the paper said that the Brentford Baseball Club should be allowed to reschedule a game with West Ham to its home park. The paper said that the Brentford team was "justified in trying to arrange for the game to be played at Brentford in order to provide some entertainment for the ordinary following of football during the winter." If the West Ham baseball team was associated with West Ham United FC one would assume it could boast the same interest.

However, the 1910 West Ham team likely had at least a loose affiliation with West Ham United. In 1906, Nelson P. Cooke, a Vermont native who had spent some 15 years in England, attempted to pick up where A.G. Spalding had left off. That year, he was able to convince five of London's top soccer clubs, Woolwich Arsenal, Fulham, Clapton Orient, Leyton and Tottenham Hotspur, to take up baseball. According to one contemporary news report, West Ham also attended the inaugural organizational meeting—held at the Charterhouse Hotel in London—for the new league, called the British Baseball League. Despite being there, the club did not join at the time. Still, an article in the 20 May 1906 issue of the *Atlanta Constitution* listed West Ham as an organization that was "already playing regulation American baseball." In fact, the 3 September 1910 edition of *Lotinga's Weekly* directly tied the famed soccer club with the eponymous baseball organization. In speaking about the two finalists for the 1910 baseball cup, the publication wrote: "Those two well-known London football clubs, West Ham United and Brentford, were represented in the final tie which was played on the ground of the Clapton Orient F.C. at Homerton." While nothing else elaborates on the relationship, it certainly points to United having at least tacit involvement in baseball.

While the lineage of the 1910 West Ham team isn't totally clear, the squad and others in the area do indicate that there was some legacy of baseball in London's East End before World War I. With five top soccer clubs already aboard in 1906, Cooke pushed forward, putting up as much as $3,000 of his own money to help his nascent circuit grow, according to the 12 April 1908 edition of the *Atlanta Constitution*.

The initial reaction to the league was strong. So much so that the 1906, British Baseball Association championship attracted 4,000 fans to White Hart Lane soccer ground (the turf of West Ham United's north London rivals Tottenham Hotspur) to watch the home team, the Tottenham Hotspur Baseball Club, win the national championship. This suggests that there was also considerable spectator enthusiasm. There also appeared to be some enthusiasm from other great soccer clubs to take up the game. The *New York Times* reported on 9 September 1906 that a number of the most powerful clubs in northern England, including Manchester United, Newcastle, Liverpool, Aston Villa, Everton and Manchester City, along with three of Scotland's greatest soccer teams, Celtic, Glasgow Rangers and Queen's Park, were poised to hit the diamond in 1907. While it appears that did not materialize, baseball in London in 1907 continued to thrive. That year a baseball season ticket for Tottenham's baseball games cost 5 shillings (25p—about £15 or something close to $30 today).

In 1910, baseball still had insular beachheads throughout London, but the size of the fan bases truly varied. An example of how organizers worked in that era to build up baseball comes in the form of that season's national champions, Brentford. This team had, in 1910, created strong ties with the local soccer club. At that point the Brentford Football Club was (like West Ham United) in the English Southern League (very much the second tier of soccer in the English game) but was able to draw regular crowds of several thousands. In April, the Brentford Baseball Club, under the stewardship of its chairman, Mr. B.L. Pyper, brokered an agreement between the baseball club and the Brentford FC in which the baseball team would have the use of the soccer team's home field, Griffin Park, for the summer. During the early season, before the soccer season was over, the baseball club played following soccer matches. This was a valuable way to entice new fans. Regular Brentford ballplayers included H.B. Franks (pitcher and second base), McCollam (catcher), Tombleson (first base), Farrall (2nd base and pitcher), Holland (shortstop), Beans (third base), Turner (left field), Pyper (center field), and Ebbetts (right field).

Brentford's performance, which saw the club at the top of the British Baseball League standings by late June, did inspire some locals to take up the game. On 25 June, *The County of Middlesex Independent* newspaper, reported that "at least five of the spectators at Saturday's game were so enthusiastic that they approached some of the officials and expressed the desire to become members of the Club." Based on that interest, the club, looking to build grassroots support, "extend[ed] to all Brentford a cordial invitation to become personally acquainted with the players, the bat and the ball, every Thursday evening at the Club's ground, Griffin Park."

The local paper was smitten by the game. *The County of Middlesex Independent* wrote, "[e]vidences that the game of baseball is making rapid headway in Brentford." Later in the summer, the newspaper lauded baseball's greater virtues:

> It is a popular misconception that baseball is a difficult and dangerous game. Now I can frankly state that it is neither. It is, it is true, a game calling for quickness of foot. Just the kind of game that appeals to the true British sportsman, who was ever a man of pluck, endurance and action. And baseball is not glorified rounders; it is a scientific game for men. Don't think it is what one would call a "kid's game," because it isn't.

But the media support, a connection to the local soccer team and the team's success could drum up only so much support. *The County of Middlesex Independent* often complained about the size of crowd, which seemed to swell only to about 200 to 300 at best. The team did its best to lure fans by upping the ante for attending games. In June, the baseball club set up a charity game to support the Brentford Football Club's "summer wage fund" (finance used to pay the soccer team's players during the sport's close season). Supporting the local soccer team should have been enough to get out a big audience to the baseball game, but *The County of Middlesex Independent* worried that the baseball organizers would be embarrassed if they could "hand over only a very few shillings" from the event. There is no report in *The County of Middlesex Independent* that the charity game, which was scheduled for July, ever went off, suggesting that fan support never increased to the necessary level.

It is important to note that public support for baseball was burgeoning in other communities. Clapton Orient, which was affiliated with another successful soccer club, pulled better crowds than Brentford, and Tottenham, as discussed above, was also making a good go at baseball. The bottom line was interest was hit or miss depending on the community.

During the same era British books on sports were still heralding baseball's finer virtues. In 1907, *Cassell's Book of Sports and Pastimes* included nearly 20 pages on "The American Game of Base Ball." The article started by addressing the common British query: Isn't baseball just rounders?

> Cricket in its earliest phase, probably will be found to be a variety of the older game of Rounders; to this ancient English game of ball, too, does American Base Ball owe its origin. But the latter, which has become the national game of the United States of America, differs materially from the English game of "Rounders." True, both are played on a diamond shaped field and with a round bat and ball; but there is a great difference between the manly game of Base Ball, as played by the American professionals, and the English schoolboy game of Rounders.

While the material covered all the basics of baseball, it is interesting to note that although A.G. Spalding had not invested his financial wherewithal into growing baseball since the failed professional league in 1890, he still had a role to play in teaching the game to Brits.

Cassell's Book of Sports and Pastimes reprinted baseball rules by Spalding. The authors said: "We are enabled, owing to the courtesy of Messrs. A.G. Spalding and Brother, to reproduce below the greater part of the rules governing this game." Spalding actually directly profited from the effort to get baseball going again in the early 20th century. According to the 23 May 1906 issue of the *Los Angeles Times*, Cooke's British Baseball League bought at least $5,000 worth of equipment from Spalding's sporting goods company.

Despite the involvement of a number of high-profile soccer clubs during the era, the *Spalding's Official Base Ball Guide* provided a lukewarm assessment of the sport in England in its 1912 edition:

> Base Ball is played in England, but more by American players who reside in England and by English players who have played the game in the United States and returned home, than by the population in general. Yet it is evident that Base Ball is progressing in England even though the progress is slow.

Yet Spalding's assessment of British baseball might not have been a reflection of a waning interest by the British public. In fact, it might have resulted from the sport's growing popularity. Cooke's efforts may have been stymied by a political power play by the ruling elite as baseball in England—particularly in London—hit a brick wall after the 1908 season. One explanation for this came in article in 11 May 1911 edition of the

Boston Globe, which said that the London County Council banned baseball on its public commons, presumably sometime between the 1908 and 1911 campaigns. The *Globe* report said that the council was concerned that "[t]he American game is dangerous to the spectators." Still, the article pointed out that cricket, football, lacrosse and hockey were all allowed on the public commons. This effectively stopped the momentum of the sport in the country's biggest city. Despite efforts to overturn the ban in 1911, baseball's growth in that era never regained any momentum.

In the official history of British baseball, there are no national champions listed between 1912 and 1933. But during this period, in 1913 and 1914, Major League Baseball did try to spur international interest in the sport with its first world tour since Spalding's 1889 effort. If the Americans had hoped to woo the British public on their London stop, their actions did just the opposite. The London leg of the four-month tour presenting the New York Giants and the Chicago White Sox was booked for mid–February. The great sportswriter Grantland Rice presciently wrote in the 27 October 1913 issue of the *Chicago Record-Herald*: "Now we are far from being endowed with a gambling disposition, but any citizen who wishes to wager that the Giants will be able to edge in one-third (1–3) of their February London schedule will be accommodated up to our ultimate kopeck."

As Rice suggested, the weather held the tourists to a single game in London on 26 February 1914. This limited what the group, which included some of baseball's greatest players of the day including future Hall of Famers Tris Speaker, Sam Crawford, and Urban "Red" Faber and Olympic hero and baseball player Jim Thorpe, could exhibit.

Even worse, American hubris overshadowed any on-field action in the tour's London visit. Before the single contest, one of baseball's all-time greatest managers, the Giants' John McGraw, did little to ingratiate the sport to the British public. In an interview with the *Pall Mall Gazette*, McGraw said, "American soldiers are superior to the British because of the athletic discipline in the United States and because every American soldier has learned to play baseball and through that game has benefited his mind as well as his body."

The game itself, which was held at Chelsea Football Club's hallowed Stamford Bridge ground, was a success as the White Sox won 5–4 in an exciting 11-inning affair. After the game, King George V, who was in attendance, asked the U.S. ambassador to "tell Mr. McGraw and ... [White Sox owner Charles] Comiskey that I have enjoyed the game enormously." For all this, the words of McGraw probably resonated more than any goodwill the game produced. The *London Sketch* wrote following McGraw's outburst: "The impudence of the Yankee knows no limits; and their baseball visit has afforded another opportunity for the display of it."

In fact, some newspapers had called for a boycott of the game based on McGraw's statements.

Despite the major leaguers' efforts (or maybe, in part, because of McGraw's gaffes), it seems that the sport lost momentum in the United Kingdom during the second decade of the 20th century. Of course, the Great War, which had an impact on all sport and entertainment in Britain—even "king soccer" had to struggle to survive—was a major factor in the apparent demise of baseball.

Americans in London

As would later be the case during the Second World War, baseball was not deeply rooted enough to sustain interest during the wartime years of 1914–18. Although the influx of Americans into Britain during the Great War meant that there was a substantial number of fairly good quality baseball games played throughout the country unfortunately, these were, almost exclusively, contests between American and Canadian soldiers. In 1918, the Anglo-American League was organized in the London area, but it was "primarily for the entertainment and recreation of the American and Canadian Forces." According to the 20 May 1918 issue of the *Daily Mail*, there was hope that the league would "stimulate the taste for baseball in England." The league was composed of four Canadian teams and four American teams and a percentage of the receipts from the matches was devoted to the American, British and Canadian Red Cross, and Y.M.C.A. funds. The venues were certainly high profile for the circuit; regular hosts for games were Highbury, home of the Arsenal Football Club, and Stamford Bridge. This is the American equivalent of soccer being played at the New York Yankees' Yankee Stadium and the Boston Red Sox' Fenway Park. Other games were played in some county locations around the outskirts of London—Northolt (Middlesex), Epsom (Surrey), and Sunningdale (Berkshire).

Opening day at Highbury did attract 10,000 and other games pulled in high-profile spectators like Princess Patricia of Connaught, who took in a game in late May, but the sport was not without a controversy that probably dissuaded many potential British spectators from attending; soldier's rest day was Sunday and, the Anglo-American league played its games on that day. This was something that concerned England's more-religious brethren. At the time, Britain's most revered sports, soccer (the Football Association banned Sunday soccer) and cricket

refused to play on that day. For all this, baseball organizers were undeterred.

On 26 May 1918, the *Weekly Dispatch* pondered allowing the traditional day of rest to be a day of baseball:

> The war has changed our views on many things, and since it has so greatly
> increased the amount of work done on week-days it may even change alto-
> gether our idea of how we can best use the Sabbath so that on Monday we
> shall be more fitted to start another strenuous day.
>   The American soldier is waiting to know what the British public think[s]
> about it.

One religious figure, the Rev. F.B. Meyer, protested against Sunday
baseball as "a violation of the sanctity of the Sabbath," according to the
Weekly Dispatch. In addition, the bishop of Birmingham also expressed
concern about Sunday baseball. A more moderate response came from
the bishop of Winchester of the Church of England. He told the *Weekly
Dispatch* that he did not object to Sunday baseball but said the games
"should be on Sunday afternoon, so as not to disorganize or help to sec-
ularise the whole of Sunday." But even this statement would have caused
a rattle of tea cups in the dining rooms of "respectable" British society.

Other religious figures did not see any problem with the schedul-
ing. Indicating that this was more of an Anglican problem than a Catholic
issue, Father Bernard Vaughn, a Catholic priest, used the controversy to
highlight the divide between Catholicism and other religions. He wrote
during the controversy:

> The fact of the matter is that Catholics and Protestants disagree altogether
> about the meaning of Sunday.... For Catholics the Lord's Day is a day set
> apart for re-creation of the body as well as of the soul.
>   Pre-eminently it is for us a day of rest from servile work but it [is] not to
> be regarded as a Jewish or Puritanical Sabbath ... boys being boys and men
> being men, they might very easily do worse on a Sunday afternoon than play
> glorified rounders or baseball.

However, the chief rabbi, Joseph Herman Hertz, might be said to
have put the good father right as far as his assumptions about the Jewish Sabbath was concerned. Hertz made the point that the Jewish Sabbath is intended to be a day of spiritual refreshment and joy, and that
traditional Orthodoxy has never really called for the abolition of Sabbath sports. Further, opposition to athletics in the ancient world, with
its association to sadistic cruelty, did not apply to modern sport; athletic
endeavor could possibly be justified as a means toward physical fitness.
Physical fitness could be understood as an acceptable means to help Jews
undertake their religious duties more effectively, and as such be part of
the path to national redemption.

Reiterating the Church of England's more liberal position the Rev.

For more than a century baseball games in Great Britain have attracted kings and other great figures from Winston Churchill to playwright George Bernard Shaw. On 4 July 1918, King George V (above) and his family attended a baseball game between U.S. Army and Navy teams. As *The Illustrated London News* said about the event, "If Waterloo was won on the playing fields of Eton, it may be that it will be said hereafter, in the same symbolic sense, that the Great War was won on the baseball ground at Chelsea...."

A.J. Adderley, who was the rector of St. Paul's in central London's Covent Garden, saw Sunday baseball as not presenting a difficulty:

> To make the Lord's Day the one thoroughly uncomfortable, joyless day of the week seems to me to be a suicidal policy whereby to convince men that our Lord came to give us a more abundant life. To come to church because we Christians have effectually stopped all the other holes into which the human rabbits can run does not seem likely to be the slightest spiritual value to anybody.

Despite the disagreement over the league, Britain's most important figures did not turn their back on the sport. The biggest baseball event took place on 4 July 1918 at Stamford Bridge. The clash between the U.S. Navy and the U.S. Army attracted a crowd of 38,000 to the home of soccer's Chelsea Football Club including the king of England, George V, the British Prime Minister David Lloyd George and the future PM Winston Churchill, whose Anglo-American background possibly helped him explain some of the finer points of the game to the monarch. Following the contest, a representative of the king wrote to Wilson Cross, an oil executive and vice president of the Anglo-American League, who had written the sovereign to ask if he'd like to take in another game. The letter, dated 31 July 1918 on Buckingham Palace stationery, said: "The King is very keen about the game, but I am afraid at the present moment His Majesty's time is too fully occupied for him to attend a Baseball match. Perhaps later on, in the autumn, the pressure of work may be lighter."

The relatively huge attendance and a modest endorsement of the British king, who would see other games later in his life, is testimony to the continued potential of baseball in London—although the controversy of Sunday baseball might have dampened the British spirit for the game somewhat.

Another example of a "baseball presence" was the fact that in Chipping Norton, Oxfordshire, the sport had been played continuously since 1912. In 1909, Fred Lewis, who was instrumental in the development of the British Boy Scout movement, got hold of the 1908 baseball guide and over Easter read it. He then made a bat and a ball, a mask and even some gloves and became a baseball missionary in England, taking his homemade equipment to every scout camp he attended until the outbreak of World War I. What drove the commendable Fred to such lengths might be a matter for conjecture and it might have been something of a strange sight for any passerby to come across Lewis hacking away in the woods close to Chipping Norton like some intent Neolithic in his efforts to replicate baseball's tool of trade, but in his local area of Chipping Norton, he made the game a staple. Teams from Chipping Norton would often come down to London and had the temerity to beat squads of American and Canadian players.

The baseball in Chipping Norton that Fred Lewis had developed was at a high level for Great Britain. In fact, at least one player during the professional boom in the late 1930s traveled up from Chipping Norton to the Yorkshire League to play pro ball (a journey of something in excess of 170 miles—a real expedition in those days of limited road access). According to William Morgan, "Wages were very low at that time so for a player could to get his train ticket paid for to play a little baseball and still put a little money in his pocket was a good deal." Morgan has also related how the players in Chipping Norton definitely took a Spartan approach to the game. Most of them actually played in street clothes eschewing uniforms.

This is just one of a plethora of instances of the continuance of the game in Britain both before and after the First World War.

However, after World War I, baseball was unable to gain broad momentum. There are a number of different theories on why the game diminished in stature. Lewis suggested that it was a lack of ability and know-how on the part of organizers, not really having much of an idea of how to present the game. The scoutmaster wrote in 1950, when he was concerned that a similar approach was being taken post–World War II as was employed following the Great War:

> In London and Birmingham the Baseball backstop net is placed within a few feet of the catcher. Quite wrong, and will surely kill the game as it did in 1922, for you cannot fool all the people all the time. This stupid error results in the worse the catcher, the better he gets on.

According to a 1936 West Ham program, the failure of the sport to take root after World War I was "departures abroad and lack of funds."

According to the British sports historian Ronald Price, "The effect of World War I, the major loss of young life and the ensuing Depression set back the Victorian zeal for sports promotion, and many imported sports went into decline."

The sport was diminished by the war, but, as Price also argued, America's "Black Sox" gambling scandal. The Chicago White Sox were arguably the best team in baseball in 1919. After finishing the season in first place, the White Sox faced the Cincinnati Reds in the World Series. Heavily favored to defeat the Reds, the Sox lost in eight games. One year later, eight members of the team were accused of conspiring with gamblers to fix the Series. These eight players became known as the "Black Sox." For Price this "may have had an effect on the British sense of fair play and integrity."

But, again, all of this amounts to a somewhat simplistic explanation of baseball's British fortunes given the obvious grassroots interest and support. In 1918, soccer clubs had used the war to develop their sport's entrepreneurial base, doing much to dispose of the limitations on professionalism imposed by aristocratic administrators, despite the alliance between the latter, the church, and the press throughout the war years. This caused something of a retreat of the establishment into the summer game of cricket that as a consequence would be stymied for the best part of 90 years. This aside, baseball was not going to be allowed to take further ground from the establishment classes.

For all this, the struggle continued. It seems a West Ham baseball club was still in existence in the 1920s. According to John Johnson, his uncle, Percy Calligari, helped promote and run the East Londoners during the years surrounding 1923. Percy bequeathed John a ball that had been signed by the West Ham players during a period when the club had made a tradition of playing groups of Japanese seamen berthed in the Royal Docks. In the autumn of 1924, baseball supporters organized a series of exhibition games between the Chicago White Sox and the New York Giants in London, Liverpool, Birmingham, Dublin, and Paris, but the games did not command great attention or indeed much more than low priority. For instance, in Dublin an exhibition was scheduled for an afternoon start but was played instead at 11 A.M. so as to not conflict with an "important" cricket match. Only 20 people showed up for the Dublin game, according to an article in the 9 November 1924 edition of the *Washington Post.* The tour, which also included a North American leg, cost $20,000, and two games played in Quebec brought in more money to defray those expenses than the six games contested in Britain and France, the 30 November 1924 edition of the *New York Times* reported.

Overall, the media was indifferent toward the tour, although the games did receive one positive review. The British playwright George Bernard Shaw, who, though not a sports fan of any sort, was a notorious thorn in the side of the British ruling classes, remarked after a Giants-White Sox game in London: "To go back to cricket after baseball is like going back to Shakespeare played in five acts with fifteen-minute intervals after seeing it played through in the correct Shakespearean way."

Shaw was not the only British literary light to find baseball appealing during this period. Sir Arthur Conan Doyle, author of the Sherlock Holmes mysteries, was also a big fan. On 28 October the *New York Times* quoted Doyle's musings on the sport and its prospects in England:

> What is essential [about baseball] is that here is a splendid game which calls for fine eye, activity, and bodily and bodily fitness and judgment in the highest degree. This game needs no expensive levelling [sic] of the field as the outfit is in reach of any village club. It takes only two or three hours of playing, it is independent of wet wickets and the player is on his toes all the time and not sitting in the pavilion bench while another man makes his century. If it were taken up by our different association teams as a Summer pastime I believe it would sweep this country as it has done in America. At the same time it would not more interfere with cricket than lawn tennis does."

The above shows that the baseball organizers in 1936 did not do British baseball's rich history much justice. Before the sport hit West Ham Stadium, the game's history in Britain and London actually included some of America's best players, a brush with British royalty as well as at least one game that attracted close to 40,000 spectators.

Sir John Takes the Mound

In 1936, in terms of number and passion of spectators, four sports dominated East London's Docklands area of which West Ham was a part. At Upton Park, West Ham United, although recently relegated to Division Two[14] of the Football League, continued to attract tens of thousands of fiercely partisan and vociferous supporters. The West Ham area, although a London borough, still had connections to county Essex, the district having previously been governmentally and administratively part of the county. This being the case, if local people wanted to see a game that involved hitting, "bowling" and catching a ball, they would be likely to make their way to the Essex cricket matches that were staged throughout the summer at Ilford and Leyton, just a few miles from the docks. West Ham stadium in Custom House had been staging Speedway and greyhound racing since the late 1920s, being among the pioneer hosts of both sports. The silver sand track could attract close to 100,000 to its international events and the "cockney classic" Casarewitch[15] greyhound event was able to provoke the "West Ham roar" that it was rumored might be heard as far away as the City of London and Greenwich on the opposite bank of the Thames. Each of these sports had a lineage in the area. Like cricket, dog racing had been part of East End–West Essex culture for hundreds of years, while devotion to soccer and motorbike racing had a history going back to at least the turn of the 19th century. As such, it would have taken something of a gambler to attempt to bring a new and "foreign" sport to London's East End at that time.

John Moores was a man who had prospered from gambling and it is perhaps this sense of chance that prompted him to commit himself to promoting baseball in Britain. He was born on 25 January 1896 in Eccles, Greater Manchester, England. Having started out in business distributing coupons for the football pools in Liverpool, by 1923 he had founded the Littlewoods Football Pools Company.

Moores first became involved with baseball in the early 1930s. He was still building his empire and often made trips to the United States

John Moores was a successful businessman who also served as president of the National Baseball Association, which guided the growth of British baseball both in the professional and amateur ranks in the late 1930s. Although his motives for supporting baseball were never totally clear, Moores was certainly one of the most generous backers ever of the game in England.

for business purposes. Moores' transatlantic adventures had, in part, quite possibly been inspired by an association with L.D. Wood, a North American who had become involved in the import and sale of catering machines, in particular ice cream making and serving machines. Bill Roberts, who played professional soccer with West Ham United in the late 1930s, was familiar with Moores through the latter's involvement in soccer pools. Bill got to know about Moores' baseball interest when the idea of starting a West Ham United baseball team was considered and discarded.[17] Roberts was a decent batter but the idea of developing professional baseball at Upton Park did not take off as most of the players were committed to probably more lucrative summer employment. According to Roberts, Wood[18] introduced Moores to the game taking him to see saw such great baseball teams as the New York Yankees, New York Giants, and Chicago White Sox play. Still, a 23 August 1936 article in the *New York Times* suggested that Moores found his affinity for baseball on the New York leg of an around-the-world cruise. After traveling to numerous exotic locals, he spied baseball, which might have been one of the most exotic endeavors of all for him, and fell in love with the game. In any event, during his travels to the U.S. he met both John A. Heydler, president of Major League Baseball's National League, and the great Babe Ruth. Moores was smitten by baseball and after a challenge by Heydler to form a British National Baseball Association, Moores responded with an aggressive business style that would mark his impressive career.

In the 1930s, as Moores' biographer Barbara Clegg points out,

"Baseball was already played in England, but with a revised code; the American game was much faster than the English one."

This British version of the game is known today as Welsh Baseball, but was then called English Baseball.[19] It was popular in the Liverpool area and Moores, who according to one publication had actually served as the president of the English Baseball Association, thought that the organizations involved in this game would be a good basis to start American baseball in Britain.

Although two North American Major League teams (Chicago White Sox and New York Giants) had played an exhibition game at Goodison Park (home of the mighty Everton soccer club in Liverpool) in the twenties, American style baseball did not return to the attention of the British public until late June 1933. On 11 July 1933, a meeting took place at the Law Associations rooms, Cook Street, Liverpool, that would send baseball down a path to bigger things in Britain. It was chaired by John Moores and brought together the most influential members of the Liverpool baseball community. Moores was looking for the cooperation of the English leagues and offered £100 in assistance for any team that would take on American rules. He warned that even if teams chose not to take up the American game, he would form a league based on North American rules with or without their cooperation. In reality, he was giving baseball in the district an ultimatum (an offer they couldn't refuse). Backing Moores would mean that regardless of what these teams did, baseball was going to be played the American way. Seven teams from the English Baseball Union came forward to accept his offer. From that day, Moores, who had brought two Canadians to Liverpool to teach baseball and recruit players and officials from the United States and Canada, began building the sport in the British context. On Monday, 21 August 1933, the first recorded American rules baseball match played between English teams took place at Priory Road, Liverpool, between the Liverpool Amateurs and Oakfield Social. Two days later, an exhibition game was played with trained American rules players at the Littlewoods Sports Ground, Picton Road.

According to Morgan, within a few months Moores oversaw the inauguration of 18 amateur baseball teams in two leagues in Liverpool. Heydler was so impressed that he donated the league trophy.

Baseball, which at this point was still an amateur sport in the UK, grew rapidly in the Merseyside area. By the end of the 1934 season 664 games had been played by various teams.

To fuel his baseball aspirations, Moores, who had ties to more traditional British pastimes (he would eventually be the owner of the Everton Football Club for more than two decades), was quick to recruit British athletes from other sports. Most notably, William Ralph Dean, better known as "Dixie," the great Everton goal scorer, became a baseball player of some skill in the amateur ranks of the game. Dean would represent England internationally in soccer 16 times before the Second World War. He was one of Britain's greatest sportsmen of the first third of the 20th century, and as a player surely provided fantastic pulling power to the infant British baseball scene. Dean's 60 goals in the 1927–28 season have often been likened to Babe Ruth's 60 home run season in 1927. Moores' approach to building the foundations of baseball was multi-pronged. Along with recruiting soccer stars, he also enlisted the military. In the summer of 1936, despite some concern from people both inside and outside the armed forces, Moores convinced Air Vice Marshal John Babington that all the Royal Air Force (RAF) schools, camps and airdromes needed to adopt baseball as a compulsory summer game. This included Halton, the RAF's School of Recruit Training.

Moores' success with the amateur game was just a prelude. The seeds of professional baseball in West Ham really began to take root in 1935, when Moores decided to make British baseball professional by starting the North of England Baseball League, based around the Manchester area. Some suggested that like A.G. Spalding a generation before Moores made the decision to embark on a professional league purely for financial gain. After all, his Littlewoods Pools was a successful form of soccer gambling and Moores could have used the sport as a strong summer complement for his business.

This was almost certainly part of Moores' motivation; he was, first and foremost, a businessman. The following article ("Past Times," by Jim Appleby) appeared in the *Bradford Telegraph and Argus* on 17 June 1998 and seems to confirm Moores' incentive for bringing baseball to Britain was not wholly in the traditions of the Corinthian spirit:

> There might have been a shortage of work and money around in the 1930s, but there was no shortage of diversion if you were a sporting type. In summer there was cricket, and what cricket it was if you were a Yorkshire fan.
>
> In that decade, Yorkshire fielded what must have been some of the strongest county sides ever to walk on a field: Herbert Sutcliffe, Percy Holmes, Len Hutton, Bill Bowes, Hedley Verity, Maurice Leyland, Arthur Wood, Frank Smailes, "Ticker" Mitchell and the like would have given most Test sides a hard time. In fact they often did but, for form's sake, Yorkshire were usually called England when they took the field against touring sides.
>
> Just to be friendly, they allowed one or two outsiders like Wally Hammond and Harold Larwood to play, if they were good enough.
>
> But for a gambling man, cricket wasn't as good a game as football. Football, you see, had the Pools, with a promise of a fortune, a release for ever from financial misery.
>
> That's why, during the 1930s, baseball became a popular and well-attended sport in Bradford and indeed throughout the north of England.
>
> Unlike cricket, baseball could be played in the course of one evening. That way it faced no competition from cricket. And that way, there could be

a pools system organized around the game, to the delight of Sir John Moores, of Littlewoods, who was a great champion of the American game.

The Moores baseball empire soon spread via the rugby league network, with the chance of summer income through the turnstiles being welcomed across the north.

However, it seems that baseball bred the entrepreneurial ethos:

It wasn't only Moores who made a few bob[20] out of baseball. Jack Carrodus, of Birkenshaw, remembers the Greenfield Giants, who played at Greenfield Stadium at Dudley Hill, home of dog racing. He also remembers one night when they played at the Bradford Rovers ground at Lower Lane, off Wakefield Road, against a team which included the famous American singing duo the Mills Brothers.

They were appearing at the Alhambra while touring England and promoting a new-fangled drink called Coca-Cola (at least it was quite new to England), and the young Jack Carrodus turned salesman and found himself one of Britain's earliest Coke dealers. He got a halfpenny per dozen bottles sold—not a fortune, but not bad for the mid–1930s

For all this, there is some evidence Moore's affinity with baseball went beyond the profit motive.

The Moores technique—as well as the Mills Brothers' visit—are remembered by former Bradford player Harry Raynor, of Scholes. He and his pal Kenny Dennison were early recruits via Sedbergh Boys Club in Bradford. Being too old for one football side and a bit too young for another, the lads found themselves at Odsal being recruited into the City Sox.

Moores provided the kit and also two members of the team—the pitcher and the catcher, baseball's equivalent of the bowler and wicketkeeper, for each side were recruited among Canadian college players. For the rest of the team, enthusiasm and the ability to hit a ball with a bat were enough.

Young Harry Raynor was soon a star—and soon in the thick of it. One night, in a match at Hull Kingston Rovers' ground, he managed to spot the signals that the catcher was sending to the pitcher. Meanwhile the catcher spotted Harry watching. "He stood up and pushed me and knocked me over. So I smacked him back and knocked him over."

The police had to escort the visiting batter off the pitch amid a hail of tin cans and other missiles. And it didn't stop there.

"I was only 17 so I didn't go in the pub with the other lads. I waited on the bus until somebody threw a brick through the window—so I ended up in the pub after all."

This sort of sport stood Harry in good stead when he came face to face with Erwin Rommell after being captured while serving with the Royal Artillery in Tunisia during the war.

But baseball had another triumph in store for him.

Northern Lights

From the start of Moore's professional push, some, who were generally bullish on baseball, were pessimistic about going pro. "This is a daring move," wrote the *Liverpool Echo,* on the eve of the pro circuit's debut. "I know that sound judges would have liked such a development to have been deferred until [British baseball was at] a more mature moment. The time was not quite ripe."

Undeterred, Moores pushed on with the new venture. According to Barbara Clegg, Moores

> was convinced that baseball would go down well in England and decided to bring some baseball players over. The two he selected were Canadians, Alan and Jack Ritchie; they were employed at Crosby in the mail-order business, but their real job was to teach the game at Littlewoods Sports Ground at Wavertree, where the amenities now included not only tennis-courts and a bowling-green but a nine-hole golf-course as well.

Moores' strategy for his North of England League was not too different from the approach A.G. Spalding took some 30 years prior in his efforts to create professional baseball in England. He formed teams that combined Americans and Canadians with solid baseball credentials and respected athletes from other sports like soccer and rugby such as Jim Sullivan, who is regarded as one of the greatest Rugby League players of alltime.

The non-North American players were men with little baseball experience, but they certainly attacked the sport with gusto. One example was Benny Nieuwenhuys, a soccer player for one of Britain's most storied teams, the Liverpool Football Club. Early in the 1935 season, the 23-year-old Boksburg, South Africa, native was lauded following his part in a Hurst Hawks' victory for "his headlong dives for the bags were very effective if not spectacular." Also playing for Hyde was Henry Travis, a Stalybridge Celtic goalkeeper. In a game against Hurst, reported in *The* (Ashton-under-Lyne) *Reporter* on 20 July 1935, Travis made "two brilliant catches" in center field.

Other soccer men on the Hurst Hawks included Lance Carr and Ted Savage, who also played for Liverpool FC. Elsewhere there were many other able association footballers taking to baseball; for example, Alf Stewart, a goalkeeper for Altrincham, played for the Hyde Grasshoppers. Guy Wilson, a Rugby Union international, also played for this team.

Attracting players from more established sports would prove to be a mixed blessing. On the one hand, the addition of soccer players was very wise in terms of drawing crowds. According to *The* (Ashton-under-Lyne) *Reporter* on 15 June: "Autograph hunters are having a grand time at Hurst Cross [home of the Hurst Hawks].... Celebrated footballers are being pestered each week by youngsters."

Yet, it was clear that baseball was of secondary importance for the men from soccer, who made their true living and gained their greatest notoriety from their effort on the fields devoted to Britain's "heroes of winter." This was clear from opening day when Liverpool FC players Nieuwenhuys and Carr missed the first game of the season because of their commitment to soccer. It is uncertain whether Savage was at the baseball game, but it seems definite that for these athletes, baseball was primarily just a way to make a little off-season money.

As for the Americans and Canadians that teamed with the British athletes in 1935, their credentials were solid. Typical of the foreigners was Stanley Trickett, a player for the Belle Vue Tigers who was described by the British press as previously being the captain of the baseball team at the University of Kentucky. Another player in 1935 was Billy Riches, a 27-year-old born pitcher from Alabama who played for the Oldham Greyhounds in England.

As for the league's geography, the teams were mainly located in the Manchester area, not too far from each other. No club probably had to make more than a two-hour journey for a game and all except one was within the northwestern English county of Lancashire. The teams were the Oldham Greyhounds, Bradford Northern (that was situated in Lancashire's neighboring and great rival county of Yorkshire), Rochdale Greys, Salford Reds, Manchester Blue Sox–North End, Belle Vue Tigers, Hurst Hawks, and Hyde Grasshoppers.

When the league opened on 11 May 1935, the media appeared optimistic about baseball's prospects. The reaction proved a sharp contrast to the newspaper's seemingly anti-baseball position when Spalding started his league in 1890. Maybe the fact that a true Brit in John Moores was fronting the circuit led to greater acceptance, or (perhaps more likely) that the owners of the Lancastrian news industry felt it to be in their interest to align with one of the area's most prominent and influential entrepreneurs. In any event, *The* (Ashton-under-Lyne) *Reporter* wrote on opening day: "The public interest has certainly been fired and there is every reason to believe the game will 'catch on.'"

Amazingly, *The* (Ashton-under-Lyne) *Reporter* was even critical of the playing conditions when the cause for one field's sub-par stature was due to it being used for soccer, saying on 18 May 1935: "It would seem that football grounds do not readily lend themselves to playing of baseball. They are too small, whilst the ground surface, torn up by football boots, is too bumpy; the ball often bouncing head high on Saturday."

Despite the early support, fans did not universally flock to games immediately. On 25 May 1935 *The Reporter* told how "attendance was below expectations" at a game in which Hurst beat Hyde 26–10. But on 22 June the same journal recorded that "there was much improved attendance at Hurst Cross on Whit-Friday" when Hurst beat Salford 23–19.

Nevertheless, attendance was quickly building elsewhere. On 29 June, *The Reporter* let the world know that 3,200 showed up at Salford to see the Reds beat the Hawks 26–8. On 6 July that estimable Ashton mouthpiece reported that more than 5,000 spectators watched Bradford beat Hurst 26–5 at Bradford, and that on 13 July 2,000 made it to Belle Vue to see the hosts beat Hyde 9–6. Two weeks later, *The Reporter* informed that 1,100 went to Manchester's venue Blackley to watch the Blue Sox beat Hurst 14–10 and on 10 August, *The Reporter* celebrated the fact that 3,000 saw Salford—whose home field was situated at "Weaste"[21]—beat Hurst 26–7.

As for the comparatively below-average attendance issue for the Hyde and the Hurst clubs, it could be partially due to the timing of games, according to the 29 June issue of *The Reporter*:

> Would baseball prove a bigger draw at Ashton and Hyde if played in the evenings? The local clubs are the black spots of the league as for attendances are concerned and the experiment which meets with great success at Salford and Bradford [night games] would be well worth trying.

The ownership in Hurst must have read that opinion because the team moved its games to the evenings, according to the 6 July issue of *The Reporter*. With the change there was some improvement in attendance. According to *The Reporter* of 13 July, a 20–10 victory by Rochdale against Hurst at Hurst Cross had attracted 500 spectators, which "was a slight improvement on recent gates."

Even with robust attendance numbers, it was clear that a mass comprehension of the rules of baseball would not happen overnight. In the 1935 season, there was huge controversy relating to what some officials thought was excessive base stealing, which was leading to bloated scoring (a team scoring 20 runs in a game was not uncommon). The promoters considered banning stealing altogether, but the Americans and Canadians protested vigorously. The reason for the stolen bases was not a flaw in the rules, said one experienced player, but the result of English pitchers not being able to effectively hold the runners on. The English pitchers were throwing out of the windup, a no-no with runners on base, instead of the stretch.

Hiccups aside, the season provided a compelling race for the first professional championship since 1890. Three teams—Oldham, Bradford and Rochdale—were in the hunt for the championship until the final days of the season. It should be noted that the British sporting nature of Moores and his fellow organizers could not be completely eradicated by the American rules of baseball. Most notably, ties were allowed in the North of England League. But it may not have been totally about form or sporting manners. The toleration of ties is an interesting fact given the reliance of Pools gambling on tied games (the prediction of draws).

In the end, Oldham emerged as North of England champions.

Final 1935 North of England League Standings

As of 24 August 1935	w	l	d
Oldham Greyhounds	12	1	1
Bradford Northern	10	2	2
Rochdale Greys	8	4	2
Salford Reds	6	6	2
Manchester			
Blue Sox–North End	5	7	2
Belle Vue Tigers	5	8	1
Hurst Hawks	3	11	0
Hyde Grasshoppers	2	12	0

While Greyhounds fans surely rejoiced, Moores probably took pause at how the postseason emerged. In British sports, cup competitions are the norm. Besides playing in league play, teams will compete against the best in other leagues regardless of each circuit's perceived standard. For example, the Football Association Cup, which is the top prize in British soccer, allows teams, including those from the lowest minor league level all the way to soccer's "major leagues"—the Premiership—to compete. The same was true with British baseball in 1935 and, despite Oldham's victory in British baseball's only professional league at the time, Rochdale actually was the one North of England team to make it to the National Baseball Association Challenge Cup, which was considered the national championship. The result surely must have disappointed Moores; the professional team in his league fell to New Briton, a London amateur team comprising Mormon missionaries. That outcome probably played a role in inspiring Moores' decision to quickly expand his professional baseball ventures.

Moreover, the league's financial success likely whetted Moores' appetite for more pro ball. After the 1935 campaign, one newspaper observed that, "clubs produced remarkably large profits and gates were surprisingly big." Moores was elated by the first season's performance. In an interview with *The* (Ashton-under-Lyne) *Reporter* on 10 August, the Pools magnet boasted that the National Baseball Association had "already gone ahead of the five-year plan originally set out." The paper concluded that "[h]aving considerable experience of the American game, Mr. Moores is responsible for the establishment of American Baseball in this country. He is more than satisfied with the progress made."

As a result, Moores announced that he would not only continue to support the North of England Baseball League, but he was also forming two new professional leagues—the Yorkshire League[22] and the London Major Baseball League.

In making that decision, Moores charged L.D. Wood to serve as National Baseball Association vice president and spearhead the league in London. Wood, who at that time owned a works in Wembley and was a big baseball fan running three amateur teams through his business, would also place his own franchise, the West Ham Baseball Club, into the league.

Moores' Motives

Over the next few years, Moores' passion for baseball appeared to grow. But overall, Moores seemed to have a complicated relationship with the sport. It was a mixture of profit motive, philanthropic urge and a sort of super-fan status.

As a proud resident of Liverpool, Moores hated to see his local teams fall to "outsiders," especially those from his county's most ardent adversary, Yorkshire. This rivalry dated back to the Wars of the Roses (1455–87) which were symbolically re-fought each time soccer clubs like Liverpool (of Lancashire) and Leeds United (of Yorkshire) met. It was also apparent in the blood, sweat, and tears cricket matches between Yorkshire and Lancashire. The aftermath of such contests could leave county towns looking like battle fields after rival supporters vented tribal frustrations that the four days of "leather of willow" competition (together with furious boozing) was liable to generate. Bradford, a Yorkshire town which is located about fifty miles east of Liverpool, was at the top of the baseball standings in 1937 and 1938, and could attract about 2,000 to games. In contrast, Liverpool, which was not performing as well, drew far less attention.

Moores must have squirmed at the fact his local side was relatively failing in both attendance and on the field. As a result, during one game, he took executive action: He removed the pitcher and the catcher from Bradford before a game against Liverpool in the hope that his home team could beat Bradford. Alas, for the usually successful Moores, the ploy failed as Bradford still beat Liverpool 1–0.

Clearly, Moores did have a passion for the game, albeit one that had both sporting and financial aspects. Moores' financial investment into baseball was sizeable. According to British baseball historian William Morgan, he laid out £15,000 in 1938 alone (in terms of purchasing this would be close to half a million pounds today). But he also wanted other business entrepreneurs to contribute to the development of baseball. Always a savvy man, Moores was not willing to go it completely alone. According to Morgan, Moores considered launching a professional league in Birmingham during his foray into professional baseball elsewhere. The problem: he couldn't find anybody who was willing to put his own money up. "Too many people wanted to take a free ride," says Morgan. As a result pro baseball never came to Birmingham.

Not surprisingly Moores, who had invested so much money into the game, wanted those who took up playing baseball to take it as seriously as he did. The entrepreneur expressed as much when he wrote the forward to West Ham player Eric Whitehead's book *Baseball for British Youth*:

> To its readers I would tender one word of serious advice. Baseball demands complete development of mind and muscle, and only one thing can produce this, and that is PRACTICE—unless you are prepared to do this, your time will have been wasted in reading this book.

Still, Moores' seeming corporate takeover approach to baseball did not sit well with everyone. There were some detractors. As the sport began to gain a foothold in England in the late 1930s, members of the elite classes began to question the game. Exhibiting similar sentiments to those shown by the politically influential in London during the early 20th century, when baseball was banned from the city's public commons, and religious figures who had criticized baseball in 1918, the socially prominent Bishop of Liverpool railed against baseball in 1937. The Right Rev. Albert A. David professed his dislike for baseball that summer, according to the 1 August edition of the *New York Times*. "He dislikes the 'backchat and calls' between players and spectators," the paper said. David, a key figure in the Anglican Church, claimed that baseball was "unsuited to the English temperament" and, in a seemingly direct reference to John Moores, added that it suited itself to gambling more easily than cricket.

In his diocesan review, David concluded:

> In professional baseball the crowds play a vocal to an extent unknown in any of our English games. The backchat and calls of both players and spectators at a baseball match in America are something to be remembered when the play is forgotten.
>
> So far English spectators of baseball have only learned the elementary calls of the game. If they ever learn the full phraseology of American baseball we do not think it will be long before its undesirable effects are seen at association football [soccer] matches.

Even in baseball circles there were some questions. British baseball pioneer Fred Lewis, who was also an influential figure within Britain's largest youth movement, the Boy Scouts, argued that there was a downside to Moores' efforts to quickly jump-start baseball in the 1930s. For Lewis, the National Baseball Association and its foray into professional baseball had not necessarily been the best thing for the game. Questioning the NBA's efforts Lewis commented, "The formation of the N.B.A. gave some help, but on the whole it did more harm than good; free uniforms and poor equipment, easy come—easy go. When a player has to pay for his kit he takes pretty good care of it."

That, of course, was a response that might be expected from a man like Lewis whose whole British baseball experience had been self-made, but Moores was certainly intent on baseball succeeding—even beyond the British shores. In 1938, he demonstrated his commitment to the game by donating a trophy bearing his name to the international baseball community. According to the 1939 *Spalding Base Ball Guide*:

> Gratified with the interest shown in England and the friendships formed by the visit of the U.S.A. Congress base ball team of amateur players to England last season, Mr. John Moores of Freshfield, Lancashire, England has donated for international amateur competition in base ball a trophy to be known as the "John Moores Trophy," to be open to teams of all nations holding representation in the International Amateur Baseball Federation.

Moores, who had welcomed the U.S. to Britain to play in a series of baseball games against an England representative squad in 1938 (that would later be deemed the first World Championship) reflected on the experience and how it further enhanced his love of the game when he wrote to the International Amateur Baseball Federation (I.B.F.) to announce he was financing the trophy. He wrote:

> During the past few days, myself and fellow officers of the National Baseball Association have had ample opportunity to observe the incalculable amount of benefit which baseball receives as a result of amateur international contests. The public interests aroused, friendships which have been formed, opportunity for exchange of ideas for the betterment of the game, are but a few of the things which make me feel that there is a great future for amateur base ball when played on an international scale. I sincerely hope that all nations who are members of the I.B.F. will enter this competition and so help to foster amateur base ball throughout the world.

At the same time, Moores' involvement provokes some cynicism; many have suggested that he brought baseball to England to be a summer companion sport to soccer for his gambling pools. Moreover, Moores also might have felt that baseball had something of a status-raising value. Quite possibly, he thought that associating his name with a powerful American sport would provide him with some standing, perhaps providing a foothold either in the U.S. or providing a conduit for American finance into the British sporting context. Beyond baseball, Moores seemed to be willing to borrow from the United States. Most notably, the scope of the mail order business in the USA might well have influenced Moores to introduce the phenomenon to the United Kingdom in 1932.

Still, it should be noted that despite his gambling background, Moores' National Baseball Association, which oversaw the North of England Baseball League as well as the league West Ham would play in,

PRESIDENT AND FOUNDER : JOHN MOORES, ESQ.

4th TEST MATCH

ENGLAND

v.

AMERICA

AT

THE SHAY, HALIFAX

ON

Thursday, 18th August, 1938

PITCH OFF 6-45 P.M.

SOUVENIR PROGRAMME   -   -   **2d.**

Although England is credited today with winning the first World Baseball Championship, the series that earned them that honor was originally for other purposes. As this program cover suggests the event was originally a "test series" between a U.S. team preparing for the 1940 Olympic Games in Tokyo and a squad representing England. Later, England's dominating four-games-to-one triumph would be recognized as something more than just a bunch of exhibition games.

prohibited betting at the grounds of any affiliated club. This could have been to prevent dog track owners who ran the venues where most professional British baseball was played from getting a piece of the action through on-site wagering while allowing him to rake off maximum profits (the pools being essentially a form of gambling undertaken by the posting of coupons to a central checking place). But it could also have been Moores' interest in maintaining the sanctity of baseball. For that same reason, or possibly because the sport was still in its professional infancy during these years, Moores never developed a baseball pools gambling system.

Another sign that Moores wasn't in it just for the money: He continued trying to spread the sport at the amateur ranks throughout this era. Just before World War II, Moores brought amateur baseball to Wales in 1939. In Cardiff, free equipment was given to schools in an effort to grow the game at the grassroots level. Internationally, Moores also made an effort to assure a legacy by attaching his name to a trophy meant to be given to baseball's world champion. But World War II would put an end to all those efforts. American Baseball in Wales disappeared and England dropped out of the first competition for the John Moores Trophy, 12 to 27 August 1939 in Havana, Cuba, because of worldwide hostilities.

Like many others, "Mr. Moores even drifted out of the game" after the war, according to Morgan. Nevertheless, the sport did intersect with the successful businessman on a number of occasions after his efforts in the 1930s. As a director of Everton FC from 1950 to 1973, he hosted baseball games at the team's stadium, Goodison Park, on a number of occasions after World War II, according to Morgan.

In the 1950s, Morgan actually wrote Moores asking whether he might take another stab at baseball. "I received back a very nice letter from Mr. Moores," recalls Morgan a half-century later. "He said he was no longer involved with baseball but that he'd pass my letter on to Theo Kelly,[23] the chairman of the sport at the time who actually worked with Mr. Moores."

Although Moores appeared to distance himself from baseball as the years passed. He must have maintained some interest in baseball well into the second half of the 20th century as the 1960 Midlands County Shires Baseball Association Challenge Cup had the phrase "presented by John Moores" inscribed on its trophy. Moreover, his brother, Cecil, did express some willingness to try to jump-start baseball in the late 1960s. Cecil was five years younger than John, and in the 1930s he actually played a few games of baseball, according to Morgan. Some forty years later, British baseball organizers approached Sir John's younger brother about another go at a professional setup. Cecil said he would be willing to invest in baseball, if British baseball organizers could find another four or five similarly wealthy benefactors to help finance the sport. The organizers were unable to do so and, thus, Moores' money was not funneled into baseball again.

While history eventually distanced Moores from baseball, in 1935, the foundation he'd laid gave the distinct impression that all baseball could do was succeed. If Moores' own track record was any indication, it is surprising the professional sport did not fulfill its early potential. As Barbara Clegg indicates, Moores' relative lack of accomplishment with the sport contradicted his history of success.

> Surprisingly, it was in the area of sport that John had his only other failure.... It never took off. John had made one of his few misjudgments and although he persisted for a while, even he eventually had had enough. It was obviously not a game which suited the national temperament.

Although baseball may not be listed among Moores' achievements, the man, nevertheless, built quite an empire. By 2002, there were 189 Littlewoods department stores. At one point Littlewoods was the United Kingdom's largest private company, employing close to 25,000 people and Moores, with a fortune estimated at over £1.5 billion, was reputed to be the second wealthiest man in Britain and the ninth wealthiest person in the world. He was the great city of Liverpool's most famous entrepreneur. His drive, energy, business acumen, compassion, his appreciation of the arts, his philanthropy, and his commitment to his hometown ensured that during his lifetime he became a legend, and his name became synonymous with success in the city he called his own.

Moores' influence was never solely associated with business. He was made an Honorary Freeman of the city of Liverpool in 1970, and his work for youth scholarship and handicapped children brought him a CBE in 1972.[24] He was a major arts benefactor, providing numerous scholarships both regionally and nationally. In 1980, he was knighted by Queen Elizabeth II.

Sir John's business success was built upon his philosophy of the equality of opportunity for all, echoed in his classic phrase, "Men and women can, if they want to enough, do anything." The Liverpool Polytechnic took Moores' name when it was awarded university status, becoming Liverpool John Moores University and his fundamental belief that anyone can achieve their aim in life when given the opportunity to do so is reflected in the university's commitment to higher education, to access, to flexibility, and to participation.

In a life that was the classic rags to riches tale, Sir John, the archetypal self-made man, never let his wealth and power become a barrier to experience. Although he had little formal education, his whole life was a process of learning which continued well into his retirement; at sixty he learned Italian, at seventy, Spanish, and in his eighties he discovered philosophy. As he once said, "When you're tired of learning, you are tired of life." He died in 1993 in Freshfield, Merseyside, England. The Moores family sold the Littlewoods Leisure (Pools) to Rodime Plc. in 1999 for £161 million. In November 2002 the rest of Sir John's empire was bought for £750 million by LW Investments Limited.

But in the winter of 1935, Moores was still in the adolescence of his success and what was most on his mind was making the London area and the county of Yorkshire baseball havens. He had West Ham in his sights to be a key baseball home.

Mining for Passion

In developing his nascent London professional league, which would become known as the London Major Baseball League, John Moores enlisted the help of L.D. Wood, a successful businessman from Wembley, in the leafy Middlesex suburbs of northwest London, about 20 miles across the city from West Ham. Along with spearheading the league's efforts in London, Wood would also bring baseball specifically to West Ham.

To understand what a herculean task Moores and Wood were suggesting in bringing baseball to West Ham requires an understanding of the unique nature of this enclave of East London. As the powerful duo Moores and Wood, who were West Ham outsiders, were making their plans to introduce the sport to London, West Ham was increasingly being defined by two elements that could prove huge impediments to their baseball dreams: severe poverty and a populace with a nearly undivided loyalty to the local soccer team, West Ham United.

Poverty

In 1936, the year that baseball came to London, it was hard times in both Britain generally and West Ham specifically. By the mid–1930s Britain was emerging from the Great Depression, a worldwide economic slump that had decimated the industrial base of large areas of the country, leaving millions unemployed. The East End of London had always been heavily reliant on the docks and traditional industries for its prosperity and these had been affected by the Depression, although not quite as badly as parts of Scotland, Wales, and the North and West of England.

West Ham had already traditionally been one of the poorest parts of London and by the 1930s was among the most impoverished places in Britain. The development of the Royal Docks and the railways at the turn of the 20th century had created a massive influx of people over a relatively short period of time. In 1851, West Ham had a population of just under 19,000; by 1931, this figure had grown close to 300,000 (about 15 percent larger than it is today). The biggest group of workers in the borough fell into the semi-skilled or unskilled categories wherein men could find themselves working for a wage of little more than £2 a week in 1930; a woman might earn half this amount. In 1936, 15.1 percent of the working population was unemployed compared to 7.2 percent in the rest of London, and 12.9 percent in Britain as a whole. The number of people receiving Poor Law relief (welfare) was more than 150 percent higher in West Ham than the average throughout England and about 75 percent more than the London average. Infant and maternal mortality was sky high while housing conditions were incredibly low, with the majority of people living in conditions that after the Second World War would be considered unfit for human habitation.

In the 1930s, Britain was a country torn by social and economic division. On the one hand, the incomes of those with jobs were rising rapidly, opening up unprecedented opportunities for the working classes to enjoy greatly improved amenities and to take up leisure pursuits. On the other hand, a deep seam of fear ran through British society, caused by the widespread use of casual labor. This was accompanied by massive and prolonged unemployment, poverty and, in many cases despair. The widening divisions were created partly by the decline of old heavy staple industries and the emergence of new industries based on the advances of science and engineering. The transition from the old to the new was captured by J.B. Priestley, who described how, on his travels, he passed through three Englands: Old England, "the country of Parson and Squire; guide-book and quaint highways and byways"; Nineteenth Century industrial England, "coal, iron, steel, cotton, wool [and] railways"; and Post-War World War I England, "of arterial and by-pass roads, of filling stations and factories ... of giant cinemas and dance halls ... bungalows with tiny garages, cocktail bars, Woolworth's, motor coaches, wireless, hiking...."

But there was another force at work. Priestley was also aware of a fourth England, the England of the dole (unemployment) lines provoked by the worldwide economic slump, and of this he was ashamed. The decade which led up to the Second World War was also known as the "Hungry Thirties."

The seeds of an economic crisis which left millions out of work were sown in 1929, when the New York Stock Market, which had reached dizzying heights, nosedived in a huge wave of panic selling. This torrent of selling drove down share prices in what became known as the Wall Street Crash. Practically all wealthy New Yorkers saw the value of their assets tumble, and many were forced out of business, throwing large numbers of their employees into joblessness and poverty, reliant on what welfare was available. The panic spread to other stock markets across the world and the slump which followed was the most severe the Western world had ever experienced.

Although the world economy started to pick up by the middle of the 1930s, the fruits of recovery went almost entirely to those who were lucky enough to have regular paid employment. In Britain, falling prices meant that wages were worth 10 percent more in 1936 than in 1929, but this did nothing to help the unemployed. These were concentrated in areas to the North and West of England and were officially designated by the government as "Depressed Areas." These regions had been dependent on the coal mines, cotton mills and shipyards, which were forced to close down during the slump. Many were never to reopen.

The East End was not designated a "Depressed Area" by the government as it suffered lower unemployment than some of the regions worst-hit by the Great Depression. For example, while unemployment reached 23 percent nationally and 66 percent in Jarrow in the North of England, it never rose higher than 15 percent in London's East End. Part of the reason for the East End's relative success in keeping down unemployment during the Depression lay in the fact that it managed to attract some public work projects to the area. However, the district did not benefit from the new growth industries of the 1930s. These tended to be dotted around the main roads leading out of London toward the North and West. Instead, the East End remained rooted in traditional industries—the docks and related ship-fitting, clothing, shoe and furniture manufacturing, and brewing—which were severely hit by the economic downturn.

Still, the condition of a huge number of working-class families in the 1930s in West Ham as in many parts of Britain was desperate. It was a decade when many surveys of living conditions were carried out by social scientists. One survey of poverty in York in 1936 revealed that almost one-third of working-class families lived beneath the poverty line. In the same year, a separate study found that nearly half of the entire population had diets which were deficient in some respect, despite the introduction of cheap, fresh milk into schools two years earlier.

Yet against this backdrop, society was modernizing itself as rising real incomes spread wealth to different sections of the population. The consumption of alcohol continued to fall, both as a result of rising taxes on it, and as a response to wider opportunities for social diversion.

By the 1930s substantial migration out of the borough of West Ham meant that the number of people living in the area had started to fall. Edgar Lansbury, mayor of Poplar, another East London borough, accounted for this trend: "People who can afford to live out of the East End wouldn't be found dead in it."

Despite the continuous stream of people leaving the area, there was severe overcrowding. According to the 1931 census, the density of population in the parish of St. George's in the East, Stepney, was thirteen times greater than that of an outer London borough like Woolwich. Stepney was also poor. At that time, a common indicator of poverty was the average number of children per family; at 3.92, Stepney's was the highest in London.

Before the sixteenth century, the region to the east of the city of London had been a rural area, interspersed with a number of small villages of which Stepney was one (in effect East London was, and still to some extent is, a conglomeration of urban hamlets). However, with the expansion of the Port of London, London's Docklands, and the gradual spreading of the metropolis eastward from the city, the East End became a first point of settlement for successive groups of immigrants from all over the world.

Following the arrival of the French Huguenot refugees in the seventeenth century, in the eighteenth and nineteenth centuries, the Irish came. Then, after 1870, there was an influx of Russo-Polish Jews (by the 1930s Stepney was considered a Jewish area). In recent years, the East End has seen the arrival of West Indian, Maltese, Somali, and Bangladeshi communities. Toward the end of the nineteenth century much of the population was crowded into rundown, unsanitary Victorian slums. A survey in Bethnal Green after the end of the First World War showed, for example, that fewer than one in ten homes possessed a bathroom. The medical consequences of such conditions were clear and it was the minister for health in 1919 who committed the earliest government funds to local authorities for slum clearance schemes.

At first, the slum dwellers were rehoused in cottage estates on the outskirts of London. Later on, councils (local authorities) began to build their own housing, replacing the slums with blocks of flats (apartments). The new flats were strictly functional, five stories high and had little character. Shabby as these look today, they were a great improvement on what they replaced.

Despite the poverty, the thirties was a decade when much of what are today considered commonplace leisure pursuits first appeared. West Ham was not an exception to this new trend. The radio was much listened to in working-class homes even though its values and interests were those of the highbrow and devoutly religious director general of the BBC, Lord Reith. The printed word also became generally accessible for the first time. Newspapers were widely read and in 1935, with the coming of Penguin paperbacks at 5 percent of the cost of a hardback, people were able to read books which had previously been accessible only in a public or commercial library.

Concerns began to be expressed that the growth of a leisure industry meant that passive entertainment was destroying people's ability to amuse themselves on their own. In the 1920s, silent films had begun to take over from the music hall as the most popular form of entertainment (in the East End there were around fifty cinemas). In 1929, with the coming of sound, cinema audiences shot up. By 1939, twenty million people a week were watching a program—that changed twice a week—of two features, a newsreel, and a cartoon. Around the East End darker diversions were the gambling dens of the Whitechapel underworld, known as "Spielers."

Sport was still the most popular pastime for the working classes. George Lansbury, a member of Parliament, campaigned for a lido in Victoria Park and there were more soccer pitches on Hackney Marshes than on any other single playing field in the country. Boxing was always popular, and there were boxing arenas at Premierland, in Back Church Lane off of Commercial Road (one of the main arterial roads leading from the east into the city) and Wonderland, in Mile End Road. Soccer matches were played to packed stadia and the pools provided the one chance, albeit a slim one, of a dream come true. By the end of the thirties, ten million people sent in their weekly coupon and waited on tenterhooks for the results. All this made the likes of John Moores multimillionaires on the back of painful poverty. Attendance at church fell steadily. At the same time, more energetic activities boomed in popularity. Cycling clubs sprang up and weekend rides were organized. Walkers joined the Youth Hostel Association, which had been founded in 1930 and had, by 1939, 297 hostels and 93,000 members all over the United Kingdom.

West Ham United

Even before the move toward more leisure, the people of West Ham had one true love—West Ham United. Although the district of West Ham took many sports to its heart and nurtured champions in most, the area's greatest passion has always been soccer. To understand West Ham and sport and how it so nearly adopted baseball one needs to comprehend something of the history of the club that has become synonymous with the community that surrounds it. It is probably fair to say that no other sporting institution is so thoroughly part of where it was born than West Ham United; the birthplace of the Hammers, an organization existing primarily to play a game, has radically influenced the culture of the club. At the same time, the institutional cause of the Irons has radiated out into the part of the East End of London and has been part of its evolution. As such, the district has molded the club in its own image, while the club has helped shaped the district; it is a unique symbiotic relationship—West Ham, the area and the soccer club are one; that oneness is claret and blue and lives under the symbol of two crossed hammers.

No one knows where and when soccer started. But in 1848, some interested and enthused men at Cambridge University refined the rules of the game as it was then played (probably fairly violently, by the working classes). The Football Association was founded in England in 1863 for the express purpose of codifying the rules, and the world's first international, between England and Scotland, took place in 1872. In 1885, professionalism was legalized and in 1888, the Football League was formed with twelve clubs: Accrington, Aston Villa, Blackburn Rovers, Bolton Wanderers, Burnley, Derby County, Everton, Notts County, Preston North, Stoke, West Bromwich Albion, and Wolverhampton Wanderers. All were from the North or Midlands. Fifteen years later, in 1900, West Ham United was born.

West Ham actually began years earlier as the works team of Thames Ironworks, a shipyard on the bank of the Thames, downriver from London, which specialized in building iron ships. Arnold Hills, the owner, had been educated at two of England's most elite academic institutions, Harrow and Oxford. He was also an athlete having played football for England against Scotland in 1879. Hills was very keen on the health of his workers (as well as diverting them from union activity, the kind that had a few years earlier given rise to one of the greatest dock strikes in history) and in 1895 he built a sports complex that cost £20,000 (a massive sum at the time) with a cycle track and a football pitch. That first season, on their new pitch, the Thames Ironworks team managed to play some evening matches under floodlight by stringing electric lightbulbs from poles and dipping the ball in whitewash to make it more visible. It was noted that when the Ironworks were about to shoot, the lights seemed, miraculously, to dim, making it much harder for the opposing goalkeeper.

In 1898, Thames was promoted to the respectable Southern League, but a bit of wheeling and dealing had been going on, unbeknown to Hills, and the side was fined twenty-five pounds by the Football Association. Their crime had been to hire an agent to tempt players away from the Football League.

Once the Ironworks were in the Southern League, they ceased to be a purely works team (although they had hardly ever been that). They were employing semi-professionals and soon looking for a much better ground. Arnold Hills realized that he could no longer finance the club from his own pocket, not wanting such a close affiliation with distasteful professionalism. On 5 July 1900, a new company was formed called the West Ham Football Club, named after the local borough, with a capital of £2,000, to be raised by selling 4,000 ten-shilling shares. The team's colors, from its beginnings as Thames Ironworks, had been Oxford blue, the house colors of the shipyard, but it was to become claret and blue, probably to be associated with Aston Villa (the Birmingham-based side were very successful at that time) The crossed hammers on the club's badge came from the shipyard, representing riveting hammers and not from the name West Ham,[26] which is what many modern fans wrongly imagine. Even now supporters still shout in support, "Come on, you Irons" as much as "Guu on you Hammers!"

In 1904 West Ham United moved to the Boleyn Ground, Upton Park, where the railway connections were better, but more importantly it was away from premises controlled by Hills, a vegetarian, teetotaling Christian who was dead set against gambling, one of the main reasons men (and it was more or less all men) attended soccer matches. From then on, it seemed that the side had two home grounds for as many people who refer to West Ham's Upton Park home, others say that the Hammers play at the Boleyn Ground (some refer to both!). The name Boleyn came from a local house where Anne Boleyn (the second of Henry VIII's six wives) is supposed to have stayed for a time. Until 1902, West Ham had been subsidized by the Hills, but that year they acquired manager Syd King. The side was still in the Southern League, but always managed good FA Cup runs. In 1905 they lost to Woolwich Arsenal (that would become simply Arsenal) and in 1907 they reached the third round, drawn at home against the mighty Newcastle United. Newcastle offered the Hammers £1,000 in cash to play the match at the North Easterners' home ground of St. James's Park, but West Ham refused. They drew 0–0 at Upton Park but lost the replay on Tyneside. In 1913, still in the Southern League, the Irons lost at home to Aston Villa in the second round. From an attendance of 50,000 the gate receipts were £2,000, a terrific sum for the time.

After World War I, West Ham, having gained a good record playing against much bigger clubs, got elected into the Football League, joining the Second Division. They were in such a hurry to sign on to the league that they broke Southern League rules and were fined £500. Great glory came to West Ham United in 1923. For many reasons the FA Cup Final of 1923 made history, not just for West Ham fans but for most people in England. It was first time the final had been played at the new Wembley stadium that had been built at a cost of £750,000 as the focal point of the 1924–25 British Empire Exhibition. In the Final match program, Wembley was described as "the Greatest Arena in the world, the largest, the most comfortable, the best equipped ... In area, it equals the

Biblical City of Jericho." It also the so-called White Horse Cup final, a legend in its own right (see Belton, 1997 and 2005). Wembley had been built to accommodate 127,000, but about twice as many turned up for the Final between West Ham and Bolton. Many managed somehow to get in, which meant that there were around 200,000 at the stadium at one time. Trying to save themselves from being crushed or suffocated, people spilled onto the pitch, where there was soon chaos until, as the legend goes, Police Constable Storey, on his white horse, restored some order, saving hundreds from being trampled to death. The scenes were captured on film but then, as now, there had been a lot of jostling before-hand for the right to record the event. Pathe News did not win it but they sneaked in a cameraman disguised as a West Ham supporter. He was carrying a large cardboard hammer, under which he held his cam-era. In fact there was no white horse. The creature captured on film was a dirty gray beast, one of many at the event. West Ham coach Charlie Paynter would, after the game, blame the state of the turf after the tram-pling of the many police horse hooves as being responsible for making the playing surface difficult for his players (who relied on service from the wings, the extremes of the pitch most affected by the "plow"). Pos-sibly as a result, West Ham lost 2–0.

It was not until 1940 that West Ham supporters would truly receive a triumph worthy of their support. The War Cup Final that year was held at Wembley and West Ham qualified to play the Blackburn Rovers. Like Bolton in 1923, Blackburn was another long-established northern club, founded in 1875, which had won the Cup five times in the 1880s and 1890s. Alfred Wainwright, later famous for his guide books to the Lake-land fells, was a co-founder and chairman of the Blackburn Rovers Sup-porters Club. He came down by coach for the final—and saw West Ham win 1–0 before a crowd of 42,399, West Ham's first real triumph.

Later, the club would build a reputation as a place that developed talent. In 1950, Bobby Moore, aged only seventeen, made his first-team debut, replacing the club captain, Malcolm Allison, who was recovering from a spell in a TB sanatorium. In the following season Moore made only three appearances, but would go on to become one of England's greatest soccer heroes.

During this period Coach Ron Greenwood's three star players were all homegrown: Moore, Martin Peters and Geoff Hurst. In 1964, West Ham beat Manchester United in the FA Cup semi-final and Preston North End in the final 3–2 and the Hammers became the last side, made up entirely of Englishmen, to play in all rounds of the FA Cup up to the final and win. That year Bobby Moore was named Footballer of the Year. At last West Ham supporters had something real to celebrate and there was a victory parade several miles long through the heart of London's

East End. In 1965, the team went on to win the European Cup Winners' Cup, only the second British club to take a European trophy; the Tottenham Hotspurs had won it two years earlier, but with a side made up of men coming from all over the British Isles and captained by Danny Blanchflower, an Irishman. West Ham was the first all-English XI to win a European trophy, with most of the team being born within a few miles of the Boleyn Ground. Hence the Hammers became "The First and Last Englishmen."

West Ham has always been known for their lack of consistency: periods of flair, elegance and success, followed by barren times ending in relegation. Sometimes they have played as if they were the Academy of Football (a name by which the club is known nationally), giving lessons in style and tactics. At others the team seems to be made up of solid but limited artisans. But West Ham has been unusual in that during their first ninety years they had only five managers. And until the 1990s, they were consistently a local team, drawing their support and most of their players from their immediate catchment area. Other London clubs like Arsenal, Spurs, and Chelsea have always been cosmopolitan, glamorous, big-city institutions, attracting support and stars from all over the country. By comparison, West Ham has been loved and supported locally, although they have fan outposts in nearly every country of the world. Very often, as in the 1964 Cup Final, they have put out a team that was not just totally English but heavily local, with most members coming from East London or the neighboring county of Essex. At its most popular the team could attract close to half a millions supporters over forty or so home games in a season.

Even in 1936, it was this homegrown and deeply cherished institution that Moores and Wood would have to draw attention away from in order to make baseball succeed in London's East End. But in Wood, Moores had found an owner who would be willing to take on such a lofty challenge. Through West Ham United and also the borough's well-supported Speedway team (also the Hammers), the Docklands demonstrated its passion for sport. The mission for Wood was to call on this, either by wooing fans away from soccer and the leather-clad dark knights of the cinder track or persuade supporters to widen their embrace to encompass baseball. This was not as unrealistic as it might at first consideration seem. West Ham United harnessed or became used for a means of identity for what was and is a population with massively diverse roots; the club brought people together within one claret and blue nimbus. What started as a diversion peppered with the spice of gambling, became something that said this is "us"—the "we" of support melded a community of followers.

In the 1930s, as the soccer season began in the late fall, or as it concluded in early spring, the singing of the Hammers theme song, "I'm

Forever Blowing Bubbles," a melancholic, "wanting tune," premised on the need for hopes and dreams by the tens of thousands of supporters crushed into the Boleyn Ground, resonated around the East End. Young women making their way home after the afternoon shift from the Lesney toy factory would pour out in their hundreds across Hackney Marshes, arms linked as they sang along; babies in their cribs about to stir in the back yards of the tightly packed Docklands terraces would be lulled back into sleep by the lullaby; down on the river brave little tugs would hoot in chorus as the passengers on the Woolwich ferry (that in a few years would, for the first ever time, turn its bow downstream to chart a course for the hell-fired beaches of Normandy and cradle wounded and exhausted soldiers home) took up the melody; within seconds the whole of teaming East End would vibrate to a harmonious claret and blue emotion that marked "our" presence—the Water People, North of the River, East of the Tower!

It was this that Wood wanted to tap into, the kind of "pure gold" support baseball needed to breathe life into it. To that extent he was mining for passion. For West Hammers sport was more than games or contests; it was a means of saying, "We have little, but this is ours!" Winning and losing was a secondary consideration as long as the game was played with passion with a deal of defiance; there is something of the bullfighter in every West Ham supporter, a Roberto Duran, "last man standing" mentality and it exudes an intense, truculent brand of iron-hard loyalty; a hammer strike-like commitment—when all is lost, when all is forlorn and broken—"we" will still be there and the West Ham chants over the years have told their own story; "The Bells are ringing for the claret and blue," "Johnny Lyall's claret and blue army," "One nil to the cockney boys," "East London la, la, la, laa. East London, la, la, la, laa!"

The Wisdom of L.D. Wood

Any story about professional baseball in London, and particularly the West Ham Baseball Club, must begin with L.D. Wood. Wood came to England around the time of World War I and decided to stay in Great Britain, becoming a thriving businessman. Primarily, he ran a factory in Wembley that produced ice cream making and serving machines. Wood's products made it to India, which indicates that he might have come to London to gain access to the markets offered by the British Empire. Being involved in catering machines, including ice-cream makers and dispensers, he may have had connections with the American confectioners Fullers who had supported baseball in London (see pp. 18–19). In addition, British baseball historian and organizer William Morgan suggests that one of Wood's biggest forms of income was serving as a concessionaire for Frigidaire in the UK—and possibly all of Europe. Considering Wood's willingness to be a pacesetter in baseball, his affiliation with Frigidaire would not have been surprising. After all, Frigidaire was a company that over the years was known as an innovator in the refrigeration business. (Frigidaire, which was founded in 1916, created the first electric self-contained refrigerator, the first home food freezer and the first room air conditioner.) Although it's unclear if Wood originally came from Canada or the United States[27] he was without a doubt imbued with a love of baseball. As successful as he was as an owner of a works in Wembley, it was baseball that was his true British legacy.

If there was one man who made professional baseball a reality in West Ham it was Wood. He was a vice president of the National Baseball Association, the governing body of baseball in England, the owner of the West Ham Baseball Club and, in 1937, its sister club, the Pirates. Wood attacked baseball with a combination of zeal and pragmatism. He applied his acumen as a factory owner to his efforts to market the game of baseball to East Londoners, a place with a tradition of watching and participating in numerous other sports at the time. Wood's love of the game must have been palpable as Morgan suggested that at least on one occasion, Wood actually umpired a game—calling balls and strikes.

Being a savvy man with impressive professional success, Wood knew that to get the average East Londoners to spend their hard-earned money to watch a new professional game, he would need to entice them to relate his teams' professional players. As such, he endeavored to fill his team with high quality performers, working on the realistic assumption that everybody loves a winner. Wood succeeded in this regard by enticing Roland Gladu to move from Montreal to England by offering him more money than he could have made in the depressed Canadian economy of the late 1930s.

First and foremost, Wood was a salesman. Although his star, Gladu, was not Canada's greatest player, he was an excellent hitter. Wood was unabashed in his readiness to exaggerate Gladu's credentials. He sold the French-Canadian as the "Babe Ruth of Canada." This was a clever ploy: to British neophytes, Gladu would appear as nothing less than *the* Babe Ruth. In performance, baseball, like anything, is relative. Gladu would dominate and as far as West Ham fans would know Gladu was as good as the legendary Babe, whom they had never seen, and most were never likely to see play.

Woods' willingness to reify his top player certainly earned Gladu's respect. In an article on Gladu in the *Montreal Gazette* written upon his return to Canada, Gladu praised his former boss. Although the article

During World War I, baseball was a popular activity among American and Canadian GIs. These photographs recount a contest between the two countries at the prestigious Queen's Club in London. The event even attracted London's lord mayor to throw out a ceremonial first pitch.

N? 484

BASEBALL

AT

WEST HAM STADIUM

PIRATES

v.

WEST HAM

(LONDON MAJOR LEAGUE GAME)

SUNDAY, JUNE 20th, 1937

PITCH-OFF - 3.30 p.m.

PROGRAMME - - - - - TWOPENCE

In the second season of the London Major Baseball League, organizers looked to consolidate and build up local rivalries. At West Ham Stadium, that meant the creation of the Pirates, a new competitor for the Hammers. The two teams shared the stadium and supporters clubs but were marketed very differently. The Pirates were portrayed as the bad boys to the Hammers' more clean-cut image.

focused on Gladu and his chances of making the professional minor league Montreal Royals baseball team, he made sure to mention Wood. In what was almost a *non sequitur*, Gladu enthused: "Woods [sic] is crazy about the game."

Beyond eulogizing Gladu, Wood also looked to persuade the youth of West Ham to play baseball. He invested a lot of energy and time in satisfying the simple axiom that people who take an active part in a sport will want to watch it. The year before Wood and Moores unveiled the professional London Major Baseball League, they set up the East London Baseball League (and presumably other amateur leagues in London). These leagues probably served as ideal testers for baseball interest. In addition, they were a key way to generate grassroots interest in baseball before developing the professional league. As such, while Moores and Wood had given themselves a tough task in bringing baseball to West Ham, some initial groundwork had been laid in 1935.

In early 1936, Wood continued to focus on getting locals to play the game. Even before the first London Major Baseball League, he organized numerous clinics for East London children. To persuade them to participate in the game, he invited young people to play in West Ham Stadium, the same location where the professionals competed. The chance to play in a huge arena where the big boys hit home runs, using the best of equipment, must have been an alluring prospect.

Gladu boasted in the *Gazette* article:

> It is difficult to get lads living around West Ham Stadium to play cricket any more. At first, they didn't want to wear gloves, for they saw the cricketers catch the ball barehanded. But after trying to spear a line drive, they soon went in for mitts, and wondered why there wasn't more padding in them.

To sell baseball in the way he did, Wood required more than just marketing skills, he also needed tremendous confidence. An irresolute person could not have preached the gospel of America's favorite sport in the land of cricket, soccer, and rugby. Selling baseball to East Enders not only required getting over the hurdle of the relative poverty of his potential customers, but also the need to compete in an environment already full of other sporting options.

It was not Wood's background in baseball that provided him with the surety that he could convince East Londoners to watch and support the baseball. Although he claimed that he had played the sport with much success in London beginning in 1934 with other ex-pat Americans and Canadians, incredibly, before playing in London just a couple of years prior to embarking on his crusade to organize professional baseball in England, Wood had played only a *single* game of organized baseball. Obviously, participation at a high level is not required to succeed as an owner and organizer of professional baseball. Most of today's owners of Major League Baseball teams in the United States have restricted experience of active participation in the sport. Still, few of those owners with a lack of expertise would have the temerity to write a *book* about baseball techniques. Wood, on the other hand, was more than willing to write such a publication. He was clearly not content with just taking on a business role in developing the game.

Supremely self-assured, Wood believed that his partial experience of playing baseball was enough to qualify him to explain how to take part in the game. During the late 1930s, Wood penned a book entitled *Baseball for Boys and Beginners*. The work, which was sold to the public for 6d (2.5p), was published by his friend, the entrepreneur John Moores. Baseball's biggest benefactor during the 1930s, Moores must have had a lot of faith in Wood to back a publication of a book by a person who admitted in his author's note that his hands-on experience in baseball was far less than the average American's. But, in selling his book, Wood applied his talent for marketing. He wrote about his only game of organized baseball as if it were high drama. In the author's note, Wood recounted a story about his childhood days. When he was 12 years old, his school included young men up to eighteen years of age and the institution's first team was made up of the best of the more mature pupils. A second team was formed to give the first team practice. Dissatisfied at being left out of the second team, the youthful Wood formed a third team and challenged the second team. L.D. pitched for his side and had "umpteen strike-outs, allowed only scratch hits most of which I fielded, and earned a run for each time I went to bat."

In true Tom Brown–Huckleberry Finn tradition, Wood's team won the game. He went on to tell how as a pre-teen pitcher he was

> mighty tough. I had marvelous control of the ball, could throw a "drop" and a "roundhouse" with great accuracy, and could "place" a ball when batting. The hardships of life kept me from baseball until 1934 in London. I found that although I had slowed up, I could hold my own on the diamond quite easily with the best American and Canadian talent in London.

Although it might seem that Wood was just a tad precocious or even bombastic (it takes quite an ego to point to a single baseball game as the basis for a book on the sport) it is clear he understood the boundaries of his experience. In reality, his story was a way to demonstrate his expertise in a very narrow scope; it mined the feeling and enthusiasm a young man might have for the sport. He was quick to concede in his book that the work was not intended to give a complete knowledge of baseball and told of how he was not a baseball expert. The reason he was willing, as he put it in his book, "to brag" about his childhood success was not to

BASEBALL *for* BOYS & BEGINNERS

PRICE **6**^{D.}

Issued by the

NATIONAL BASEBALL ASSOCIATION

West Ham owner L.D. Wood was zealous in his efforts to grow baseball in Britain. Along with owning the West Ham Hammers and the Pirates and serving as a key executive for the National Baseball Association, the sport's governing body in England, Wood wrote this book, entitled *Baseball for Boys & Beginners*. The 88-page book illustrated Wood's flare for the dramatic, his cocky streak and his baseball acumen.

prove that he was a baseball superstar, but that he was knowledgeable enough to lead readers to "believe that I am an authority on my subject—boys' baseball."

According to Wood, "When any one writes a book he should be an authority on the subject. Babe Ruth's name attached to this book might be convincing, but he would not convey the message I want."

For Wood, the leading lights of baseball knew too much about the sport and as such were more suited to advising on the finer, more technical points of the game. He argued that having played boys' baseball only, completing his playing experience as a 16-year-old, he was "highly proficient" at that level, and as such was ready to share the methods he used for training himself through the pages of his book. He wrote,

> There has been added the usual stock baseball plays, etc., and the subject has been influenced by my experiences with newcomers to the game in England. Having told you all this, I hope you have been led to believe that I am an authority on my subject—boys' baseball.

Wood's book was a pragmatic and insightful overview of the game. In much of the work, the sanguine Wood opted for directness over tact. In a chapter entitled "Baseball and Cricket," which was, according to Wood, written with the specific purpose of improving the fielding skills of those new to baseball, he told of how he based his views on personal experience in teaching baseball to the young people of England. For him, every boy in England played cricket and tended to approach baseball from a cricketing perspective. Wood claimed that cricketers were poor fielders. In the first paragraph of the chapter, he candidly wrote, "In spite of the fact that cricket calls for fielding, the English youth makes a poor fielder when compared to his contemporaries, the Canadians and American youths."

Wood told how this was not just his conclusion but reflected opinion on both sides of the Atlantic, including one of "England's greatest cricket players" (he did not say which one).

Despite being a foreigner with seemingly little experience with cricket, Wood was bold enough to explain what cricket fielders lacked. Wood argued that while cricket focused on the battle between bowler and batsmen with the fielders playing a secondary role, baseball, when played at its highest level, required greater skill on the part of the fielders for a team to consistently succeed (the great Australian[28] cricket sides of the past 15 years, who have brought fielding to the fore, have perhaps proved Wood right, but they of course hail from a country that has come on leaps and bounds in baseball over the same period). As Wood saw it, the baseball pitcher is not the chief obstacle to the batting side.

People who have seen games in this country are apt to believe that the pitcher represents 75% of the defensive strength of a team. That is because when a team is formed, the Canadian or American on the team is selected as pitcher inasmuch as he invariably has the best throwing arm on the team. But he is really playing in a lower grade of baseball than he is used to. These mediocre pitchers loom up imposing and terrific with their numerous strike-outs against novice batsmen. When pitchers face batsmen of their own caliber, however, baseball presents a different aspect. The batsman hits the ball more often than he is struck out; the pitcher is not the chief obstacle of the batting side.

In making this statement Wood was almost suggesting that his readers avoid playing the way in which teams in London Major Baseball League approached the game. He claimed that the fielders, including the pitcher acting as a fielder, were responsible for putting out more than 60 percent of players, and as such it was the fielders in "balanced baseball" whom the batsmen needed to fear most. According to Wood, fielders in cricket did not have the same opportunities to stop runs as they have in baseball. In countries where baseball is played regularly, boys know that they have these opportunities and are likely to concentrate a greater part of their training on fielding. However, Wood believed that the boys in England knew that there is more advantage in being a skilled batsman in cricket than a good fielder. This being the case, for Wood, "we have the cricket mind applied to baseball—i.e. it is more important to get runs than to stop them, or, fielding a ball is a very secondary and inconsequential matter."

He went on to counsel that the claim "offense is the superior form of attack" might be well applied to cricket, but he insisted that players should reject this maxim when playing baseball. Children needed to learn an axiom known to even the average fan in North America: Defense wins ballgames. Wood instructed,

It is easier for newcomers in baseball to bat a ball than to field it correctly. In view of this and the fact that fielders in baseball are presented with plenty of opportunities, the first efforts of the novice must be to take advantage of his opportunities by good fielding.

He added that a final score of 45–35 in baseball—the kind of score not atypical of some amateur and even a few professional games in England—did not indicate good batting but in fact suggested poor fielding.

Because of Wood's philosophy that in baseball defense was more important than strength at the bat, his book focused intensely on elements of throwing, catching, and battery work (catcher and pitcher). For Wood, in baseball, an impermeable defense was the pre-eminent goal of any side that had ambitions to succeed in the game and a contest might be won and lost by a single mistake on the part of a fielder; he pointed out that the professional American teams fined players heavily for fielding errors, but that they were not fined for failure to hit the ball.

> An error by a fielder in good baseball will most likely allow the opposition to score a run, and in a game where runs are scarce, this run is apt to be the deciding one.... Tighten up your defence. If your opposition has a poor defence you will have no difficulty in getting 35 runs. Keep him from getting any. You have the opportunities for doing so.

In addition to his somber and somewhat critical view of cricket, Wood was very realistic about how to grow British baseball at the grassroots. Before writing about how to conduct a regulation baseball game, Wood encouraged "Scrub Baseball," a version of the sport that could be played with as little as five players. He recognized that it could be hard to find enough players for a conventional game and wanted to encourage children to learn the techniques and skills of baseball, even if they couldn't enjoy the sport in its traditional form.

To that end, Wood used his West Ham team and other professional clubs as examples of how even playing "Scrub Baseball" could lead to success at the game. According to him,

> Indeed, it might surprise many people to learn that many of the Canadians who played in the professional leagues of England during 1936–1937 were experiencing their first taste of organized baseball.... Yet they were ball players. They were efficient at throwing, batting and fielding, all the product of their boyhood—playing scrub baseball on the back lots of Canada.

When discussing playing the actual game, Wood was equally as straightforward about British baseball. A balk was not something that the nascent British baseballer could quickly grasp. Wood or other North Americans could describe it as a sanction for pitchers who illegally try to deceive a runner on base in which the umpire can rule that the runner is allowed to advance to the next base; but that would simply not fully convey the nuances of a balk. Therefore, Wood suggested that such a complex concept should not be contemplated by English baseball umpires. He wrote, "In juvenile baseball, and in fact, almost all amateur baseball in England, umpires should refrain as much as possible from calling 'balks.'"

Wood also recognized that, for the uninitiated, baseball must be played at a fast pace. On that matter, he pulled no punches. He wrote,

> Umpires in England fail to enforce the delay rules, with the result that the game often drags. Between the innings after the pitcher has thrown the fourth warming-up ball, the umpire should call "play ball" or "batter up," whether the fielders have reached their positions or not. He should also enforce the rule that the pitcher cannot hold the ball while in play more than 20 seconds, the penalty of which is that a "Ball" is called on the pitcher. Umpires should also enforce the rule that a batsman is out if he fails to take up his position within one minute.

Understanding that too much technical writing could be tedious, Wood did not just explain baseball's finer points. He also wanted to build up baseball beyond dry rules and simple sports clichés and homilies. For example, he emphasized the "manliness" of throwing to inspire boys to play baseball. He described throwing as

> one of the latent instincts of all mankind.... Babies are born with it and before they can walk or talk they begin hurling objects around.... These are really manifestations of that instinct, bred into our race during prehistoric eras. Throwing was man's first weapon. Created without the strength, physical equipment, nor fleetness of foot of the animals, he resorted to throwing stones in order to bring down his prey.

As for hitting a baseball, Wood was honest about what many have called one of the most difficult feats in all of sports. For him, "To tell some one how to bat is almost as difficult as telling them how to wriggle their ears or close their eyes if they have never done these things."

Always practical, Wood's first concern about hitting was making sure that a batter could find a proficient enough pitcher to throw accurate batting practice.

While some young people might have been deterred by Wood's willingness to disparage the game of cricket, his book would have served anyone who read it as a good primer for baseball. It taught important

West Ham owner L.D. Wood was quick to use his players for marketing purposes. This picture is from Wood's book *Baseball for Boys & Beginners* and depicts an unnamed member of his team following what appears to be successful contact with the ball.

basics, including using two hands when catching, striding the front foot toward the pitcher when swinging a baseball bat, and stepping toward the target when throwing. These are all suggestion that teachers of baseball today would still offer to beginners. *Baseball for Boys & Beginners* also provided good explanations on such baseball elements of the game as bunting, stealing bases, and picking off runners. While Wood's experience as a player may have been restricted, his book strongly indicated one important fact about the man: he was an astute learner and an equally proficient teacher.

Baseball for Boys & Beginners outlined all the elements of baseball. It taught how a player could improve his throwing arm through undertaking certain drills and the ways to grip the ball and how to stand when throwing. Information was also given on taking care of one's arm. Wood quite accurately stated, "From a baseball point of view, throwing can injure the arm as well as develop it." He cautioned, as any good coach would in the modern-day game, that "throwing with a cold arm ... too violently before gradually getting the arm warmed up" could lead to great damage.

As for batting, Wood described how to hold a bat ("the grain of the wood in the bat is held upward and the ball is hit against the grain"); how to choose one's batting hand ("the greatest advantage of the left-hander ... is that after hitting the ball he is about four or five feet nearer to 1st bases than the right-hander"); and batting stance ("Stand far enough away so that when the arms are extended full length over the plate the end of the bat just covers or overlaps the plate by about one or two inches.").

Wood also outlined how to pick positions, offensive tactics (such as the hit and run play and bunting), defensive plays (including signals and ways to pick off base runners on base), and different grips pitchers should use when throwing in a game.

Although Wood intermittently extolled the professional virtues of players in England between suggesting that young people try not emulate them too literally, in the pages of his book he did make the most of the more recognizable members of his team. *Baseball for Boys & Beginners* is an interesting publication from a historical perspective as it includes a number of photographs, some of West Ham players in uniform illustrating various elements of the game. For example, there is a two-page, eight-picture spread of a West Ham player demonstrating how to field a baseball. The pages of the book also house images of players hitting at West Ham Stadium.

L.D. Wood worked hard to inculcate baseball into the sporting traditions of East London, but, ever the realist, he never invested all his efforts in West Ham. Like Moores', Wood's baseball interests were framed

A Good Swing — Arms Extended

An actual photograph of the ball. Note:—Batsman is looking at the ball as it is hit by the bat

L.D. Wood showed off some baseball action in West Ham Stadium in his book *Baseball for Boys & Beginners*. Note the crowd—baseball attracted attendances in the thousands in West Ham.

on a national scale. In 1937, along with his ownership of the West Ham clubs, he also served as a promoter of the Hull Baseball Club, which won the 1937 British Baseball Championship. While Wood's support with West Ham ran deep, Wood may have also had a financial stake in the Hull club, says Morgan. During this era, Wood also put together a baseball exhibition in Bristol at the Somerset County cricket ground.

Despite these far-flung ventures, Wood invested most of his time in developing baseball in London. Beyond the professional game, Wood also worked hard to push the sport at a grassroots level. There were two teams in Kingsbury, northwest London (in the same district wherein his business interests were based) that used his name as part of their moniker. It is possible these were two of the teams affiliated with his factory. In addition, there was a trophy named after him in the Metropolitan League and he remained the patron of the East London Baseball League—the league he started before bringing the pro game to West Ham—until World War II.

Wood's work with amateur baseball left a mark on the players who competed in those leagues. In the July 1950 issue of *Baseball (in Britain) Monthly*, a Mr. A. Sims recounted his experience playing amateur baseball in 1937 and how a run-in with Wood was a highlight of the season.

> In 1937, we [Sims' team] were joined by some players from the Streatham Ice Rink ... and we had a very successful season. We were then playing on the Streatham Town Football Ground and competing in the Metropolitan League. We managed to win the Pennant that year which was presented to our team by Mr. L. D. Wood, who many baseball players and fans will remember.

According to Roland Gladu in 1938, after professional baseball in West Ham ceased, Wood's ambition was to "stage an International championship tournament embracing teams from the United States, Canada, Australia and England." World War II would end any aspirations that Wood or any other supporter of British baseball might have for the game.

So what became of Wood? What happened to the East End patron of baseball is a mystery. William Morgan, who first got involved with baseball in the United Kingdom at the end of the 1930s, suggested that it was not uncommon for people involved with baseball before the Second World War not to return to the game following the hostilities.

"He might have drifted out of the game as so many people did," says Morgan. However, it should be noted that Wood's book did resonate with British baseball organizers long after the man had left the scene. In 1939, Morgan, who, for a time, was involved in organizing British baseball, obtained a copy of Wood's book. Impressed with the publication, he considered reprinting the work in the early 1970s for British baseball enthusiasts of that era. He even asked the Moores family, which had published the manual, whether they would allow it. (They told Morgan they had no record of the book being published.) Ultimately, changes in the rules over the years dissuaded Morgan from trying to bring Wood's tome back into print.

Alas, for historians of baseball in Britain, the name of L.D. Wood is hardly remembered and much of the detail of his life has been lost in the mist of time. John Moores, who put forward the majority of financial support for professional baseball in the 1930s, is best remembered as the game's key British baseball supporter. But Wood, a genuine fan of the sport, who marshaled all his skill as a businessman in the name of baseball in East London and beyond, was one of the true adventurers of the game. He was an entrepreneur with a passion for one of the world's greatest athletic entertainments and L.D. sincerely wanted to make a gift of it to his adopted land. His nobility is worthy of record.

The Birth of West Ham Baseball

Despite a brief period when baseball seemingly was taking a toehold in East London before the First World War, it is clear that by the 1930s baseball in the West Ham district was either played in limited pockets or wholly dormant by the time John Moores and L.D. Wood came on the scene.

When Moores and Wood decided to bring professional baseball to West Ham in 1936, they must have known that they had their work cut out for them. At the time, there was not really much depth in terms of local talent in the Docklands. This was unavoidable: as soon as anybody showed any athletic propensity he would almost immediately be conscripted into cricket, soccer, or boxing. Although other pockets of London had played continuously since baseball was introduced to England in the 19th century, West Ham could not boast such lineage.

Given the contextual problems Wood went to North America to recruit the nucleus of his team.[29] Roland Gladu, who turned 25 in 1936, was a top player in the Quebec province of Canada. A third baseman and outfielder by trade, he had already played for the Montreal Royals, the area's top professional team, when he was contacted by West Ham about moving out to England to play ball. Gladu, who would show later in his baseball career a willingness to take risks, jumped at the offer to be a baseball pioneer in Britain. He would serve not only as West Ham's top player but he was also head coach, field architect, and chief recruiter. Before he left the shores of North America, he had convinced a handful of fellow Canadians to play for West Ham. Among those players were Jerry Strong, George Etheze and Pamphile Yvon. The latter was the most accomplished of the ballplayers who accompanied Gladu to London, according to Quebec baseball expert Christian Trudeau. Yvon was a veteran infielder, probably well into his 30s by the time he went to England. For all this, he was still one of the top players of the late 1920s and early 1930s in Quebec. Strong, who was 23 years old in 1936, had won the championship of all Montreal in 1935, according to one British newspaper account. He was from St. John, New Brunswick, and Etheze, from Brockville, Ontario, also had respectable credentials. Both appeared to have had brief careers in Quebec's Provincial League. A player named "Ethese," who was most likely George, appeared for a team in Granby in 1935 and Strong played briefly for Drummondville in 1938. These men were seasoned players and as such represented a robust foundation on which to build a team to compete from a London base. The Provincial League, during the period these players appeared, included some who had Major League experience as well as high-caliber American university players looking for good competition during the summer months.

While not every West Ham member was to play at the level of Gladu, Etheze, Yvon and Strong, every member of the team had an abiding love of the game. Eric Whitehead exemplified that zest for baseball. Although not one of the team's stars, Whitehead was a two-year member of West Ham who played a solid outfield and second base. (John Moores, who wrote the forward to Whitehead's book, said the player had "ability on the ball field"—an indication of West Ham's depth.) Still, Whitehead made his greatest contribution to the game in Britain in ways other than leading West Ham in hitting. In 1939, he wrote *Baseball for British Youth*. Not to be outdone by his team's owner, Whitehead's book was described by Moores as "bright and breezy." The conversationally written 116-page publication not only offered a take on the game's basics but also offered a more detailed look at the sport's "slanguage" and baseball's origins.

Whitehead, who based on his detailed knowledge of baseball must have at least spent considerable time in either Canada or the United States, also knew British custom and sports as well. Interestingly, unlike many British baseball writers, he was more than willing to embrace the ties between baseball and rounders. "Stripped of its embellishments, [baseball] is simply old English rounders; beaten and sweated into one of the world's most highly skilled and intricate sports, yet nevertheless still the rounders that you all used to play with four bases, any kind of a ball, and an old stick," he wrote. Whitehead's involvement with West Ham was probably a selling point—or at the very least a point of tremendous pride—as accompanying one of the few series of pictures of the right-handed hitter was the mention of his affiliation with the team. The caption also heralded the team's successes.

For Gladu, Whitehead and rest of the team West Ham was to be an entirely new baseball experience. First, they had to get over the culture shock of living (and as such eating) in London's Docklands, and acclimatize themselves to the weather that the East End spiced with all the pollution that the easterly wind that sweeps over London could dump on them. Then they had to contend with putting together a baseball diamond at the spacious West Ham Stadium.

West Ham Stadium

The West Ham greyhound and speedway stadium on Nottingham Avenue, E16, just off of one of the main roads to the great Thames docks complex, Prince Regents Lane, was the largest of fifteen purpose-built greyhound tracks opened in London during the period 1927–35 (not including Wembley, White City, and Stamford Bridge, which also embraced these new track sports).

Roland Gladu must have been staggered when he got his first look at West Ham Stadium, the place that would be his baseball home for two seasons. It was situated in the Custom House area of West Ham, a district east of Beckton where the great gas works stood and west of Canning Town and Silver Town, close to the Thames and of course the East London docks, one of the poorest areas within a deprived district. The arena, also known locally as Custom House Stadium, was opened in 1928

West Ham Stadium, Custom House, 1938. During the two years before this photo was taken, the stadium was the home of East London's Hammers of baseball. Thanks to team leader Roland Gladu, it boasted one of the best-configured baseball diamonds in the London Major Baseball League. Used with permission of Areofilms.

and was originally designed for greyhound racing that was among Britain's most popular sports by the mid–1930s. It was one of the first of the London tracks, and with Stamford Bridge one of the fastest and the longest in the United Kingdom. Before the great East End arena was built the site had been a traditional location for local sports, particularly whippet racing, for many years, and was known as Custom House Sports Ground. Narrow soil embankments surrounded an oblong playing area with a small enclosure centrally located on the south side. The ground was surrounded by allotments, mostly rented from the local authority for rents amounting to not more than a few pence a month and used by local people to grow vegetables to save money on food and flowers for weddings and funerals.

For all its glory and influence, the genesis of West Ham Stadium is unclear. It appears to have been financed by a consortium of businessmen led by Sir Louis Dane, a former lieutenant-governor of the Punjab. When completed the central area was surrounded by two banks of different levels of concrete terracing. Two enclosures, located on each side of the ground and extending partly around each end, had seating, but these accommodated only about 5,000 people.

The huge edifice was designed by one of Britain's leading architects, Sir Archibald Leitch. He was a Scottish engineer and one of the most prestigious and prolific designers of sports stadiums in the early modern period. Millions of spectators sat or stood in Leitch's structures, built for such famous soccer clubs as Arsenal, Manchester United, Everton, Tottenham, Chelsea, and Aston Villa. But while his criss-cross steelwork balconies and pedimented gables were emblematic of the man, Leitch was virtually anonymous during his lifetime and after the modernization of stadiums in the last quarter of the 20th century few of his buildings survived.[30]

West Ham was the only greyhound and speedway stadium known to have been designed by Leitch. At the age of 63 Archibald Leitch returned to soccer, a territory that seemed more familiar to him. At the end of 1928 he was completing what is perhaps considered to be his finest work, the "New" Ibrox Park, home of Glasgow's Protestant-supported Rangers Football Club, the deadly rivals of the Glasgow Celtic. It is perhaps fitting that Leitch's greatest achievement was with the team closest to his heart.

Perhaps part of the reason Leitch turned his back on greyhound racing was that the new industry (due maybe to the sport's origins in coursing) was full of ex-majors, captains and brigadiers, men quite unlike the business people Leitch was accustomed to dealing with in soccer. But these military men were adventurous. Sir Louis Dane expressed the desire of himself and his partners for West Ham Stadium: "We wish it to be a stadium in every sense of the word and so provide a great centre for all sports in a densely populated portion of the metropolis which has been sadly in need of such a place of recreation."

Although officially it never hosted a crowd more than 64,000, for a Speedway international between England and Australia in 1933, it was filled to capacity on a number of occasions, the turnstiles and entrances to the stadium being notoriously insecure. Speedway, which opened the stadium on 28 July 1928, attracted the largest attendances, the best of which was a remarkable, if unverified, 82,400 for that Test Match against Australia in 1933. In the late 1940s reports of crowds of over 50,000 were also common. The fourth decade of the twentieth century was the most successful for the West Ham Speedway team. They won the National League in 1937 and the following year, the Hammers most masterful rider of the 1930s, Australian Bluey Wilkinson, the "Custom House Comet," became the first West Ham rider to win the individual World Championship at Wembley, in front of a 100,000-plus crowd.

The first greyhound meeting, on 4 August 1928, drew an equally amazing 56,000 (then a record for that sport) followed by regular crowds of 15–30,000 in the years that followed.

West Ham's greyhound track was 562 yards in length, longer than any other in Britain. The length of the speedway track meant that there was more space in the infield than most other tracks. This may have been why West Ham had better dimensions than the other baseball fields in the London Major Baseball League. Uniquely it was made up of Swedish matting laid over wooden boards and raised 12 inches above ground level. This facilitated fast times in all conditions and meant that fewer meetings needed to be canceled due to the weather. Another new idea was that each of the traps (positioned

While West Ham baseball had tremendous success, it was another West Ham athlete in another sport who brought hardware to East London. Speedway star Bluey Wilkinson became West Ham's first world champion speedway rider in 1938.

on the starting line) were color coded to make identification easier for punters[31] in the stands.

Greyhound and speedway racing were the great pioneer sports of the inter-war period. Driven by technology and commerce, their arrival in 1926 (from America), and 1928 (from Australia), respectively, sparked a plethora of speculative stadium building that had the potential to lead Leitch's company into a completely fresh area of the growing leisure market. Instead it seems that after West Ham, Leitch avoided any more involvement with the new stadiums, while dozens of investors were soon involved in loss-making arenas; only about 25 percent of them would endure the test of commerce and time.

West Ham was by far the largest of the new stadiums, estimated to have a capacity of 120,000, mostly under cover, which was 20,000 more than the massive Empire Stadium at Wembley and larger than White City (both in west London). The West Ham Stadium was similar in profile to the original Wembley Stadium. Every spectator at Custom House had a clear view of the whole center field. The speedway track was made of fine silver sand rather than the usual hard cinders. This being the case, on speedway nights, when the stadium lights were dimmed and all illumination was concentrated on the track and the revving motorcycles, the leather-clad gladiators were seen to compete for glory over a gleaming ribbon of speed.

The stadium boasted in its advertising that it had "An excellent restaurant and refreshment bars in each enclosure." Just after it was built West Ham Stadium was one of the finest sporting edifices in Britain and certainly far in advance of its neighbor, West Ham United's Upton Park, which just a few years before had been consistently responsible for flooding the streets around its environs; the soccer home of the Hammers lacking sufficient urinals forced supporters to use an alley under one of the stands and thus generated what came to be known as "Green Street's Green Creek."

As well as speedway and greyhound racing, West Ham Stadium had been home to the Thames Association Football Club, making it the largest venue used regularly by a Football League club in England. The playing area was the enormous oval of the center field.

The first Football League match at West Ham Stadium attracted 7,000 paying customers that saw Thames win 4–1. But soccer failed miserably. The Dockers won fame as the worst supported team in the league. Attendances quickly declined and when Luton Town visited on 6 December 1930 only 469 fans turned up to watch the game. How lost they must have felt in the vast enclosure. This was the one record that Thames managed to set in their brief existence however, and it's one they still hold: the lowest league attendance for a single game; the glut of local sides (Clapton Orient was also no more than a short bus ride away) meant Thames never really cut it on the east London scene. In contrast, at the time the Speedway club was attracting crowds of around 25,000 on a regular basis.

Thames' final season started well when a new record gate of 8,000 cheered their side to a 0–0 draw with Exeter City on 29 August 1931. After a run of defeats the club found themselves at the bottom of the league where they stayed. The season had been a disaster with Thames tasting victory in only seven of their 42 matches. On 3 June 1932 a press release stated that the club had decided to withdraw its re-election application. Secretary Mr. H.R. Milbank stated: "Lack of funds prohibits us from continuing in the League. Indeed we are disbanding altogether and will not compete in any competition."

During April 1964, West Ham United's England center-forward, John "Budgie" Byrne (a keen supporter of greyhound racing), persuaded his manager, Ron Greenwood, to use West Ham stadium for the Hammers' preparation for their FA Cup Final appearance of that year. The size of the central playing field and its lush turf offered conditions similar to those they were about to face at Wembley. It paid off. West Ham beat Preston North End 3–2.

But for all of West Ham's innovations and scale, with no easy subway (known in England as the "tube") or rail connections close by, and with no chance of staging regular soccer, the stadium's chances of long term survival were always slim, as were those of a dozen other similar greyhound and speedway ventures dotted around the capital (including the New Cross Stadium, next door to Millwall FC's Den). Today only two of London's greyhound stadiums remain in business—at Walthamstow and Wimbledon.

The West Ham Stadium survived until 1972, when the site was sold for redevelopment and a housing estate was built where once the great crowds combined to create an East London sporting culture. The last Speedway event took place on 23 May 1972 and the final greyhound meeting three days later. No trace of the stadium has survived apart from the titles of a few roads recalling the names of West Ham's Speedway stars. The great Docklands arena, with its soccer, greyhound racing, Speedway, stock car racing, and baseball represented a definite challenge to the sporting establishment that dominated its times. The rambling edifice was a great battleship of entrepreneurial spirit that attempted to exist without the kind of aristocratic patronage that controlled the administration and legislature of other British sports, from horse racing to boxing, from rugby to cricket and even huge elements of soccer via the Football Association. West Ham's ethos owed much to the search for unfettered enterprise in sporting business than some Olympian notion of "taking part" or philosophy of "personal betterment." However, this does not mean that people would not have found the same in any or all of the sports that the stadium gave a home to; it is just the case that was not what it was primarily for and it was always honest about that. To that extent it could be argued that there was no better home for the American sport of baseball; it was big, it was brash, it was up-front and it looked to establish a kind of independence of endeavor, founded on the will and effort of individuals operating in competitive cooperation. But it was a phenomenon born before its time and as such probably never had much chance of surviving. Its greatest asset, its sheer size, in the last analysis became its greatest enemy. In the end, it just fell apart in a state of semi-abandonment.

But in 1936, West Ham Stadium was still a shining monument to British ingenuity. Upon his arrival in England, one of Roland Gladu's first responsibilities was to turn West Ham Stadium into a playable baseball field. This was no easy task as the oval nature of greyhound stadiums, like the one at West Ham, did not lend themselves to the dimensions of a baseball field. For many of the teams in the London Major Baseball League, fathoming how to create the correct size and angles was nearly impossible. For instance, the organizers in Romford, a side that also played at a greyhound stadium, set up their field in such a way that the greyhound track was directly in centerfield. Instead of the normal 400-feet-plus distance from home plate, a center field fence had to be set up considerably closer to prevent players from running on the greyhound track.

But Gladu and his team put their expertise to use in developing West Ham Stadium. Although it is not clear how he did it, Gladu figured out a way to have dimensions that were at least somewhat akin to a normal field in America. According to Terry O'Farrell, who attended London Major Baseball League games during the 1936–1937 seasons, West Ham Stadium was the only field configured to avoid the easy home runs. Albert King, who attended West Ham baseball games as a teenager, estimated the dimensions as follows: "A home run to the left field boundary (the speedway safety fence on the back straight) would have been about 330, to center field some 360 feet and right field about 330 feet."

With a handful of top players in place and a field fit for competition, Wood focused on seducing and cultivating a fan base. Along with holding baseball clinics at West Ham Stadium for youngsters curious to take a try the month before the season started, Wood also offered local people a vested interest in the side by allowing them to choose the team's nickname. The Hammers was overwhelmingly the most popular of epithets, the same sobriquet used by nearly every sports team in the area; the speedway team, the Boxing and Soccer Clubs, there were even "Hammer" dogs, kenneled and trained at West Ham Stadium. When it came to choosing the team's colors there were, once more, no surprises. Like West Ham United, the baseball club chose crimson (claret) and blue. Prizes were also used to further entice fans to games; at one game, gifts were given to lucky spectators whose program matched winning numbers in a draw. The auspicious winners received one of six complete sets of razors with blades from Ever-ready Razor Products Ltd.; four gift boxes containing Palmolive and Colgate Products from Colgate-Palmolive-Peet Ltd.; and two "richly enameled" magnifying make-up mirrors from E.B. Meyrowitz Ltd. This was a literal treasure hoard in the poverty-stricken East End of London at the time.

Wood also endeavored to give the fans a sense of community with his team. There had been a tradition of a supporters club at Custom House from the earliest days of the speedway team that at one point was the biggest of its type in the world. In the summer of 1936 the baseball club followed suit, and in August of that year it was reported in the *Echo* (under the heading *Baseball Social Club*).

> During the comparatively short existence of the West Ham Baseball Supporters' Club Social club, members have enrolled in such numbers so as to necessitate larger headquarters being taken.
>
> Meetings are held at the Greengate Hotel, Greengate-street, every Thursday when ball, homers, dances and social functions are discussed. Arrangements for forthcoming matches in the way of transport also receive attention.
>
> It has been decided to hold the first dance at the Stratford Town Hall on August 29, and tickets are moderately priced at 1s 6d single and 2s 6d double.
>
> Stan Linstead's band will be in attendance, and an enjoyable evening is assumed.

But prizes and clubs alone weren't going to bring the crowds to West Ham Stadium to watch baseball. A quality team had to be assembled. Gladu and the other Canadian recruits were going to star, but it takes nine players to field a baseball team. While little is known about many of the other members of West Ham's 1936 side other than their names, many were probably already in England working in other jobs. During the era, milk bars[32] where popular places were young adults would congregate. Foreigners often worked at these establishments, and, according to O'Farrell, a baseball fan from the area at the time, many players were recruited from such locations. It is an interesting fact that one product that L.D. Wood manufactured in his works in Wembley was ice cream making and serving machines, the likes of which would have been used in such establishments. Although it's unclear whether he was a milk bar employee, Bill Turner, who according to the *Hull Daily Mail* of 4 August 1936 came from Philadelphia, was among the Americans who would play for West Ham. According to William Morgan,

Turner actually had some minor league experience before plying his trade with West Ham.

Salaries for the West Ham players are a bit of a mystery. Like the major leagues, each player negotiated his own salary. While Gladu and the other imports probably received a decent wage as the West Ham stars, the rest of the team were likely to have been relatively modestly compensated for their services. According to William Morgan, players in the London Major Baseball League were paid £2.50—£3.00 per game, whereas in the Northern Leagues £1.50 was common, according to British baseball historian Ian Smyth.

Morgan makes the point that while players competing in Britain were considered professional, they would probably have been thought of as semi-professional by American standards as many of them had other jobs that supplemented their pay from baseball. However, numerous soccer and cricket professionals in Britain would have had similar employment patterns to many men who were paid to play baseball.

O'Farrell agreed with Morgan, confirming that players received 50 shillings (£2.50) a game, however this was a fair sum for an afternoon's work in those days, not too far from the basic income of a professional soccer player. A top baseball player like Gladu would undoubtedly have made even more (there was no maximum wage as was the case in soccer) and would have received accommodation and additional employment. But the likes of Gladu were doing much more than just playing—they were also teaching the game.

Along with the base salary, it appears that British baseball was also a trailblazer in the concept of incentive-laced contracts. According to Gladu, players received money based on their performance in a given game. A 1938 article on Gladu in the *Montréal Gazette* explained that players were also paid fixed amounts for a home run, a triple, a double or a single. A maximum of $12.50 (Canadian) could be earned from a stellar performance. This was about £3, so it is likely this sum would be added to a basic wage of from £2 to £4. An additional bonus, according to West Ham baseball supporter Albert King, was given if a player hit a home run over the covered stand, which was about 440 feet from home plate. The prize: £25. (No one performed the feat, said King, though George Etheze hit four-baggers onto the stands roof twice.)

All the elements were in place for West Ham Baseball Club to face the future. The team had set solid foundations and as the curtain opened for their first season it seemed that West Ham would have to work hard to fail.

Sizing Up the Competition

Moores and Wood worked hard to recruit owners and venues for the 1936 inaugural season of the London Major Baseball League. Going into that first year, the London circuit comprised six teams other than West Ham. Around eight miles from Custom House, heading into the county of Essex were the Romford Wasps; the Hackney Royals were about five miles from the Docklands, still in East London, but at its northern extreme; Harringay (contemporarily spelled Haringey) was solidly in the north of the capital; the Streatham and Mitcham Giants, representing the southwest of the metropolis, would have given the Hammers their longest trip, perhaps an hour or so; the White City Citizens played in the westerly district of Hammersmith and Fulham; and the Catford Saints plied their trade in the southeast of London.

As the 1930s was a time when the financial means of the average Londoner was restricted and there would have been some care taken (in terms of getting value for money) about how money was spent on entertainment, baseball organizers needed to create a spectacle. To that end, all the teams were to play in large, established stadiums. In doing so, it would add a bit of a wow factor—as opposed to playing at smaller venues—and would add credibility to the fledgling league. For example, greyhound stadiums were used not only by West Ham but also Romford (Romford Stadium), Catford (Catford Stadium), and Hackney (Hackney Wick Stadium).

In addition, White City played at one of London's most prestigious venues of the time. White City Stadium also hosted greyhound racing among numerous other sports.

With high-profile locations for its games, the next step was to attract prospective fans. At the time the London Major Baseball League was formed only a few nascent amateur baseball leagues were established in the area and the game was certainly not considered a spectator sport. The key was to get Londoners to both understand the game and try it out. Compared to soccer, at the time the most popular of British

The 1936 White City Citizens were West Ham's fiercest rivals. The two teams battled down to the wire for the London Major Baseball League championship. White City prevailed and would go on to win Britain's national championship. West Ham did top White City in two respects that season: The Hammers beat the 1936 U.S. Olympic baseball team, while the Citizens were soundly beaten by the Americans, and West Ham had larger attendance numbers than White City, which folded after the 1936 campaign. For those true supporters of the Citizens, the reward was this charm (above), which was worn around the wrist.

spectator sports (as is the case in contemporary Britain), baseball is a complex game with so many nuanced rules. While people might appreciate the spectacle without understanding its finer points, the league's organizers believed that sustained interest would require at least a basic understanding and grassroots participation. In June 1936, for example, supporters of Leyton FC were invited to Hackney Wick Stadium to try out baseball. Elsewhere, an anonymous benefactor, probably an organizer of the league, donated £1,500 to help youngsters play baseball. The money was enough to organize and equip 24 boys teams in and around London and the provinces. Efforts to recruit fans were not limited to men. Teams in the league, including West Ham, set up female squads. Women with no experience were encouraged to come out and play the sport and games were publicized as part of the action at the stadiums. Like the other clubs, West Ham also worked diligently to make the game appealing to spectators. Before the inaugural 1936 season began, the Hammers held camps for children to learn how to play baseball; according to a local West Ham newspaper, *The Express*, "a very large number of London youths" were taking to baseball. "Every day for the last month [April 1936] different

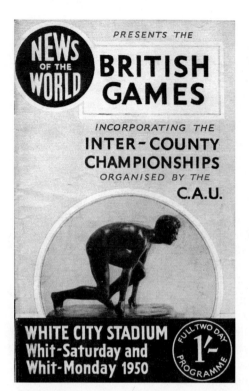

Left and bottom: **White City, home to the London Major Baseball League's White City Citizens, was far more than just a baseball stadium. The famed location hosted countless other sports for more than 60 years.**

enthusiasts have turned up at West Ham Stadium and without exception every one of them have been given a trial." While these players wouldn't make the West Ham senior side, the hope was to create youth teams affiliated with the parent club. In addition, amateur adult leagues were also nurtured. Two amateur leagues, the Metropolitan League and the East London League, were developed in London.

From the beginning the league's marketing goal was to sell baseball as something new and different. An advertisement

in *The Express* from 16 May 1936 lists prices as 6d. 1s.3d. and 2s. (to watch *"London's Thrilling New Sport"*) which was quite a reasonable range and at the lower end affordable to most working people in the West Ham area and about on a par with what admission to a cinema would have cost. What they paid for was for many akin to cricket, but was also a game that had "pep" (a word John Moores used to describe the appeal of base-ball), and could be played in an afternoon as opposed to the four-day encounters of cricket. There were no "one-day" matches then and "20–20," the most contemporary form of the game involving contesting sides bowling 20 overs (120 balls) each, would have been something close to a blasphemy. For better or for worse, L.D. Wood and fellow London organizers emphasized the "Americana" of baseball, stressing the loose culture of encounters within the diamond. Exemplifying this approach, the West Ham program highlighted the "Morale of Baseball." "You will perhaps notice in some baseball games a tendency on the part of the players to 'rag' and tease their opponents," an article on the topic began. "It is difficult to say how this custom became associated with baseball, but it has become almost part of the game." This practice was something like "sledging" in cricket (up to the last decade or so more associated with Australian "colonials" than the gentlemanly conduct of English play-ers) and the reason for this unorthodox, possibly (from the British point of view) unsporting act was "to make the opposition all hot and both-ered," or in the local vernacular of the East End at that time, "all of a flu-flar." The result would be "bonehead" plays. A "bonehead" was a term for a player who made errors in the field and suggested that "the skull of the player is composed entirely of bone, leaving no room inside for anything to think with." The program also suggested that "ragging" the opposition could lead to one team losing all confidence that it could win, even if it had the better team. Although this analysis might have been true of more patricianly or less rebellious environments, how many of the cockney audience would have been convinced that a team might be defeated by banter, given the local culture of using language as a weapon, as a means of defiance, attack and defense, is a matter of conjecture.

Hammers outfielder Eric Whitehead also heralded the importance of what he called "slanguage" in his book *Baseball for British Youth.* "Why do the boys out on the diamond jabber incessantly at one another and bark out such strange phrases?" he wrote. "Without 'infield chatter' as it is called—a stream of encouraging words from the men in the infield position—and occasional words from the outfielders, a baseball game would probably lose half its keenness.... Those who watch ball games know the fun a crowd can have at a game by just for once in a while for-getting their every-day reticence and formality and exerting their right to free speech in the full." Although Whitehead's book came out in 1939, his sentiments undoubtedly reflected the attitude among foreigners bringing the game to Britain in 1936.

For all this, explanations of facets of the way baseball was played would have been important for fans that were not used to this approach to sporting contests. The "ragging" certainly rankled fans in the north. "The big difference over [in the US] is in the shouting," the *Scarborough Evening Post*, which covered the Scarborough Seagulls baseball team in the Yorkshire League, wrote on 16 May 1936. "The Yanks make such a hubbub, both on and off the field that it's like listening to a wagonload of escaped baboons." Ellis Harvey, who attended games in West Ham's London Major Baseball League in 1936 and 1937, found that British baseball fans were also more reserved than those who attended football matches at the time. In contrast, Whitehead wrote that the British took to "slanguage" (although one must remember that he was trying to sell the sport in his book). "English crowds have certainly wasted no time in coming a style of their own to express their appreciation or otherwise," he wrote. "And always the 'rooting' is good-humored."

Whether fans took to baseball chatter or not, the idea of selling baseball as a game where teams would get on opponents by "ragging" was a quite different approach than how the sport was being presented to the British populace some 30 years earlier. In the 1907 edition of *Cassell's Book of Sports and Pastimes*, which was published for the UK audience, the section on baseball emphasized the gentlemanly nature of the sport of baseball. The book explained:

> There is no habit fielders have that is more characteristic of mere schoolboy ply in the game, or which leads to more ill-feeling in a match, than that of openly finding fault with those who commit errors in the game. Every man on the field tries to do his best for his own credit's sake.... We must enter our protest against the fault-finding, grumbling, and snarling disposition which continually censures every failure to succeed, and barely tolerates any creditable effort that does not emanate from themselves, or in which they do not participate. Such men as these constitutional grumblers are the nuisances of a ball field, and destroy all the pleasures which would otherwise result from the game.

For the professional baseball fans in England in 1935–1937, such civility was not the goal of organizers.

Even with these efforts, the British fans had a relatively limited knowledge of baseball. But it was probably also the case that people were unsure how to react, perhaps suspecting the etiquette of the sport to be something like that which applied in cricket, a game where anything beyond polite applause would be seen as crass or uncouth. According to Harvey he went to games because "British folk tended to dismiss it" and he wanted to see what attracted so many thousands of Americans. He was a cricket fan and, while his knowledge of baseball grew with each game he attended,

The people of West Ham were willing to show their support to the causes that mattered to them. A year before professional baseball came to the area, the West Ham faithful are seen celebrating the royal silver anniversary of the king and queen.

it took a while before those who came to watch games got to a point where they felt comfortable badgering the umpires for bad calls.

Along with the language of the game, whimsical player nicknames were another way to give the league a bit of a Wild West, American feel. Wood was quick to dub his best player, a French-Canadian named Roland Gladu, "The Babe Ruth of Canada." The Romford Wasps, a club whose home field was not too far from West Ham Stadium and therefore a local rival, took to this approach with great vigor. A sampling of nicknames from the Wasps squad demonstrates the extent to which the west Essex side habituated its own baptisms: "Lazy Bones" Macphail, "Sleepy" Bradbeer, "Rajah" Ormsby, "Old Maestro" Woodland, "Schoolboy" Dawber, "Mud Hawk" Creamey, "Poison" Asbell (who also played briefly for West Ham), "Slugger" Cranstoun, and "Swifty" (the American sobriquet for the mechanical hare in greyhound racing) Peterson. Using nicknames so widely not only gave baseball a unique angle in the British sporting community, but it was also a way to market individual players. If you liked the moniker "Lazy Bones" maybe you would become a fan of "Lazy Bones" Macphail.

As for the players behind the nicknames, many were North Americans sent over by Leslie Mann, a 16-year veteran of the big leagues, who took it upon himself to push for the international expansion of baseball.[33] At 5 foot, 9 inches and 172 pounds, Mann had been an excellent athlete who had a solid playing background and, as a champion of amateur baseball in his later years, he worked hard to help recruit top baseball talent for England. It is possible that Wood personally utilized Mann's services in recruiting Roland Gladu, as Gladu himself would later mention Mann as a key figure in helping bring North American players across the Atlantic to England. Along with Mann's efforts, players with baseball experience who were already in London were identified. At the time, ice hockey was also becoming a thriving sport in Britain. For many of the Canadians who came to England to play hockey, baseball was a good way to make money in the off-season.

With a fair pool of solid talent, the first season was shaping up to be a competitive one. Wood and his West Ham team would certainly have their work cut out for them in 1936. Although each team surely received centralized help from Moores' National Baseball Association, the organization under which the London Major Baseball League played, each team in the London league had its own identity in 1936, playing in unique stadiums and boasting somewhat different compositions.

Romford Wasps

In the first part of the 1930s Romford was a more rural (but by no means rustic or pastoral) area than its nearest baseball playing neighbor,

DIAGRAM FOR GROUND RULES

BALL OVER FIRST FENCE ON TO GREYHOUND TRACK – 2 BASES
FLY BALL OVER SECOND FENCE – HOME RUN (4 BASES)

Not all teams in the London Major Baseball League could configure their fields into traditionally shaped ballparks. Because many of the "ballparks" were actually greyhound stadiums, special ground rules were created at some locations. The Romford Wasps, which were run by the flamboyant businessman Archer Leggett, had a particularly unorthodox setup.

with fewer of the social problems associated with urban living at the time. Although the district could not be said to be wealthy, it was more of an artisan environment, serving small local manufacturing and part of the farming community of Essex. However, with the coming of the massive Ford Motor Company plant in 1931 on the Dagenham shore of the Thames estuary, just a few miles south of Romford, by mid-decade the whole face of west Essex was beginning to change. New roads and service industries kick-started the area's evolution toward what it is today, the most urbanized area of the county with a number of former parishes conscripted to create outer London boroughs—for example Barking, Dagenham, Ilford, and Romford itself which is now part of the London Borough of Havering.

While West Ham owner L.D. Wood was quite a salesperson, his counterpart in Romford, Archer F. Leggett, was at the least a worthy competitor for the estimable Wood. Unlike Wood, Leggett's legacy in Romford remains to this day. One Wasps supporter, Ellis Harvey, remembered the founder of his side more than 65 years after the Wasps disappeared from England's sporting firmament: "Mr. Leggett and a Mr. Baldwin were partners in a small manufacturing confectioners with a factory in Queen Street Romford. I believe the former was one of those instrumental in introducing greyhound racing to Romford...."

Leggett was a successful Romford-based entrepreneur and a keen sports fan. From the 1920s, greyhound racing had become a popular diversion in Britain and Leggett, while seeing the financial opportunities offered by the "doggies" also loved the spectacle and the crowd-induced aura of the pursuit. Being an adroit and energetic capitalist, Leggett found a site for greyhound racing in Romford in 1929 and convinced a local landowner that he should build a track. According to Harvey, this track was a monument to modern technology. "The [mechanical] hare was pulled around by the motor of an old bus," remembers Harvey.

Brian Evans tells of the humble beginnings of the Romford stadium in his book *Romford, Collier Row & Gidea Park*:

> This is the south side of Elmhurst, Collier Row. Archer Leggett, the founder of Romford Greyhound Stadium began to hold races in a field behind this house in the 1920s. In 1929 a site was found in London Road, Romford, beside the Crown inn and on the opposite side of the road to the present stadium.

Within two years of the tracks opening, greyhound racing became incredibly popular and, maybe having learned a little from Leggett, the landlord tried to raise the rent on the stadium. However, the shrewd Leggett saw that it did not really matter where greyhound racing took place, the gamblers would go. So rather than remain at the behest of an unpredictable patron, without hesitation or consultation, he bought a rhubarb patch across the street from the original stadium and, in partnership with one Michael Pohl, moved the track to the where Romford Greyhound Stadium stands to this day—now part of the Coral corporate empire.

Organized greyhound racing, as a mass spectator sport, like the speedway racing (another massively popular sporting attraction in Britain from the late 1920s) was an imported phenomenon; greyhound racing was born in the USA. As such, Leggett's willingness to house baseball at his stadium should not have been a surprise. He loved the dramatic exhibition that baseball must have been for Londoners in the 1930s. For all this, unlike Wood, who was a true baseball fan, Leggett was not too discriminating about what sports he supported as long as it brought people through the turnstiles and the "King's coin" into his coffers. Indeed, in its dazzling history his stadium would play host to entertainments as diverse as whippet racing to a Wild West show.

The Romford Wasps, which continued to play even after the disbanding of the London Major Baseball League, were a major attraction at Romford Stadium. Although the "ballpark" was primarily used for greyhound racing, this aerial photo of the stadium indicates just how central a place baseball had in Romford. Photograph originally appeared in *The* (Romford) *Recorder* newspaper; used here with permission of Archant.

Perhaps the most outrageous proof of Leggett's penchant for experimentation in the realm of public entertainment for pecuniary profit was his attempt, in December 1937, at racing cheetahs at his Romford track. Brought to England from Kenya by a sportsman named K.C. Gander Dower, a regular visitor to Kenya and the Indian sub-continent, the dozen cheetahs were described as "tame" and it was claimed that the cheetah racing at Romford Stadium would be the first event of its kind in English sporting history.

Gander Dower was keen to introduce the British public to the speed, grace and beauty of the cheetah and maintained that the cheetahs had been trained for a year before making their debut in Romford. But Leggett was not really bothered by logistical matters. For example, cheetahs, unlike the greyhound that usually ran the track, didn't have a taste for racing each other. These animals were hunters and, therefore, a piece of meat had to be attached to the electronic hare in order to get the animals to run properly.

As a promotional exercise Leggett (a stocky, round-faced man with soft features and a short haircut that was very closely cropped on the sides) had his photograph taken with a cheetah. But it seems the publicity was a double-edged sword. It led to speculation that the cheetahs were being imported to course wild game, and there were questions in Parliament about the whole affair. Sir John Simon, the home secretary at the time, was asked to take action to prevent "new forms of cruelty." Following an inquiry by the Royal Society for Prevention of Cruelty to Animals, the true nature of the venture emerged and, with public concern assuaged, the necessary permission was granted.

Following six months' quarantine and a further half a year of training at the Staines and Harringay tracks, the cheetahs were prepared for their debut.

The big cats were truly a spectacle but the racing did not last very long. One local resident named George Bowler, who actually saw the races, told the *Financial Times* in 2004 that he thought that complaints by local residents shut down the races. Still, the *Romford Times* at the time shed light on why Leggett would run cheetahs—and possibly why baseball was such an attraction for him. The paper wrote: "Mr. Leggett is in a happy mood, for has not Romford Stadium received one of the most gigantic advertisements in recent years? In more ways than one Mr. Leggett and his colleagues have placed Romford on the map."

Leggett's example demonstrates that promoters of times past were not lacking innovation relative to today's sporting entrepreneurs. Like modern-day owners, Leggett knew that a key way to induce people to consistently attend baseball was not only to provide a good experience at the ballpark but also to get the attention of the local media. Before Romford even played a game, on 1 May 1936, *The* (Romford) *Recorder* asked, "How will baseball fare? Thousands of pounds have been sunk in the venture to popularize it in the country." A columnist for the paper then concluded: "I see no reason why baseball should not succeed."

Although Leggett could be outlandish, he was also pragmatic when it came to baseball. His game programs, for example, included many clear explanations of the game of baseball. Most notably, a 5 July 1936 program had a brief story called "Baseball is related to cricket." The piece claimed:

> In the dim past these two games no doubt had a common origin. The ball is practically the same. Baseball players at one time used a cricket bat. The man with the bat is called "batsman" in both games, the pitcher acts as the

bowler, and up to only a few decades ago the pitcher used to run with the ball like the bowler does. The pitcher spins the ball to take effect in the air; the bowler to take effect on the ground. The catcher act[s] as wicket-keeper. The bases act as creases.

Despite his flare for creating a sporting scene and some willingness to try to relate baseball to more a more recognizable British sport, Leggett's approach to the actual game of baseball, at least in the first instance, did not have the same *savoir-faire* as that displayed by Wood at West Ham.

Leggett certainly didn't have much aptitude for setting up a field. In contrast to Custom House, where a hitter would be required to actually crush a ball for a home run, the configuration of Romford Stadium made big hits relatively easy. The stadium's greyhound track ran directly through mid-center field. A fence was erected in front of the track and behind the track and the following ground rules were set:

Fly Ball Over First Fence—3 Bases.
Fly Ball Over Second Fence—Home Run (4 Bases)
Ball Bouncing Over First Fence—2 Bases.
Ball Bouncing Over Second Fence—3 Bases.

Based on Leggett's approach to creating excitement at his sporting events, these complex ground rules and the unconventional field configuration could have been by design. After all, more runs and more big hits would come from shorter fences.

Whatever Leggett did, it worked as supporters like Ellis Harvey followed the Wasps from the team's inception. Harvey recalled that his initial interest in baseball was fed by curiosity and a hint of non-conformity: "I first went to watch baseball because many British folk tended to dismiss it as a game similar to the rounders played by our children but I wanted to see for myself what attracted so many thousands of Americans."

This attitude was quite indicative of the reputation of Wasps fans. Unlike West Ham supporters, many of whom had come to baseball via the home stadium's association with the speedway, the Romford faithful had no such bridge to the sport and had to be won solely by the appeal of the diamond game with its American and modernist associations and difference from anything traditional British sports had to offer, as Ellis elaborated; "I was impressed by the speed of thought and accuracy of the throwing, the variations employed by the pitchers, and the nature of the various plays."

Supporting baseball also offered a more intimate experience in terms of spectator relations. Soccer, speedway and cricket generated attendances often numbered in tens of thousands, frequently packed into cramped and dilapidated stadiums. These crowds were almost wholly made up of working-class men and boys. In contrast, Wasps games could be viewed by the whole family in a new stadium in relatively comfortable conditions.

While the Wasps' performance in the London Major Baseball League would be mixed (1936 was underwhelming, but 1937 was impressive), the team would have the distinction of lasting the longest of all the teams from the circuit, surviving until the outbreak of World War II in 1939.

Catford Saints

Professional players competed on every team in the London Major Baseball League with the exception of one organization: the Catford Saints. From the top of the lineup to the last player on the bench, Catford was comprised of Mormon missionaries moonlighting as amateur baseball players. While the team was made up of mostly unknowns, the squad must have had some importance because it included a second baseman named Brigham Young, who was a direct descendant of one of the founders of the Mormon faith.

The Catford Saints (shown here circa 1936) were the London Major Baseball League's only amateur team. Composed of Mormon missionaries, the team, at one time, boasted a direct descendant of Brigham Young, one of the religion's founders. The organization played the 1936 season at Catford Stadium and then moved in 1937 to Nunhead Football Club's grounds. Used with permission of Robert Shearer.

Of all the teams in the London league Catford was perhaps the most unconventional. Robert Shearer was a supporter of the Catford Saints who continued to think fondly of the side the best part of seven decades later. Robert was born on the west coast of Canada, in Port Coquitlam, British Columbia, on 21 September 1914, but had moved to London from Glasgow in 1936.

He was riding a train one day that took him past the Catford race-track and he saw a group playing baseball. He recalled,

> To my surprise and delight on returning from work at the Elephant and Castle [in South London] I spied from the railway carriage window a number of figures in baseball uniforms. This had to be investigated and my journey home was interrupted whilst I paid a visit to Catford Stadium. There, the baseball players seen from my train were, I learned supporters of the Catford Saints Baseball Club.

Robert soon became friendly with both players and supporters.

> This club comprised of young Mormon missionaries spending a customary period in the field with the object of spreading their message. I got to know some of them and they took to me. I was soon introduced to the Mormon story.... They were encouraging some of the fellas to become Mormons ... I was told the story of Joseph Smith ... and encouraged to take part in their evening practices at Hither Green ... they played good baseball.

As William Morgan has pointed out, the Catford Saints were not the only Mormon side to have graced British baseball:

> The Saints were a Mormon team and its players described themselves as amateurs; as New London [also known as New Briton] they had beaten another Mormon team, the Rochdale Greys, to win the National Baseball Association Challenge Cup in 1935. [That Cup represented the national championship].

So it seems that Catford players and Mormon involvement in baseball may have had another mission beyond selling the game; although Robert Shearer did not convert, he was quite definite about his own motivations:

> My whole interest lay in baseball and not with religious conversion. I must compliment those Saints whom I met who steadfastly refused either to drink alcohol or to smoke. I still retain several of their signed photographs. So 1936 became the year in which I was to be introduced to baseball in the UK.
> Interesting years of play were to lie ahead broken unfortunately by the years of War 1939–45.

Despite not taking on the faith of the Catford men, Robert got to know the players well and said that they were a good group of guys. According to Robert the Catford supporters were a fervent group. He recollected, "It was a fairly enthusiastic audience."

It appears that the Saints fans had a team worthy of their support as exemplified in their 1936 National League visit to Custom House. The following article from the *East Ham Echo* gives insight into how the British media covered baseball and used language not normally seen in baseball game reports, but appeared to be more akin to a journalist's take on a cricket match:

Catford were no match for the "Babes in Red" in the National League match at the West Ham diamond on Saturday, the home team only failing to score in their second and finishing victory of 12 clear runs. The score box showed that Catford managed two runs in their sixth through Ellis and Badger....

Home Hits

Jerry Strong scored a home run in the "Hammers" first, and his example was followed by Pam Yvon, with one man on and Bill Turner, both in the eighth.

On the mound, Turner had six strike outs to his credit, while for Catford, Fowler had seven and Homer, who pitched for Fowler from the eighth had one.

Gladu Can Run

Art Dunning was given a hand by the spectators when he took the plate. It was his first game since he met with an accident when attempting to slide first base at the start of the season. A bad error on a simple catch let Gladu to the first base and allowed him to steal second in the "Hammers" eighth. Gladu was so sure of being out an easy pop-fly going to the second baseman that he trotted along the line with his bat in hand. But did he turn on the heat when the ball was dropped and on the throw another fielding error saw him slide the second bag. Yvon slugged a ball into the far stand clearing the speedway and dog track fences for a home run and scored Gladu and after two long hits onto foul ground, Turner put the ball away for a home run.

Reserve Pitcher

Homer took the ball from Fowler and Irvine scored a single off the new pitcher, and stole second before a hit to put Whitehead out of the inning. Durant tapped one down towards the third baseman. Irvine drew the play between third and the plate, while Simpson and Durant were safe on second and third, but Rawlings was struck out with both men on.

The Catford last inning finished with three catches, by Whitehead, Simpson, and Rawlings.

It seems that it was the players' commitment to religion that finally ended the Saints. According to Robert Shearer, "The Catford Saints refused to play [on Sundays] and that brought it to an end."

Shearer became a top player in Britain in his own right. He played for the Eltham Dodgers between 1937 and 1958 (excluding the war years 1939–45) as a pitcher and first baseman. The Dodgers could attract up

Following World War II, baseball struggled to regain the momentum it had created with professional baseball in the late 1930s. Although much of the baseball played in this era occurred among North American servicemen, there were a number of true British teams. The Eltham Dodgers (above) were among those organizations. Led by Robert Shearer (front row, far left), the Dodgers were based in the London suburbs and were a very competitive ball club for a number of years following the war. The Dodgers are shown (standing, left to right: Alan Bradley, unidentified player, Ken Quinn and Tom Price; sitting, left to right: Bob Shearer, Charlie Stokes and Jack Forbes) here in the early 1950s. Used with permission of Robert Shearer.

to 500 spectators when they played at Bromley Country Club. Alas when the country club changed ownership, the team was forced to move and attendance dropped considerably.

For Shearer in the post-war era, the large number of North American GIs playing baseball intimidated some potential locals interested in playing the game. "Some of the British players who would have been keen would be discouraged by the Americans and Canadians," he said.

One who was not put off was Terry O'Farrell, another Catford supporter. Born 6 December 1918 in Brixton, London, O'Farrell followed the Saints in both 1936 and 1937 and played on their scrub team. O'Farrell went on to play for the Wandle Cubs for two years before the war ended baseball for him from 1940–1946. He then returned to play baseball in London first for the West London Pioneers (1947–1949) and then the Mitcham Tigers (1950–1955). It seems the Catford Saints left something of a secular legacy in addition to any converted souls in South East London.

The Saints started their first season at Catford Greyhound Stadium. It was a prestigious venue for the team. The area was very mixed in terms of social conditions. Being on the extremities of London, Catford had appeal to the lower middle-class, but it is close to Lewisham, the Old Kent Road (one of London's original prizefighting centers) and New Cross, which in the late 1930s had its fair share of urban poor. The stadium opened on 30 July 1932 and was one of the most popular and picturesque tracks in the country with more than 6,000 people visiting the venue in its 1950s heyday when it used to call on the services of as many as 80 bookmakers. The rich and famous, Hollywood stars, and those from the world of sport all visited Catford. The Gold Collar trophy, its most prestigious race, regularly had a "personality" to present the winning trophy. In 1934, film star Tallulah Bankhead greeted the successful dog owners. In later years the likes of boxing champions Henry Cooper, Lennox Lewis, Frank Bruno, legendary jockey Lester Piggott, and even Grand National winner Red Rum have stepped across the famous sand track to the presentation podium, where star-struck owners, trainers, and well-wishers celebrated before being joined by their heroes in a lap of honor. The late Roy Dwight, a former professional soccer player and cousin of Reg Dwight (Sir Elton John) who famously scored and then broke his leg in the 1959 FA Cup Final for Nottingham Forest against Luton, was assistant racing manager during the mid–1980s.

The greyhounds stopped running at Catford when the Greyhound Racing Association (GRA) closed the track on 5 November 2003 and the site was bought by a developer for a large housing scheme. The stadium had been extensively refurbished throughout its history and lost most of the original 1930s features. The managing director of the GRA, Clive Feltham, said: "This is a sad day for everyone, myself included as a south London boy who first worked at Catford." The track had been losing money for years because of declining attendances, the result of a lack of investment while new tracks were being planned in Coventry and Scotland.

When the stadium closed it was getting less than 1,000 gamblers through the turnstiles for its twice weekly racing events and only four bookmakers were operating in the main ring in Catford's last days. The popularity of greyhound racing had waned following the legalization of betting shops in Britain during 1961.

The Catford Saints baseball team would move from the stadium for unknown reasons for the 1937 season, but the relocation could not have been based on performance. While Catford wasn't at the top of the league, the circuit's one amateur team was certainly competitive,

Dean Francis (pictured here circa 1936) was one of the team leaders on the Catford Saints. A solid team in the London Major Baseball League, the Saints, led by players like Francis, also tried to teach the game to local youths. Teenagers would be welcomed to Saints training sessions to learn the finer points of baseball. Used with permission of Robert Shearer.

making it to the finals of the National Baseball Association Professional Cup, which was one of the side competitions beyond league play in 1936. But as Latter-Day Saints reject all forms of gambling as a pernicious evil to society, it may be that their continued use of Catford Stadium, as a place that celebrated, encouraged, and existed because of gambling, became incongruous in terms of their beliefs.

White City Citizens

In 1936, White City would prove to be a powerhouse of London baseball. It all certainly started with the stadium, which would have been the pride of any organization. It was originally built for the Franco-British Exhibition of 1908 which was eight times the size of the one held at Crystal Palace in 1851. Twenty gigantic palaces were built on the site and 120 exhibition buildings. The development covered 140 acres and about 120,000 men were employed in the work. Millions of people came to the exhibition. All the buildings were whitewashed, this being the root of the site becoming known as White City.

   The site also played host to the 1908 Olympic Games. The event was originally to have taken place in Italy. However, when Rome failed to raise the finances to build a stadium, the Games were offered to London, and an Olympic stadium was added to the exhibition plans. The White City stadium was opened by the prince and princess of Wales. It housed running and cycling tracks, a swimming pool, and a pitch for soccer, hockey, rugby, and lacrosse. The grandstands accommodated 93,000 spectators. The modern marathon distance was established at the 1908 Olympics when the starting line was moved to Windsor Castle to allow the royal family a good view: the distance between the castle and the White City stadium—26 miles, 385 yards—was adopted as the standard.

   The White City was a huge edifice with a 24-foot-wide, 3-laps-to-the-mile running track with a 35-foot-wide, 660-yard concrete cycle track outside it. In 1922 there was an unsuccessful attempt to sell off the stadium but the track was used in 1924 by some athletes training for the Olympics.

   In the 1930s, the exhibition site was partially used for the development of public housing—the White City Estate. It was used also used for exhibitions and textile fairs until 1937. During the First World War, some of the larger buildings were used for the manufacture of airplanes and, in the Second World War, they were used to make parachutes. Later, film scenery was built in the wide open spaces of the stadium.

   The stadium was taken over in 1927 by the Greyhound Racing Association (GRA). Although it is unclear who the actual owners of the White City franchise were, it would make sense that the GRA might have owned this and some of the other teams in the league. With such large stadiums, the GRA was often searching for other sports to fill the seats when the dogs were not running. Speedway was another popular sport that utilized dog tracks. If the GRA were the owners of the Citizens, they did make an effort to give the team a separate identity from the other sports competing at White City. Most notably, the stadium received a special moniker when the Citizens took the field. For baseball games, White City was referred to as "The Citadel."

   But baseball's involvement with White City actually predated the start of the London Major Baseball League. In the early 1930s representative all-star teams from John Moores' burgeoning Liverpool leagues would come down to London to play the best the capital had to offer. White City hosted all of London's home games.

   As a result, the Citizens had a potentially strong fan base even before the start of the 1936 season. Being in west London, a relatively wealthy district of Britain's capital city, some of White City's supporters would have come from better-off middle, even upper class background. However, there were areas of Chelsea and Fulham (locations not too far from White City) that were strongly working class and it seems likely that the

Citizens' support would have been relatively diverse socially. "Jessie" is probably one of the team's last living supporters; she was a sprightly 90-year-old in 2005. As a daughter of a member of the House of Lords, she came from a very privileged background. As a result, even today, she asks that her full name not be divulged because of her wish to avoid any potential embarrassment to family with regard to her "wild days" watching baseball some seven decades previous. "The appeal of baseball to young women was obvious, and at that time things like that were just not approved of. Cricket and Rugby Union were kind of protected by all the gentlemanly stuff," Jessie says. "With speedway, baseball was a breath of fresh air. They had independence about them; not starchy—not English I suppose."

A big selling point for White City fans like Jessie was the approachability of baseball players in comparison to some other sports. Even today, top soccer players in England tend to be far less approachable than Major League Baseball players who are expected to answer media questions from throngs of reporters before games and then sign autographs. The elite of soccer players employed in the English Premiership do not have the same requirements; press and fan access is mediated by agents, clubs, and the personal predilection of individual players.

The fans got to know the baseball players of the 1930s, but this seemed to be particularly the case at White City. "The baseball boys looked slick, clean, and smart and that's what I liked," recalls Jessie. "'Bozo' Fisk was one of the side's best players. He was a shy young man, which apparently is unusual for a pitcher. [But] we walked out together on a number of occasions. It is funny, but everyone called him Bozo and that's the name I remember him by."

Behind the pitching of the shy Bozo Fisk, White City would prove to be West Ham's most formidable opponent in 1936. Even after baseball left "The Citadel," White City stadium remained a center for dog racing for nearly 50 years. In 1984, the stadium was demolished, taking with it the home of one of the finest British baseball teams.

Hackney Royals and Harringay

According to William Morgan, the London league's association with greyhound racing may also have been related to a financial connection between baseball and the dogs:

> Its clubs played in greyhound racing stadiums in London and some of the clubs were financially backed by greyhound racing concerns. The backbone of players in this league were Canadian ice-hockey players. The Greyhound Racing Association, which backed at least two of these ball clubs, also operated two ice-hockey teams at Harringay arena.

The latter comment is probably referring to two of the sides that played in 1936, Harringay and Hackney Royals, as they both had ice hockey teams at that time. Like White City, the two teams played in stadiums run by the Greyhound Racing Association. This further emphasizes the definite connections between 1930s British baseball and the "gambling fraternity." Given the game's associations with greyhound racing and the Pools empire of John Moores, it would not be unreasonable to speculate that this "community" may well have had aspirations for baseball—in the British context—to become something of a cross between a sporting attraction and a gambling opportunity; unlike soccer, it would be totally in control of big gaming enterprises, and as such, unrestricted by interests other than profit. From the start, the likes of Moores and Leggett were manipulating the rules of baseball to suit both the British context and the profit motive, something the likes of Moores could never have achieved in soccer or cricket, those sports being ring-fenced by controlling bodies deeply committed to the Corinthian ethic of sport for its own sake.

Like West Ham, White City, Romford, Hackney, and Catford, the Harringay baseball team played in an arena that was principally a greyhound and speedway stadium. Harringay Park—as it was first called—on Green Lanes, was the second track owned by the Greyhound Racing Association in London, White City being the first. Constructed by Messrs. T.G. Simpson of Victoria Street, London, on the miniature hills of the Harringay Dump, comprising spoil left over from the construction of the Piccadilly tube line to Finsbury Park, the course was opened in late 1927. It was equipped with extensive kenneling and training facilities.

The location was convenient to both trams (trolley cars) from the Finsbury Park tube (subway) and what was then the London Midland and Scottish (LMS) station at Harringay on the Kentish Town to Barking line. Expecting more mobile patrons, the promoters advertised its good parking capability. Reportedly costing some £35,000 to construct, the stadium could accommodate around 50,000 spectators. Knowledge of greyhound racing was not great, and the promoters went to great lengths to educate their customers about the difference between the new greyhound racing, which made use of a mechanical hare, and coursing, which by the last part of the 1920s was seen by many as cruel. They also promoted the social side of racing, claiming that "titled people" were enthusiasts, including "ex–Queen Sophie of Greece, widow of the late King Constantine" (mother of the present-day Duke of Edinburgh, husband and consort of Queen Elizabeth II). For all this, the early facilities seem to have been fairly basic in comparison to what was available at West Ham.

The greyhounds race on a separate track outside the speedway circuit, with the hare running on the outside. Over the years, the Harringay area became associated with the stadium, its greyhounds and speedway team, and it became a center of local community activity. The shale speedway surface was sometimes used for schools' athletics meetings in the late 1940s and early 1950s, one event being the North Middlesex Schools Sports in the late 1940s.

Harringay Stadium was demolished by the early 1990s and the site where the great sporting edifice once stood is now occupied by a budget superstore.

The support for the Hackney Royals was very much akin to the fan base of West Ham, and while the Wick Stadium hosted baseball, the Royals were probably West Ham's greatest rivals, picking up on the intense feelings that existed between Hawks and Hammers Speedway supporters. Opened in 1932 for both greyhound and motorcycle racing, the Hackney Wick Stadium in Waterden Road, situated just north of the border between West Ham and Hackney and close to the "soccer-pitch-world" of Hackney Marshes, was a much smaller arena than the great construction at Custom House. The Wick's stands could hold 10,000 and terraces a further 15,000. Greyhound racing was reintroduced after closure during the war, but speedway did not make a comeback until 1963. The Kestrels, a speedway team among the founding members of the British league in 1965, raced weekly at Hackney Wick in 1989.

After an ambitious modernization program, the stadium was used purely for greyhound racing for a short time, but in the early 1990s it fell into disuse and has almost evolved into a vast informal outdoor trading area that has become known as Hackney Wick Market. The unusual and rather abstract location deprives the market of the usual references associated with London and as such has evolved its own diversities of language, cultures, and values.

The site of Wick Stadium was a contender for a new arena as part of London's bid to host the World Athletics Championships, but was beaten by Picketts Lock, a few miles farther north. However it is back in the limelight as a possible venue for the 2012 Olympics.

Neither Harringay nor Hackney would mount much of a run at the championship in 1936. The teams were also somewhat lackluster at the gate, much like the White City Citizens. Not surprisingly, since all three were most likely operated to some extent by the Greyhound Racing Association, lack of a decent show of income meant that they closed operations after the 1936 season. It appears that there was some expectation that the greyhound racing public would somehow pick up on baseball, but the activities would probably have attracted a quite different clientele; baseball appealed more to families and younger people who could relate to things American likely through the movies, while few who went to the dogs attended for the love of watching canine athletic prowess; they wanted a bet! At the same time baseball offered a link with what were likely to have been seen as modern aspirations. As such, its main appeal might have been to upper-working and lower middle-class groups, the numbers of which were relatively low to some of the dog tracks. But even in places like White City and Catford, where there would have been a higher proportion of people from and in these social classes, it is unlikely that they would have been drawn to locations associated with greyhound racing. The pursuit was generally seen as "low-life," to the extent that some local newspapers (either because of their fears about respectable opinion or because of the snobbery or religious convictions of the owners) totally ignored even the biggest greyhound races that took place on their patch. This being the case it might be said that the failure of the experiment with professional baseball in Britain in the late 1930s may well have had its roots in the means of its existence at that time: it was staged primarily in greyhound stadiums.

Streatham and Mitcham Giants

The London league worked hard to translate baseball as an innovation in British sport and to some extent this was its main, if somewhat ephemeral appeal. For all this, within weeks of its inaugural 1936 season, the Streatham and Mitcham Giants folded.

Reading between the lines of local newspapers of the time, it seems that the Giants might have done more than other clubs that started out in the London league to draw on and develop local talent to play in their big games. They played their baseball at Herne Hill Stadium in Burbage Road, south London, and the arena still hosts various cycling activities more than 100 years after it came into being in 1892.

The stadium was built by Peacocks of Water Lane, Brixton, who held the lease until 1945. There was a cinder track on the inside of the cycle track which was used for athletics. In 1896 concrete track was completed; three and a half laps were equal to a mile. The circuit, which had good banking at each end, was 30 feet wide.

The big events of the first years of Herne Hill included 24-hour bicycle races that took place from 1892 to 1894 and attracted crowds of around 20,000 people. During World World II, the grounds were used exclusively by the RAF as an anti-aircraft balloon base and the old cement track broke up. However, after the war it was made good and the track was covered with bitumen to make it fit for the 1948 Olympic Games cycle events.

In 1945 the lease of the stadium was purchased from Peacocks by the National Cyclists Union and the Greater London Council took over the stadium in 1959.

Herne Hill Stadium is now London's only stadium with a track specifically for cycle racing and is England's oldest cycling track. It was totally redeveloped in 1992 and is now a fine 450-meter banked oval, constructed of all-weather concrete. It is reputed to be the fastest outdoor track in the United Kingdom. Alas, perhaps partly because of the lack of backing from an organization like the GRA, that was not enough to make it a mecca for baseball.

The Hammers Start Hammering

In early May 1936, on the eve of the start of baseball in West Ham, the sport got a surprisingly warm welcome from the media. In the past, the British press had disparaged baseball, saying it would never succeed. But the local press in West Ham was far more optimistic. On 2 May 1936, West Ham's *The Express* wrote: "The probability of baseball becoming a popular summer game now that it is going to be run on properly organized league lines this year has encouraged" local young people to take up the game. Years later William Morgan would sum up West Ham baseball at the start of the 1936 season as having "good publicity and talented players."

Excitement about the sport increased when West Ham traveled to Hackney to open its season against the Hackney Royals on 9 May in front of 4,000 fans. West Ham dominated winning 12–2, despite the fact that the Hammers' star player, Roland Gladu, broke his nose in an exhibition match and did not play. Even with the rather one-sided result, following the game, *The Express* wrote with glee: "To the uninitiated at first sight, the game may appear a pointless one, but when the rules have been mastered and the finer points of play understood, it is easy to realize that it is a game requiring steadiness of nerve, physical fitness, quick thinking, and a quick eye."

The sport was warmly welcomed as well on opening day at other ballparks in the London Major Baseball League. For the Wasps' opening game on 2 May, the industrious Romford owner, Archer Leggett, managed to persuade some distinguished celebrities (at least by Romford standards) to attend the game against the Streatham and Mitcham Giants. Among the dignitaries at the match were Irish heavyweight boxer and contender for the British title Jack Doyle, and his wife, Hollywood actress Judith Allen, whose brief spell with Paramount saw her as the leading lady in Cecil B. DeMille's *This Day and Age* (1933). She also made a gently satirical portrayal of the daughter of two-bit impresario W. C. Fields in *The Old Fashioned Way* (1934). Her bid for stardom forgotten by the mid–1930s, Judith nonetheless remained in films into the 1950s. Another VIP was Mr. Chas. H. Allen, chairman of Romford Council, who according to *The* (Romford) *Recorder*, was very sanguine about baseball's prospects in the area. Allen's optimism must have been bolstered by the home team's performance as the Wasps were victorious 25–7 in front of its "celebrity" crowd.

As the season gathered momentum it appeared as if West Ham would have no peer. After dismantling Hackney, West Ham easily dispatched the Streatham and Mitcham Giants 20–7. Etheze and Strong hit home runs in the victory. The sound defeat was probably more than the Giants, who were described by *The Express* as "particularly weak in fielding," could handle. The team folded not long after this contest. West Ham then took on the Romford Wasps at West Ham Stadium. Some 5,000 spectators were in attendance to see the home team win 15–1.

WEST HAM'S BASEBALL TEAM. —The sporting public are to be given a new thrill in sport at the West Ham Stadium, where on Saturday, May 2nd, the West Ham Stadium Baseball team meet Hackney Wick in the London Major Baseball League match. Our photo. shows (left to right) Roland Gladu, capt., who incidentally is known as the Canadian Babe Ruth, Jerry Strong, George Etheze, Ellis Lydiatt, Bill Irvine, and David Asbell. ("Express" Photo)

West Ham's lineup in 1936 was formidable. Along with Roland Gladu (first from the left), Jerry Strong (second from the left) and George Etheze (third from the left) led the squad. Like Gladu, Strong and Etheze were both Canadians. Gladu had convinced the pair to cross the Atlantic with him and play for West Ham. Gladu's choices were excellent. Strong went on to be one of the league's top pitchers, beating the U.S. Olympic team in 1936. Etheze proved to be an elite catcher and hitter. Photograph originally appeared in *The Express*; used here with permission of Archant.

Etheze followed up his single home run performance against the Giants with two home runs in the contest with Romford. Proving that baseball is a contact sport, *The Express* of 16 May reported that West Ham left fielder Art Dunning broke his ankle sliding into first base. (Why he was sliding into first base is unclear, but shows that a mastering of the game was still a work in progress for some players.)

On 23 May, the Catford Saints visited West Ham and quickly took a 4–2 lead in the first and held it for four innings. But West Ham was undeterred and scored 10 unanswered runs in the next four innings to seal the victory. Roland Gladu made his West Ham debut in style, hitting a three-run home run in a 12–4 victory over the Saints.

Going into the last week in May, West Ham still looked as if it would run away with the league, but the team had yet to face the White City Citizens and their star pitcher "Bozo" Fisk. When the teams finally met at the end of May, Fisk "against whom the West Ham batter could do little," according to *The Express*, gave the Hammers' hitters reason for concern. White City was victorious 10–2.

West Ham, or the "Babes in Red" as the team would come to be known, refused to panic after the setback and remained a tight defensive unit. An adage in baseball is that pitching and defense wins baseball games. The West Ham Baseball Club showed its defensive prowess in a 4–3 win against Hackney in early June by turning three double plays. Strong, pitching a shutout, was impressive in a 12–0 triumph over Catford and followed that performance by striking out eight batters in a tight 2–1 win against Hackney. In a 12–6 victory against Romford, Gladu also demonstrated West Ham's offensive firepower. He hit two home runs as the Hammers came back after being behind through four innings. Despite the setback against White City and another loss to Romford, by mid–June, West Ham was at the top of the standings with a dominating 8–2 record. However, the Babes in Red, like any professional club, were unwilling to stand pat with their roster; despite the side's success the Hammers looked to keep the team dynamic and strove for even greater achievements. During the early part of the season, the team released Jimmy Blackwell. A sign of the strength of West Ham was demonstrated when Blackwell was quickly snapped up by the Hackney Royals. Thus, even a Hammers outcast could find work elsewhere in the league.

While uninitiated West Ham fans could cheer and take pride at their team's dominance, more knowledgeable spectators might have seen certain flaws developing in the league during its early days. It became clear that the umpiring was not at the same skill level as those playing. This led to arguments between the umpires and the experienced North American players. Umpires' often glaringly inaccurate calls were leading to questionable results. In a 4–3 West Ham victory over Hackney, Gladu got

into a heated quarrel with an umpire in the third inning after being
called out at first base. A week later, it was Hackney's turn to question
the umpiring. The Royals lodged a complaint, claiming that West Ham's
two runs in a 2–1 win were not valid. The issue was whether Etheze and
Gladu had legally advanced on a fly ball hit by Strong. The complaint
did not change the outcome of the game, but it was a sign of continued
tension. The questioning of umpires was not confined to matches
between West Ham and Hackney. The Royals also had a similar run-in
with White City at The Citadel. Hackney players tussled with the umpires
and the umpires retaliated: the upshot was that the whole Royals team
was ejected and White City was declared the winner.

This would remain a central problem throughout the life of the
league. "Homer" in the *East Ham Echo* was commenting on the issue in
June 1937. The growingly influential hack argued,

> Umpire—a person chosen to enforce the rules!
> So says my dictionary. And in view of this, it seems obvious that the per-
> son chosen to enforce the rules should know them as well as you know your
> twice-times-two.
> My views on this umpire and argument business are still the same as last
> year. Not until the N.B.A. put men in charge of the game who know the
> rules and know them well, and can apply them in a practical manner, and
> above all, will not enter into arguments with the players, will the game go
> over without these unfortunate incidents.

The conflicts between the players and the umpires were so bad that
the National Baseball Association, which oversaw the London Major Baseball League, suspended one of the Royals indefinitely. The league's concern about this problem was encapsulated when it announced that
"discipline is becoming more stern" in the Romford Wasps' 5 July program. To that end, the league took two steps. First, coaches, who regularly stood in the foul territory near first and third base, were instructed
to remain in their specially assigned box and at least 15 feet away from
first or third base. If the coaches did not comply with this regulation an
umpire would order the coach to the bench. Second, a hitter, after making fair contact with the ball, was obliged to run the last half of the distance to first base within the regulation three-foot lines. Although this
was common practice in North America, in Britain players must have
been inching out of the area they were allowed to run in, trying to dis-
tract fielders attempting to throw the baseball to get them out. If a runner failed to do this the umpire was ordered to call him out. The league
explained: "This allows the 1st basemen to field the ball without any
chance of interference [sic], and minimizes the chances of him being
accidentally spiked by the runner."

Through the end of July the standings changed little and West Ham, sporting a gaudy 12–3 record, was atop the standings essentially neck-and-neck with White City, which was 11–2.

The "Tour of the North"

Recognizing the talent of the West Ham squad, the National Baseball Association wanted to showcase them to fans in the north of England—particularly in the new Yorkshire League, which, like the London league, made its debut in 1936. In the north, baseball had taken off tremendously, but no team could boast the level of talent that the West Ham club was able to call on. Unlike many of the contests in the north of England, London Major Baseball League games tended to be low-scoring affairs and when teams in the league did compete against their northern rivals, the London clubs dominated. The difference in class between the Hammers and their northern opponents was clear on 1 August when Liverpool traveled to West Ham Stadium to be unceremoniously crushed 16–2. It was after that victory that the Hammers took what was then the long journey north (it would have take the best part of a day to get to Yorkshire from the East End of London) to show fans how good baseball could be in England.

There was a mixture of psychological warfare and bluster as soon as the tour was organized. The Hammers had offered Sheffield a 15-run handicap for their scheduled match, but the Dons refused. Sheffield's *Sports Special ("Green 'Un")* of 1 August 1936 reported:

> The West Ham team play[s] Hull and Yorkshire as well as the Dons on their tour, and have agreed to play the three teams and give £10 to any charity if they are beaten in any match. Shows what they think of their prowess, for they are also willing to give 15 points each to the Dons and Hull, and 10 points to the county side.
>
> The Dons say they don't want those 15 points. "West Ham will be wanting them before the finish," says Jim Calderwood [the Dons' top pitcher] and his boys. The Poor Children's Outing is the fund to which the money goes if the Dons win, and the Owlerton[34] boys are going all out to send some smiling little kiddies on a trip.

For all this, the *Sports Special* refused to underestimate the Londoners:

> West Ham are considered to be England's No. 1 side, and they are out to show their "stuff" in the north. Roland Gladu, one of their "stars" is the Canadian "Babe Ruth" of baseball, and considered the best baseball player in the country. Other stars besides the 23-year-old French-Canadian are Jerry Strong, who has been pitching since he was 15 years of age, and George Ethese [spelled elsewhere as Etheze].

The writer concludes his cautionary words with the inaccurate yet almost shrill warning: "This West Ham team is composed entirely of Canadians."

The "Visit of West Ham," as it was called by the influential *Hull Daily Mail,* began on 3 August 1936 with an exhibition match against Hull in front of between 4,000 and 5,000 fans at Craven Park.

The life of Craven Park started in 1922 when one of the city's Rugby League teams, the Hull Kingston Rovers (the Robins), moved from their Craven Street home to the newly built Craven Park ground farther along Holderness Road in East Hull. The ground witnessed many great matches, cavalcades of fine teams and a plethora of highly talented players live out their hopes and disappointments on the lush turf, the site of many glorious and famous victories for Hull's roving Robins.

Craven Park was to be the Rovers' home for 67 years. However, because of the constantly rising cost of renovation, the club moved to a new stadium that was built close to Preston Road, an area not too far from its former home, which is today known as New Craven Park. It is also the home track of Hull Vikings speedway team. A Morrisons Supermarket (part of a chain of "budget" convenience stores) now stands on the site of the baseball diamond on which Hull met the men from West Ham.

Hull was a solid team in the Yorkshire Baseball League that could out-hit most of its opponents. The East Yorkshiremen had dominated many of their opponents leading up to the West Ham game. On 9 May, they had beaten the Dewsbury Royals by a score that appeared more like an American football result: Hull 38, Dewsbury 21. A week later Hull blasted the Leeds Oaks 21–11. The team then beat the Sheffield Dons 13–12 on 23 May. On 6 June, a 21–7 pummeling was handed out to Wakefield, and, on July 25, the Scarborough Seagulls received a 28–2 thrashing. However, an improving Sheffield team took two games from the Hull club, including a 14–2 triumph in the first round of the Yorkshire Cup and by the season's end, Hull had to be content with also-ran status behind the Greenfield Giants and the Dons.

Nevertheless, Hull would have believed they had a strong side to face the Hammers. Ellis Lydiatt was Hull's leader on the field; a left-handed pitcher for the team, he knew something of the West Ham club having played briefly for the Hammers. He was respected enough in the North to be named captain of North Yorkshire in a North Yorkshire vs. South Yorkshire All-Star game played that summer. The Hull team also included Dave Farrell, a catcher from Canada, who, like Lydiatt, was a starter for the North in the North Yorkshire vs. South Yorkshire game. Fred Miller, another North All-Star, also donned the uniform of Hull to meet the Hammers. He was also a Rugby League fullback for Hull. Miller was physically typical of a player in the Rugby League, a game with many of the facets of the gridiron (but provides more of a mobile and fluid spectacle) which demands both strength and speed, being a much faster, more aggressive (and far more exciting) adaptation of Rugby Union. It is a sport of hard men and, in the English context, very much a northern game. Although in the contemporary period the Australians are the acknowledged masters of the "League code," in the late 1930s English Rugby League, played without armor and with only the protection of muscle, speed and personal courage, was unchallenged and understood to be the most violently contested organized team sport in the world. The league might properly be seen as the last echo of the gladiatorial group battles of the Roman arena; it has been said of the sport that it has no winners and no losers, only victors and survivors; Fred Miller was characteristic of his creed in that he was both.

As things turned out, Hull must have been shocked by the power of the Hammers, the final score, 22–12, being a testament to the Hammers' mastery of their hosts. As the *Hull Daily Mail* said in its 4 August edition, "West Ham is to Hull in roughly the same ratio as Arsenal is to Hull City." This was praise indeed as the Hull City Football Club at the time was something less than a modest provincial soccer side while the Arsenal Gunners of north London dominated the association football world. However, Hull would get its revenge against the South. At the end of the season, the former Hammer Lydiatt sailed for Canada and he told the *Hull Daily Mail* on 21 August, "I'm determined to make Hull the centre of a real crack team next season." He was true to his word. In 1937, Hull would win the national championship, defeating the London league's top team that season, the Romford Wasps.

West Ham also competed with an East Yorkshire All-Star team as part of a baseball festival arranged to benefit Scarborough—home of the Seagulls baseball club. Scarborough, on Yorkshire's northeast coast, beyond the county's capital, York, was (and is) a popular "Tyke"[35] holiday and day trip destination—the festival may well have been timed to draw on the patronage of these "tourists." The event also included a game between all-star teams from the east and the west of Yorkshire and provided good insight into the cross-section of players competing in the north of England. The contest featured a number of high-profile Leeds players including Barney Cruise, a pitcher who originally hailed from Hamilton, Ontario, Canada; Matt Sanderson, a well-known Yorkshire Council Cricket player; Dick Auty, a Rugby Union player; and T.M. Mitchell, a soccer national team player.

The *Scarborough Evening Post* rightly feared the Hammers, explaining, albeit not completely accurately, in its 1 April edition that "West Ham is composed entirely of professionals, men who have played baseball since their childhood days and they are all Canadian." However, the paper's fears proved accurate as West Ham dismantled East Yorkshire 14–4 in front of more than 700 fans on 5 August, thanks to home runs by Roland Gladu and Bill Turner. The Hammers also planned to meet the Sheffield Dons in a game the day before, but it is unclear if that game was ever played.

Next up for the Hammers (two days later) was an all-star team representing Yorkshire, England's largest county. West Ham had played and defeated a Yorkshire all-star team at Custom House on 19 July; the 18–8 score line indicates something of a rout. The team that traveled down to London had included some solid ballplayers like Roland Brown, an American medical student at Edinburgh University, who was a prodigious home run hitter, and Jack Smith, a top athlete who also played professional soccer as a goalkeeper for the prestigious Sheffield United club. But West Ham was confident—so much so that when they came north, the Hammers spotted that team 10 runs in the first inning.

After the defeat in July, Yorkshire officials wanted to be certain that they would be putting the best their league had to offer against West Ham when the Hammers came visiting. The game was really about pride. Both the Yorkshire League and the London Major Baseball League had started at the same time. There was no reason why a team like West Ham should dominate against the best that Yorkshire had to offer. As a result, Yorkshire chose to shuffle their team's lineup to assure they were at their absolute best for the game. Instead of the likes of Brown and Smith, some new blood was added to the Yorkshire lineup. Along with Lydiatt and Miller, another Hull player Don "Chet" Adams was drafted in. Two of Sheffield's best players were also in the lineup: J.W. "Jim" Calderwood and Bill "Doc" Lubansky.

Calderwood had been the starting pitcher and team captain for the south in the North Yorkshire vs. South Yorkshire contest in 1936. He had previously played for the Rochdale Greys and according to the 30 May edition of the Sheffield *Sports Special*: "The young player coach [Calderwood was a] native of the Western States. Good at ice hockey, basketball, football, jumping, pole vault, swimmer." Calderwood was also a deft coach as he had led the Rochdale Greys to the runner-up spot for the National Baseball Association trophy of 1935 (New Briton had taken the trophy). He could both hit, proving his worth at-bat on 18 July by slugging a home run against the Bradford City Sox, and pitch, showing his acumen on the mound by striking out 12 in a third-round win in NBA Cup action against the Greenfield Giants on 8 August.

Like Calderwood, "Doc" Lubansky started for the south in the North Yorkshire vs. South Yorkshire game. Beyond the baseball fields, Lubansky was a scholar. He had earned his moniker "Doc" because the American was a third-year student of medicine at Edinburgh University. The 24-year-old had previously earned a B.Sc. from New York University and was very optimistic about the future of baseball in England. "I think the game of baseball is going over great in this country," he told the *Sports Special* on 30 May. Handy with a bat, he had hit a home run against Wakefield on 1 August. He was also versatile in the field, playing both catcher and a variety of infield positions.

Along with foreign imports, the Yorkshire team also called on top local talent. Most notably, Reg Mallinson, who played in the outfield against the Hammers. Mallinson was a boxer and a Northern Union Rugby player for Bradford Northern.

Despite the impressive force that faced the Hammers, West Ham prevailed 21–12. Yorkshire actually scored only two runs in the seven-inning game but the final tally reflected the 10-run handicap.

The loss must have been of particular embarrassment to the Dons' best pitcher, Jim Calderwood, who before West Ham had started their tour had been supremely confident that his own Sheffield side—let alone an all-star team—would beat West Ham.[36] The promises of quite substantial pecuniary outlays on defeat made before the tour had begun shows confidence (or maybe bravado) on both sides, but in those days, when sportsmen in the north of England reveled in slandering their counterparts in the south as "a load of Jessies,"[37] being proved very wrong on the field of combat must have been a bitter pill for the estimable Calderwood to swallow.

The tour of the north cemented West Ham's place as one of the elite baseball teams in all of England, but the glory the team brought home from Yorkshire may have cost them their standing in London. The Hammers' season had been dramatically extended by their glorious drive north. To insure more lasting fame as a championship side West Ham would still need to better their toughest rivals, White City, in two matches over consecutive days. The games would prove to be among the most exciting played in England to that date.

Back Down South—White City Blues

West Ham's success in the north of England had come at a price: the exhaustion of travel and playing more games in a week than the players were accustomed to. Nevertheless, the Hammers rose to the challenge when they faced off with White City immediately upon their return. There would be two games in two days—one that would be crucial in terms of the London Major Baseball League championship and the other that would go a long way to deciding the separate cup championship that the London teams were competing for. The two games would be among the best that England had seen and West Ham supporters were prepared for them. "We'll show those high-hat Citizen supporters that we mean business and know how to put the encouragement business across down our end of little Old London Town," wrote Richard Hardy, West Ham's Supporters' Club Secretary in a West Ham program before the match-up.

In first match-up involving White City and West Ham, both teams battled inning by inning for supremacy of the London Major Baseball League. There were some 10,000 fans watching at Custom House as going into the ninth inning the score was tied 3–3. In the top of the final frame, White City exploded for four runs and seemed to have an insurmountable lead. But West Ham refused to give up and scored three runs of their own. Alas, it was not enough. The final result: White City 7, West Ham 6.

Despite the score, *The Express* told its local readership that baseball had been the biggest winner on the day: "If all matches were as exciting and interesting as the one on Saturday, there could be no doubt about the popularity of the game."

The next day, the two teams squared off again, this time at White City Stadium. This game was the first leg of the London Cup Finals, which was an event that ran simultaneously with the race for the league championship. Despite the loss the day before, West Ham came out strong and led 7–6 late in the game, but the fatigued Hammers ultimately fell 11–7. The loss to White City in the league game would prove to be West Ham's downfall in the race for the London Major Baseball League title. The Hammers would finish the season without losing again, although they did have a tie with Harringay. As with the North of England League, the allowance of a tie was something that might be assumed to have been influenced by a notion of "British fair play" or something imbued from soccer where drawn games were common. However, there were other possible reasons for ties: The unpredictability of the English summer weather (that often forced cricket matches to be declared "draws") and, if baseball was ever to be inculcated into John Moores' pools framework (that was premised on the prediction of results, the possibility of three results provides more wager potential than two) the option of tied matches had a certain pragmatic and financial attraction.

Citizen's arrest

The Hammers finished their first season with a record of 15 wins, four losses, and a tie. But White City had been unstoppable down the final stretch of the schedule and would finish the year with a dominating 18–2 record. West Ham did still have one more hope of silverware: the return match for the London Cup. White City was "plus-four" after the first Cup final game on its home field, but West Ham had high hopes for the match at Custom House. To win, they would need to beat White

City in cumulative runs combining the two legs of the final. That meant a victory of more than five runs would seal the title for the Hammers. The Babes in Red's fans were equally keen to see the home team fulfill the promise they had shown all season with a trophy. An impressive crowd of 13,000 came out to watch the match but ended up leaving with nothing but disappointment; White City prevailed 6 2. The Citizens would ultimately claim the London baseball treble by winning the National Baseball Association Professional Cup, beating the Catford Saints.

North of England League—1936

While West Ham dominated the Yorkshire League and White City won all the major hardware, the North of England League, Moores' first foray into professional baseball, was quietly making progress in the Lancashire area.

Rather than keep the lineup of teams currently in the league, Moores looked to shed weak franchises and move into new territories where backers appeared ready to support baseball. For example, a new team was installed in Blackpool. According to the 9 May issue of *The* (Ashton-under-Lyne) *Reporter*, "Blackpool officials spent more than £1,000 getting St. Anne's Road greyhound racing track ready for baseball." The *Oldham Evening Chronicle* reported on 25 April 1936: "Officially the season does not begin until next Saturday, but already the clubs of the Northern League have been spending money improving their teams to reap the benefit of the phenomenal success which professional baseball enjoyed in its first season last year."

Elsewhere two marginal franchises, the Hyde Grasshoppers and the Hurst Hawks, were merged to create the Ashton Hawks. This was a wise move: at the season's start a decent attendance of 800 spectators saw the Hawks lose to Belle Vue 19–5 at National Park, the Hawks' home field. As the team got better later in the season, Ashton attracted more fans—1,100 in a game against Oldham in July and 1,500 at a game against Bolton reported in August.

With the move to more competitive markets and a willingness to invest large amounts of money came more cutthroat efforts to win. For instance, *The* (Ashton-under-Lyne) *Reporter* said on 3 July that "Ashton complained [to league officials] that Oldham Greyhounds had illegally approached two of their players, [Ross E.] Scott and [H.J.] Richardson, their Canadian stars, with a view for transference."

Even when teams weren't trying to poach opposing clubs' players, they were aggressively searching for foreign talent. The Liverpool Giants, which was Moores' hometown team and a new addition to the league in

1936, had "6 players with American playing experience," according to the 30 May edition of *The* (Ashton-under-Lyne) *Reporter.* This thirst for North Americans didn't end as rosters were set at the start of the season. In fact, teams were willing to bring in players from abroad at any point—often with worthy results.

The Ashton Hawks were battling to stay out of last place in the North of England League when the team imported a Canadian pitcher in mid–June named Ross E. Scott. Scott had solid baseball credentials, having pitched in the semi-pro Toronto Viaduct League and Canadian Senior League. The results on his arrival in Ashton were immediate. In his first four league games, Scott struck out 58 batters (an average of 14 per start) and the Hawks finished the season well clear of the cellar.

Although teams were taking a decidedly Machiavellian approach to the game that seemed more American than British, there were still elements of the British sporting culture that appeared to be sneaking into the league. Most notably, the North of England League planned to set up a relegation and promotion system with the bottom team in the first division going down, according to the 19 June issue of the Ashton paper. Although such a structure was never realized, it would have been just like the system that has been and currently is employed in British soccer.

Another sign that baseball was making inroads in British culture was the willingness of established organizations to recognize the sport. Probably the greatest sign that baseball was becoming entrenched in the northern cultural panoply occurred on 17 July when *The* (Ashton-under-Lyne) *Reporter* broke the big news that BBC radio would be broadcasting a North of England baseball game. Eric L. Turner, who was the popular secretary of the Manchester County Association, was commissioned by the BBC to broadcast a running commentary of a league contest between top teams the Oldham Greyhounds and Rochdale Greys at Spotland, the home field of the Greys. The 15 August match-up was the first domestic baseball game broadcast in the north.

Despite these successes, both the London and Yorkshire leagues matched, and in some cases, surpassed the North of England Baseball League in interest. While top North of England teams like the Greyhounds could attract 1,500 fans, the other leagues' top teams surpassed them. In London, West Ham could draw crowds in excess of 4,000 for a regular league game and Essex rivals Romford attracted 3,000 for some contests. The Yorkshire League was the most financially lucrative baseball operation in Britain; Hull could bring out 9,000 for a marquis match-up, and Sheffield's first home game attracted a crowd of 6,000. According to the *Scarborough Evening News,* in 1936 Hull, had an average gate of £70 a game, whilst Sheffield took a regular £50 to £60 a game. A carpenter on a good wage around this time could have expected to earn about

£1.50 a week. Today the same worker might look to make around £1,500 a month based on a 38-hour week. Given this a £70 gate would have been equivalent (approximately) to £70,000 today. A ticket for an Essex 20/20 cricket match in 2005 would cost around £15, so a crowd of 10,000 would raise a total of £150,000 at the gate.

Maybe the novelty in London and Yorkshire led to the larger crowds than those in Lancashire. Still, the issue was not that the North of England League was failing, but teams like West Ham were independently gaining toeholds in the consciousness of local sportgoers. With the 1936 season, Moores, Wood, and others had proved baseball could be a winner in diverse pockets of England.

The Bigger Picture

The successful emergence of the London Major Baseball League and the Yorkshire League were only two examples of what a golden year 1936 was for baseball. In America, January saw the election of the first class of the Baseball Hall of Fame. The five players chosen were Babe Ruth, Ty Cobb, Honus Wagner, Christy Mathewson and Walter Johnson. On America's major league fields, baseball enjoyed a mini-renaissance as the sport saw its highest attendance number in a half-decade (since 1931) with some 8 million fans attending games that year.

That season also witnessed the start of one of the game's most remarkable careers. On 3 May, as the Hammers were beginning their season, "Joltin" Joe DiMaggio made his debut for the New York Yankees. The 21-year outfielder connected for three hits in six at-bats and would finish the season with 29 home runs. During the year, DiMaggio would capture the imagination of Yankees fans. In July at Boston's old Braves Field, he became the first rookie ever to play in an all-star game and along with first baseman Lou Gehrig (who despite the presence of Joe remained the star of the team that season) would lead the Yanks to their first World Series championship since 1932. This was a time before baseball players could earn ridiculous sums of money for playing the game. In fact, DiMaggio's salary in 1936 was $8,500 (still far greater than Roland Gladu's wage), but he would ultimately become baseball's first $100,000-a-year player in 1949. For many, DiMaggio was the epitome of what was great about baseball, a true professional who played hard every day.

Under DiMaggio's leadership, the Yankees would win four straight World Series between 1936 and 1939. In 1936 the Yankees won the Series by four games to two; DiMaggio batted .346 in his first Series appearance. He was an American hero, and, for a generation, he was a sign of simpler times.

Elsewhere, in Japan, the Japan Professional League, later known as the Japan Pro-Baseball League (JPBL), was formed. The circuit comprised the Yomiuri Giants, which had been established in December 1934, and six new teams: Osaka Tigers, Hankyu, Dai Tokyo, Nagoya Kinko, Nagoya and the Tokyo Senators. Most of these ball clubs were sponsored by either newspapers (Yomiuri) hoping to boost their circulation or train lines (the Tigers and Hankyu) seeking to increase travel on their lines to their team's home ballpark. With the outbreak of World War II, the league went into hiatus, but 1936 was the beginning of the sports professional history in Japan.

Despite all these notable events, the year's most amazing baseball event—in fact, one of baseball's greatest events ever—occurred elsewhere in 1936. That summer, at the Olympic Games, U.S. players competed in front of the largest crowd *ever* to witness a baseball game. More than 120,000 watched America's game—albeit under the less than appealing venue of the Nazi-run Olympics. Still, it was a record-breaking event and one that further sealed West Ham baseball's stature as a top baseball team as the Hammers would eventually play the American Olympians from that famous game.

The Olympians

While athletes and sports people all over the world prepared for the 1936 Olympic Games, the geopolitical composure of Europe was quickly changing. In Britain, King George V died on 20 January. Two months later the Nazi Party won 99 percent of the votes in the German elections. In May, the Italians occupied Addis Ababa following their invasion of Ethiopia. Two months later, the Civil War in Spain began following a military revolt, while at Fernhill Colliery, Wales, miners emerged after a 12-day stay-down strike by 60 men over a minimum wage dispute. The idea of such a protest came from Hungary where in 1934, 1,000 men stayed underground, refusing to come to the surface until their grievances were heard.

But politics were probably a long way from the minds of many of the world's athletes. For the first time in decades baseball players were among those preparing for the Olympic Games. The sport had played bit roles in previous Olympics,[38] but in 1936 plans were underway to push baseball onto the main stage of international sports.

Although there had been world tours of Major League Baseball teams in the past, baseball promoters were looking for a more permanent platform to develop the sport internationally. The most obvious and high-profile way to meet this objective was the Olympic Games. At the time, no one could have predicted that America's baseball pilgrimage to Germany in 1936, within days of the conclusion of the Olympics, would have consequences for West Ham and its ballplaying pioneers.

Leslie Mann, who had played a key role in staffing many teams in England, was also at the forefront of the effort to build baseball globally. As a player, Mann's claim to fame was knocking in the Boston Braves' winning run in game two of the 1914 World's Series to help his team sweep the Philadelphia Athletics. He was an individual who would act decisively when he made a decision. After the 1914 World's Series, Mann made the controversial move of jumping to the outlaw Federal League. Although he returned to the Major Leagues the following year, in 1918 he again was in the eye of the storm as a member of the National League champion Chicago Cubs, leading a group of players fighting for a better share of the 1918 World Series. Mann and Harry Hooper, a representative of the Boston Red Sox, negotiated unsuccessfully with baseball's potentates—American League president Ban Johnson, National League president (and acquaintance of John Moores) John Heydler and Cincinnati Reds president August Hermann. Despite Mann's efforts, the players reluctantly took the field after delaying game five of the World Series for nearly an hour. Years later, the *Boston Globe* reported that according to a statement given by Boston mayor John "Honey Fitz" Fitzgerald, the grandfather of President John F. Kennedy, Mann and his cohorts were convinced to play "for the sake of the public and the wounded soldiers in the stands." Mann's gambit truly failed as the fans at game five booed the players and only 15,238 showed up for Game Six (compared to 24,694 in Game Five). Still, it was that sort of tenacity that spurred the native Nebraskan on to help develop international baseball.

As an organizer, Mann was a tireless supporter of amateur baseball and the development of the sport internationally. He would eventually become the first head of baseball's inaugural international federation. But before that, his first victory for the sport's international development was successfully lobbying for baseball's inclusion in the Berlin Olympic Games. The plan was for baseball to be a demonstration sport. While there have been reports that an unrecognized baseball game was played at the Olympics as early as the 1904 Games in St. Louis, the sport officially first took the mound in an Olympic competition as an exhibition sport in Sweden during the 1912 Stockholm Games. Vesteras, a Swedish amateur baseball club, was scheduled to meet the American team. However, after taking in the American warm-up the Swedes decided that they would not be able to compete with the skills of their visitors. It was decided that a pitcher and catcher from the U.S. side would play for Vesteras. For all this, the Swedes were beaten 13–3. But the plans for the 1936 Games were far more ambitious than a single-game demonstration. Teams from throughout the world were invited to compete against an American squad comprised of the top amateur players drawn from across the United States.

The Nazi Olympics

While plans were still being finalized for the Summer Games, Nazi leader Adolf Hitler was already churning the propaganda machine for the Winter Olympics. They had taken place between 6 and 16 February 1936 in the twin Bavarian towns of Garmisch and Partenkirchen, as a sort of propaganda "dry-run" for the Summer Games. The anti–Semitism that would play such a violent and devastating role in the years to come was apparent as Hitler ordered that all anti–Jewish signs be removed from the southern Bavarian region. Still, the Nazis made some efforts to hide much of the abject hatred that was to come. Hotels in the area were ordered to show extreme tolerance to all visiting foreigners, regardless of race or religious affiliation. German planners had to take special care to prevent harm to Spanish athletes, who because of their darker skin complexions (having a passing resemblance to stereotypical portrayals of Jewish people) were often singled out for insult, ridicule, or even physical injury. The German press was instructed to not print anything that might embarrass anyone and refrain from commenting on the racial and religious make-up of any national team. At the same time, the Nazi rag *Der Stürmer* was not to be circulated in the greater Garmisch region and the *Stürmerkasten,* the newspaper vending machines, were removed. Military uniforms were to be worn only when absolutely necessary. Despite all these precautions the foreign press reported that Garmisch could be likened to a military camp.

There was controversy from the very beginning of the Games. The official Olympic salute, which involved extending the right arm, in the fashion of the *Hitlergruss* or *Deutschlandgruss* (the Nazi salute). The British team decided to use the official Olympic salutation as they marched into the stadium, but they were to be admonished for making the Nazi salutation. The American team elected to dispense with any salute, instead they made a straightforward eyes-right gesture as they passed the reviewing stage. They did not dip the Stars and Stripes.

Estonia and Finland also declined to make the Olympic salute as it might be seen as saluting Hitler and replicated the U.S. team as they passed the *fuhrer* and the IOC officials.

For all this, there seemed to be little evidence of German officials and referees favoring their fellow countrymen or working against particular racial groups. Overall, they were seen to be very fair in their decision making. Few complaints were made regarding bad calls.

In competition, the Winter Games proved momentous for the British. For the only time in Olympic history, Great Britain won the gold medal in ice hockey. The team had been led mainly by Canadians who held dual passports, but the victory over perennial power Canada in the finals was still a source for celebration. That team also had a British baseball connection: Jimmy Foster, who would star as the British goalie, would go on to play in West Ham for the Hammers' sister team, the Pirates, in the London Major Baseball League in 1937.

When the 1936 Summer Olympic Games took place between 1 and 12 August, Hitler and his Nazi followers had learned political lessons from

Baseball

AT

WEST HAM STADIUM

PIRATES BASEBALL CLUB

UNLESS OTHERWISE STATED ALL
SATURDAY AND SUNDAY GAMES
PITCH - OFF 3.30 P.M.

The Pirates, which were West Ham's second entry into the London Major Baseball League in 1937, struggled during their one year in operation. The team did feature a number of great athletes including Sam Hanna and Frank Cadorette, who would both go on to be members of the 1938 England team that won the first world baseball championship. But injuries and the untimely departures of some the team's North American players limited the squad's success.

the Winter Games. They worked even harder to hide the racist character of the German fascist state. Paradoxically, there was great confidence that the spectacle would be the ideal opportunity to demonstrate their claim that the German people were racially superior. The *fuhrer* himself had directed that the equivalent of $25 million be spent on the finest facilities, making the streets immaculately clean and ordering the temporary withdrawal of all outward signs of state anti–Semitism. By the time the 4,000 plus athletes from 49 countries arrived for the Games, the stage was set.

USA Olympic Baseball

The development of a U.S. Olympic baseball squad began in 1935. That year, General Foods—through its popular cereal brand, Wheaties— launched a promotion for international baseball. Purchasers of Wheaties could vote for one player from each state to be recruited for tryouts in Chicago for an American amateur team that would be selected to play Japanese amateur teams. The response was robust. For example, Les McNeece, an infielder who would play on the 1936 Olympic team, received 50,000 votes to be Florida's representative. The following year, Mann invited a number of the top players from the 1935 squad as well as the best college baseball had to offer to a tryout camp. It seems that there were some (what might have been) preliminary tryouts in Maryland; Palo Alto, California; and Kalamazoo, Michigan, but the main camp took place in Baltimore. Herman Goldberg was one of twenty-one players selected to go to Baltimore.[39] The Olympian catcher and outfielder recalled: "Work at the Olympic tryouts in Baltimore carried the same spirit throughout.... The coaches [were] Harry Wolter from Stanford, Leslie Mann from the Boston Braves, and Judson Hyames from Western Michigan College."

It seemed Herman's Jewish background was not an issue. He commented that the camp staff "showed me no favoritism and no antagonism. It was hard work; it was getting down behind the plate every day; it was my hitting and throwing that led to my selection on the team, not my name."

The list of players at the trials contained top collegians from all over the country, including Stanford (California) University standouts Fred Heringer, Dick Hanna and Gordon Mallatrat; the University of Georgia's team captain, Henry Wagnon; Temple (Pennsylvania) University pitcher Carson Thompson; University of Maine outfielder Clarence Keegan; and the University of Nebraska's Paul Amen. The squad also included a young man by the name of Dow Wilson.

During an interview with Wilson on 1 May 2005, he told of how grew up in Dow City, Iowa, but his family raced greyhounds and so he spent time in Miami, Florida. During his time in Florida, he attended a baseball school run by Mann. The camp was geared to honing excellence and included instructors from the major leagues including Hall-of-Famer Paul Waner of the Pittsburgh Pirates and nine-year major league veteran Jo Jo White of the Detroit Tigers. A middle infielder, Wilson impressed Mann enough to get an invitation to the Olympic baseball trials in Baltimore. Wilson was excited by the opportunity and pleased that his friend from Mann's baseball school, Les McNeece, was also invited to the camp.

In Baltimore, the competition was fierce, according to Wilson. "Everybody could play," he said. But Wilson, who at 19 would be the Olympic squad's youngest player, stood out. A shortstop with speed, Wilson was a top athlete who would go on to play both baseball and basketball at the University of Nebraska. Both he and his buddy McNeece showed the athleticism necessary to make the squad headed for Berlin.

Despite the sport's demonstration status, the U.S. baseball players were treated like any other U.S. Olympic athletes on the eight-day voyage to Germany on the ocean liner SS *Manhattan*. Dow Wilson quickly made friends with the man who was to be the most celebrated athlete at the 1936 Games and one of the all-time greats of track and field: Jesse Owens. Wilson recalled: "Jesse Owens was a real gentleman. He was very nice and so down to earth. We had a good time together." The baseball player had nothing but fond memories of the track star. "He was a special man," said Wilson, recalling his brush with one of the world's greatest athletes at the time. "He'd be running on the boat every day and exercising. He was very nice."

The pair, along with other athletes, played bridge constantly throughout the trip to Germany. Although Owens and the other players kept a running score, Wilson could not recall nearly three-quarters of a century later who prevailed, still the competition between the top-class athletes was surely congenial, if not a little competitive. "I don't remember who won, but if you asked any one of us we'd all probably say we won."

According to Wilson, the running score for the "bridge-athon" got up into the 80,000s, meaning the athletes must have played non-stop. Owens and Wilson developed a real bond on that Atlantic voyage as after the Olympics, the two young men kept in touch for some time.

Owens would single-handedly dispel Adolf Hitler's "Aryan supremacy" propaganda by winning four gold medals in the sprints and long jump and, by being snubbed by Hitler because of his color, further exposed the racist nature of the Nazi government. When Wilson and Owens got to Berlin, Wilson made time to watch Owens run in every one of the sprinter's races.

Jessie Owens was the star of the 1936 Berlin Games. He also had a tie to baseball. Dow Wilson, a U.S. Olympic baseball player who would go on to compete
against West Ham, became friends with the sprinter on the trip to Germany. The
two were among a regular group to play bridge throughout the voyage.

The baseball team was also in close proximity to one of the voyage's biggest scandals. Among those they shared passage with was swimmer Eleanor Holm, who won an Olympic gold medal in the 100-meter back-stroke at the 1932 Olympics and later had a brief acting career playing "Jane" in the 1938 movie *Tarzan's Revenge*. The attractive and vivacious water baby was kicked off the 1936 team for drinking champagne in pub-lic and shooting craps. According to baseball player Dick Hanna, the baseball team was seated next to the women's swimming team in the ship's dining room, and some of the ballplayers were actually with Holm when she was drinking the illicit champagne.

How much the American athletes cruising to Germany contem-plated the politics of their impending competitions varied by individual. By 1936 there was certainly not complete ignorance about Nazi Ger-many's treatment of its Jewish population and the possibility of a Jewish boycott of the Games had been contemplated and then rejected. A wide range of influential figures, of all political shades and none, were involved in this proposal.[40]

A number of organizations and publications also supported the idea of boycotting the 1936 Olympics. These bodies included the likes of the NAACP, the American Federation of Labor, the *New York Times* and *The Nation*.

Herman Goldberg, the US Olympic baseball team's catcher, had dis-cussed the merits of boycotting the game with other Jewish players and athletes. In Louis Jacobson's compact and informative *Herman Goldberg: Baseball Olympian and Jewish American,* Goldberg recalled: "There were five or six Jewish athletes out of the three-hundred-plus on the team, and some of us were considering whether we would boycott. We came to the conclusion that if the entire team would boycott, we would also do so."

Herman's position was a noble one, based on the attitude that he was a person before a given category;

> But we were really American athletes of Jewish religion. It didn't make sense to us to be the only ones to boycott. We were not Jewish ballplayers ... we weren't Jewish sprinters [Sam Stoller and Marty Glickman]; we weren't Jew-ish basketball players [Sam Baiter]; we weren't Jewish pistol shooters [Mor-ris Doob]; we weren't Jewish weight lifters [David Mayor]. We were American athletes, selected by the team to represent our country.

In Berlin

Goldberg told Jacobson that when the team reached Germany, he was met with politeness and civility and did not see any evidence of Jews being badly treated: "Nothing had come to my attention as a nineteen-year-old youth.... Perhaps if I had dug more, I might have known more. I was unaware as a young man of all the things that, perhaps, I should have been aware of."

But some aspects of Goldberg's experience in the Germany of 1936 did reveal a level of institutional prejudice. Herman recalled to Jacobson,

> When they listed the house of worship in some of the publications, there was no mention of Jewish synagogues. They had all the others, but never these. I was especially concerned when I read in an American newspaper that Hitler had forbidden the use of the word hallelujah at all religious services in all churches because it was a Hebrew word.

A book entitled *Germany* had been placed in each player's room. An insert at the start of the book was a welcoming message from Field Marshal Von Blomberg, the reich minister of war. Its content demonstrated the wide-ranging vision of the Nazi government, based on hostility and anti–Semitism. For Goldberg, elements of the book seemed threatening, as he explained to Jacobson: "This book was a massive propaganda production showing Adolph Hitler in his search for Lebensraum, 'more room' for Germany and for Germans...."

A range of the *fuhrer* is declarations were reiterated in the pages of the book, including the one of 16 March 1935, in which Hitler proclaimed, "According to the German belief, a people without protection is a people without honor. The German army is the expression of the common will of the people and the supporter of the national standing and honor."

The text detailed the assignment of the most able children in German schools to the Hitler Youth Corps. Goldberg recollected his response to this publication:

> Taking the time to read this book carefully, I could sense the beginnings of their war machine, epitomized on one page by the red white and black Nazi insignia, the swastika, winning allegiance from the German people. They were telling us, throughout this book, that they were getting ready for war, although they didn't call it that. They just called it the "preparation of Germany for expanding its borders." It went on and on, and we were somewhat disturbed by it.

Bad news

Just after arriving at the Olympic village the U.S. baseball team was given some bad news. According to Nebraska native and top hitter Amen, who recounted his experience for the 1984 Olympic baseball program:

> There were supposed to be a number of nations represented in baseball, even though it was just a demonstration sport.... But when we got to Berlin, we learned that they had all dropped out, most of them because they

couldn't afford to send teams. There was a world-wide depression going on at the time.

The Americans were disappointed with the prospect of not being able to compete. Most of them had made substantial sacrifices to get to Germany. Although all the players in the final try-out camp were esteemed athletes, some of whom would ultimately have professional careers in baseball's minor leagues, the squad was limited by financial constraints. Players had to pay in order to play. Stanford's Dick Hanna recalled in 1984:

> We had tryouts in Baltimore, but they wouldn't send you to Berlin unless you could show you could come up with $500 for expenses ... I remember there was a fellow from Chicago who spent his last $30 to ride a bus to Baltimore for the tryouts. He was probably the best player in camp, but he didn't make it. He couldn't come up with the money.

Hanna's U.S. and Stanford teammate Gordon Mallatrat recollected that the amount needed to go was $300 and confessed that he had to borrow the money to go from Hanna.

Dow Wilson could not recall exactly how much money he was required to have in order to go to Germany, but he did remember how much he brought with him and how much he had left when he returned to Iowa:

> My father gave me spending money. It was $1,000. I don't know where he got it from, but I'm pretty certain he had to borrow it. I spent all that money. I bought everything I could get my hands on. I was disappointed that I gave some money to an umpire, who was going to Ireland. [The Americans brought an umpire to Germany with them]. I wanted him to buy a gift for my mother, but I never saw that money again. When I returned to Iowa, I had only 35 cents left. But what a great time!

Given the situation the Americans decided to provide something for the paying public and an exhibition game between the members of the team was set for the final day of the Olympics in the massive Olympischen stadium. During the days leading up to their planned match, the team practiced, attended other Olympic sporting events, and organized clinics focusing on introducing baseball to the German audience and developing playing skills. Some members of the team, which was made up of young adults mainly in their early twenties, struggled to comprehend that Germany was staging the Games for little more than propaganda purposes. American second baseman McNeece, who was 20 years old at the time remembered that "when the Olympic teams marched into the stadium there were thousands of Nazi S.S. troops lining the road.... We thought they were honoring us."

Although baseball had only demonstration status, Hitler and his mistress, Eva Braun, were very interested in sport. Dow Wilson met the pair and told how "they both had this fixation with American ballplayers ... I never figured out why."

However, the German psychologist Dimitri Uznadze had a notion that baseball is rare in the sporting realm in that it is a game that offers the individual an exceptional level of opportunity to exhibit individual prowess—against another individual—within a team performance. This, together with baseball's nuances, subtle discipline, and numerous strategies appertaining to both the individual and the team, perhaps makes it understandable why it might appeal to someone whose life was premised on the notion of "one strong man." However, the German leader had never been a sportsman and also tended to see only that which he wanted to see (perhaps a trait of a mind inclined to fascism), the complexity of truth having the propensity to confound prejudice. As such he would almost certainly not have been able to comprehend how baseball relies on all team members supporting and working for each other; the batter and the pitcher being, only temporarily, the first among equals and constantly reliant on those around them; and the innate and detached justice of the rules of the game—the original meaning of democracy—*rule of the people, by the people, for the people* ... and the bit that sometimes gets forgotten ... *all the people!*

Wilson, who was oblivious to the political climate in Germany, talked to Hitler every day for quite a few days. Unaware of the Nazi leader's abhorrent beliefs, Wilson made small talk with the dictator about little things. Looking back almost 70 years after his encounter with the man who would bring so much suffering and hatred to the world, Wilson tried to explain why he was so nonchalant about the experience at the time. "I was 19, what do 19-year-olds talk about?" he said. "[Hitler] was polite and seemed like a nice man who obviously became a very bad man."

The baseball fascination was also very apparent with Eva Braun. At one point during the games, Braun sought out the U.S. team's captain. Pitcher Carson Thompson was chosen to meet her because he spoke some German. "She told me that Hitler had given her exclusive rights to do [a documentary on] the event and since baseball was an important event, she wanted background on the game," Thompson recalled in 1984.

The pitcher admitted that he was smitten by the attractive Braun. "She was the most fascinating woman I ever met," said Thompson. "She was beautiful with reddish brown hair. I couldn't figure out what she saw in that Hitler."

Herman Goldberg also met Hitler. The chance encounter occurred at a swimming event. Aware of the big picture, Goldberg would say years later, "[Hitler] was constantly grinning and raising his hand, obviously wanting to make the most of the Olympics to promote his cause."

The Olympic Game

On 12 August, at 8 p.m., the U.S. Olympic baseball team finally got to take the field. This one-game exhibition was the culmination of more than two weeks of demonstrations and clinics conducted by the Americans.

The squad was split into two sides, the World Amateurs and the U.S. Olympics. The weather was chilly for an August night. Herman Goldberg said years after the exhibition that the weather "turned chilly ... we didn't have jackets to go over our uniforms, so we were given blankets to keep us warm on the sidelines." Despite the unseasonal coolness, the first thing many of the players noticed was that the playing conditions were less than optimal. "The lights only went about 50 feet into the air," recalled U.S. outfielder Hanna. "I remember one ball went into the air and I had no idea where it was. It came down right into my glove."

In addition to this, there was no outfield fence and a cage was put around the home plate to minimize the chance that foul balls would hit unsuspecting spectators. The field also lacked a mound and the dimensions of the diamond were odd. Like the stadiums in Britain, the layout of the baseball field in Berlin had to be shoehorned inside a track. As a

At the 1936 Olympic Games in Berlin, baseball was a hit. A demonstration game on the final day of the event drew an estimated 125,000—the largest ever to a baseball game. (Each in attendance had a ticket like the one above.) Originally planned as an international tournament, the baseball demonstration ended up drawing just an American Olympic team, which competed in an intrasquad game for the German audience. The Americans did eventually get international competition, playing two contests in England—losing to West Ham but beating White City.

result, it was approximately 200 feet down the right field line while left field ran the full length of the stretch run of the 400 meter track. The strangest element to the setup was that Hitler's box was located ten feet inside fair territory in right field. Year later, U.S. pitcher Bill Sayles said that

> Before the game started a whole gaggle of German generals came down—I later recognized Goring as one of them. We were told that under no circumstances were we to hit a ball into right or right-center field. Well, being Americans, you never saw so many line drives hit to right in warm-ups.

Although many in attendance had little knowledge of the game, the crowd has been called the largest ever to watch a baseball match; an estimated 125,000 people were in attendance as the game was only one of the events that day at the stadium. To enhance the enjoyment of the spectators, the game's umpire, a Miami, Florida, man by the name of Tiny Parker, was very animated in calling balls and strikes thrown by the pitchers. But Parker didn't need to sell the game too much as the players put on a pretty compelling show. The exhibition was played for only seven innings rather than the usual nine-inning affair and was deadlocked 5–5 going into the final inning. Les "Rabbit" McNeece, the Florida write-in candidate of 1935, came to the plate and hit a ball past the outfielders. With no fence, the fleet-footed McNeece (hence the nickname "Rabbit") quickly ran around the bases to register an inside-the-park home run, giving the World Amateurs a 6–5 victory.

"The German crowd was not quite sure what had happened," McNeece told the *Sunshine Magazine* in 1994. "But they knew it was something good, so they applauded."

Following the match Dr. Carl Diem, the secretary of the German Organizing Committee, came down to the field to congratulate the players. He announced,

> I have come officially to advise you that this has been the finest demonstration of any sport that any nation has ever put on at any Olympic Games.... We congratulate you and speaking for my people, you have made over 100,000 friends here tonight and as you go home America's baseball players' praises will be sung by all.

Although baseball would not become an official Olympic sport until the 1992 Barcelona Games, it had been a true spectacle in 1936 and the players like Amen, McNeece, Wilson and Goldberg had made it so.

London's Pride

The 1936 European odyssey of America's Olympic baseball team did not end in Germany. Before the young men led by Leslie Mann returned to the United States, they visited in England to play a couple of exhibition games in London. It is unclear when these plans were made. Quite possibly, Mann—disappointed with the lack of competition in Germany—wanted to give his boys some real competition. As a key person in recruiting players for the London league, he had the connections to set up games and knew the caliber of the players his squad might come against. It is likely that he was curious to sample the best baseball England's embryonic professional leagues (something he had a hand in creating) had to offer. That meant playing the London Major Baseball League's two finest teams: the White City Citizens and the West Ham Hammers. Given the lack of a competitive challenge in Berlin, there is little doubt that by the time the American players got to London, they were literally looking to get their money's worth of competition.

But not all the Olympians would get that opportunity. Mann and his staff did not take the whole of the Olympic squad to Britain but picked a select group to make the trip to the British capital. Dow Wilson and Les McNeece, his friend from Mann's Miami baseball school and roommate throughout the European adventure, were both chosen. Wilson recollected: "It was a lot of fun. We went from one stadium to another. The games were well-attended. The games were good because the players who were over there from Canada could really play."

Wilson was not sure what the criteria was for picking the players to go on what the squad was to think of as a barnstorming tour of England, but he was not asked to be part of the team that went to London until the end of the Olympics. It is a matter of speculation, but Mann may have premised his choice on the likelihood of any given player to take on a contract in the British game—he was, after all, effectively an agent for John Moores' baseball ambitions and as such something of a midwife to the sport in England. After all, at least one player from the U.S.

132

team, Carson Thompson, would go on to play professionally in England the following year.

The Olympians saw little that was impressive in their match against White City and the home side was trounced 18–1. Part of the reason for this was perhaps the fact that the Citizens' top pitcher, "Bozo" Fisk, was unavailable. So it was that the Hammers were left to uphold the honor of London and British baseball. After such a one-sided victory against White City in the waning days of August 1936, the Americans must have felt confident when they entered West Ham Stadium in London's East End.

From the start it was clear that the U.S. team was not going to take it easy on West Ham. Mann's team selection included Fred Heringer, Stanford's star pitcher who had also pitched in the demonstration game in Berlin; Heringer would start the pitching for America. McNeece, who hit the game-winning home run at the Olympics, Jesse Owens's friend Wilson and Amen, the University of Nebraska standout, were also in the U.S. line-up. West Ham countered with its impressive starting nine. Jerry Strong, a top pitcher in the London Major Baseball League and Gladu recruit from Canada, was on the mound and future major leaguer Roland Gladu himself anchored the middle of the Hammers line-up.

The *East Ham Echo Mail and Chronicle,* a popular local newspaper in the East London area where the West Ham team was situated, reported the game on 28 August.

"HAMMERS" TOO GOOD FOR U.S. OLYMPIC BASEBALL TEAM
Brilliant Fielding
Prevents Runs
Victory of 5 to 3 Gives
Yankees A Headache
Jerry Strong "Fans" Four
By Homer

If you missed seeing the ball game at the West Ham diamond on Thursday when the all-star American team who had taken everything before them in the Olympic Games, were sadly trounced by the home town boys to the tune of five runs to three, it is a pity and your loss. Many a day will pass before another game of such high standard is seen.

The victory put West Ham on top of the baseball world and proved them to be an "ace-high" team, and coupled with the English Amateur Ice hockey victory in the Olympic Games, puts England in a position to claim the title of World champions at both hockey and ball.

What made the victory more than satisfactory was the fact that the Americans had put it across the White City side on the White City diamond in no mean fashion, the score box recording an eighteen to one victory in favor of the overseas visitors.

Free from arguments with either base or chief umpire, the game went along in the best style and in the opinion of several American visitors who came over with the team from Berlin, was on par with ball in America.

Pitching dominated through the first three innings as the Americans' Heringer and West Ham's Strong held opposing hitters scoreless.

In the fourth inning, the offensive fireworks began. McNeece hit a double and, after getting one out, Strong yielded a walk. With two runners on, Amen came to bat and didn't wait long to make an impact. On Strong's first pitch, Amen hit a home run to give the Olympians a 3–0 lead. But West Ham would not be intimidated by their opponents. The Hammers rallied to score three runs of their own thanks mainly to a single from Pam Yvon, the Hammers' French-Canadian second baseman, scoring two runners. The West Ham defense took over in the fifth inning. Yvon, the hitting hero an inning before, snagged a hard line drive for the first out and then Hammers outfielder Eric Whitehead, author of *Baseball for British Youth*, made two incredible plays. First, he ran some twenty yards to make a diving catch on what appeared to be a sure hit and then, a batter later, caught a second ball off his shoestrings in nearly the same spot as his first catch.

The *East Ham Echo* described the events:

> It was not until the fourth inning that the US Olympics went to the fore with three runs. The "Hammers" tied the score in their fourth, pegged another two in the fifth, and superb pitching, fielding and team work was rewarded with a string of eggs against the US line on the score board for their remaining inning.
>
> McNeece opened for the US in their fourth and hit a two bagger to centre field. In the previous visit, he had hit Strong for a three bagger. [Wilson], who followed, died at first, but the play advanced McNeece to the third, and a walk for Hubbard, saw Amen, the Yankee big hitter up with two men on.
>
> Loosening up at the plate, Amen made no mistake with the first delivery, slugging it way out into the far stand for a home run, scoring both McNeece and Hubbard.
>
> A strike out by Strong on Wagnon and a "shoe-sting" catch by Eric Whitehead, taken on the run in the deep, closed the US inning.

Yvon "Cleans-In" Two

> Turner, who had a perfect day at bat, set the home team going for their three in their fourth, scoring a single off a hit to centre field, but was forced out at second when Etheze hit to the third baseman. Roland Gladu made a mighty hit to the centre field, the ball falling short of the home run flag by inches, advancing Etheze to third. Both players took big lead-offs when Yvon, who has been doing such good work lately as "clean-up" man, took the plate. The "Hammers" second baseman drove a ball hard with a clean hit to the centre field to score both Etheze and Gladu and make first himself.
>
> Jerry Strong could not find the ball, and a short hit along to third base saw him out at first. Yvon making second on the play, to come home when a wild throw after a bunt by Irvine was made, the batter sliding second. The third out came when Whitehead failed at first, and the inning closed with scores tied.

Great Catching

Three miraculous catches put the US team out in as many minutes in their fifth. Yvon took the first, a hard line drive. The ball traveling between the left and centre field from Keegan saw Eric Whitehead run twenty yards and hold the catch as he rolled over, and as if to test the left field, Carlstan put a ball in practically the same spot, to find to his sorrow that the first was no fluke, and that his hit could be taken cleanly by Whitehead off his "shoe-strings."

Benefit of Errors

After a strike out on Eddie Gladu an error by short stop Wilson Dow [sic] allowed Simpson to make first in the second half of the fifth. He was advanced when Turner made a single base hit to centre field. Turner wisely returned to first when a Etheze hit was smartly gathered by the right field Clarence Keegan, but Simpson watched the throw and stole third. A run was clocked in when R. Gladu's hit to the right advanced Turner to second, and another error by short stop off Yvon's hit let in Turner, Gladu (R) sliding in safe at third. A long fly to the left field was held by Emmett Fore off Strong, and the side retired for two.

The momentum had shifted and the Olympians seemed to be shaken. West Ham had been quick to capitalize. In their half of the fifth inning, a key single by Roland Gladu and two errors by the American shortstop Wilson led to two runs. With the score now 5–3, West Ham had secured its first lead of the day. The question now was could they hold on?

"Homer" of *The Echo* further described:

More Brilliant Fielding

Simpson and Roland Gladu shone in the US sixth, Harry putting McNeece and Hubbard back on the water jug with catches at centre field, and Roland took one over his head from Amen. He repeated the performance in the following inning when Keegan made a similar hit. It was in this inning that Eddie Gladu twisted his ankle when endeavoring to take a catch on the run at right field from Heringer.

A Double Play

In their eighth and ninth visits the US boys tried everything they knew to tie-up the game but the home town boys were too hot in the field. A smart double play by Yvon and Turner saw the side retired in their eighth after McNeece had died at first. Amen hit hard along the carpet to Yvon, who gathered the ball, touched out the advancing Hubbard and threw in to Turner at first, cutting out Amen.

Great defense by the Hammers had demonstrated that the impossible could happen: A British side—granted, made up mainly of Canadians—could beat the Americans at their own game. The running catches by West Ham's Harry Simpson and Gladu in the sixth and then a double play in the eighth gave the West Ham faithful hope. In the ninth, onlookers held their breath as two long fly balls were hauled in the outfield as far as the stadium's speedway track. With two outs, Jerry Strong, who had pitched brilliantly all day, focused intently as he faced his opposing pitcher Heringer, who was now batting and had recorded a hit in his two previous at-bats. Strong proved too powerful, striking out the American to secure the victory. The *Echo* recorded the end: "Another catch by Eric Whitehead way out on the speedway track off Wagner and Fore and Heringer fanned by Jerry Strong, closed the US ninth for nil, leaving the 'Hammers' two runs ahead with the second half on the ninth in hand."

Box Score:

US Olympics

	AB	R	H	1st	2nd	3rd	TB
Keegan	4						
Carlstan	2						
McNeece	3	1	1		1		2
Wilson	3		1		1		2
Hubbard	3	1	1				4
*Amen	3	1	1				4
Wagnon	4						
Fore	4						
Heringer	3		1		1		2

Amen hit a home run in the 4th with two men on

West Ham

	AB	R	H	1st	2nd	3rd	TB
Simpson	4	1					
Turner	4	1	4	4			4
Etheze	3	1					
Gladu, R (capt.)	4	1	2	1	1		3
Yvon	4	1	2	2			2
Strong	4						
Irvine	4		1	1			1
Whitehead	4						
Gladu, E	2						

Runs brought in. Etheze and Gladu in the fourth by Yvon. Error off Irvine's bunt scored Yvon in the forth. Simpson by Gladu in the fifth and Turner by Yvon in the same innings.

Sacrifice hit by Etheze in the seventh.

Rawlings came in for injured Eddie Gladu in the seventh, but did not bat.

Pitching: Jerry Strong four strike outs, Heringer three strike outs.

US Olympics	0–0–0	3–0–0	0–0–0—3
West Ham	0–0–0	3–2–0	0–0–X—5

It is true that the Americans had won the hearts of the German fans, but they lost on the field in West Ham. At the same time, the Hammers had at last gone one better than White City. Both teams had played the 1936 United States Olympic baseball team, but West Ham had prevailed 5–3 while the Citizens were soundly defeated 18–1.

Young Americans in London

Both the games in London had been entertaining events and Dow Wilson remembered the London fans being highly amused on one specific play.

> The field we were playing on didn't have a dirt infield. It was all grass in between the bases. I decided to steal second base and started sliding pretty early because there was no dirt to slow me down. I must have started sliding halfway to second base. It was probably the longest slide in baseball history.

Wilson did not recall (unsurprisingly, seven decades later) at which venue this incident took place, but the description fits West Ham's famous lush turf. The British audience loved the show and greeted Wilson's seemingly awkward effort with thunderous laughter. Wilson was unsure about the level of baseball knowledge the cockney spectators had, so when he came up after his slide, he was not at all sure whether the fans had enjoyed the slide because of the pure spectacle it had offered, or because it was so different from a normal slide.

Although Wilson had no memories of fraternizing with any of the players on the British teams, he did remember the pitching he faced was good. He also remembered the unique nature of the baseball field configurations of the stadiums he and his colleagues visited. The fields were all grass and there were greyhound tracks running through the outfield. He had fond memories of hitting a home run over a fence onto a track. (Presumably, this occurred at White City since Wilson didn't hit a home run against the Hammers.) Wilson's family being in the greyhound business helped him to immediately recognize the fields as greyhound stadiums. Growing up he had "cooled down" many a dog. While in London he did watch a greyhound race and described it "as the same as out" in the United States.

Beyond playing baseball, Wilson and his teammates made the most out of their time in England. They were all young men; the oldest were in their early 20s. They were intrigued by the energy and excitement of London and in particular Piccadilly Circus. The players sampled the London nightlife in groups of five or six and on several occasions were out on the town until the crack of dawn. For an Iowa boy like Wilson, London must have seemed like another planet:

We all wanted to go to Piccadilly Circus. At the time, there were "women of the evening" around there. They would start following you and see if you wanted them to go to your room with them. One night, one of them was following me. I was with some of the other ballplayers. We stopped at 5 a.m. to get a milkshake, but she wouldn't leave me alone. All the other players were laughing. I had to tell her I wasn't taking her any place.

World Champions?

West Ham had done well but the idea that England could claim to be both baseball and Ice Hockey World Champions is not terribly convincing. At the Winter Olympics the Canadian and British ice hockey teams indulged in an all-out brawl, which had to be broken up and there was a serious question lingering as to why most of the British hockey players were actually Canadian. It is true that some were born in Britain like Scotland's Jimmy Foster, who would play for the West Ham Pirates baseball team in 1937 and also the Romford Wasps, but it seems the majority of the squad were French Canadian. This made the claim by *East Ham Echo* for England (not even "Great Britain") being the ice hockey world champions slightly spurious.

The American baseball team that met the Hammers included players who would play professionally in minor league baseball and university level stars. In fact, one of the Olympians, pitcher Bill Sayles, went on to appear in 28 games in the major leagues (although it's unclear if he joined the team on the England leg of the trip). The U.S. Olympic team was a top-level amateur squad and West Ham fans could be justifiably proud to have bettered them. Following the 1936 Games and the subsequent trip to London, the U.S. Olympians returned to America with great fanfare. Although there were no medals awarded in Berlin to the U.S. side because baseball was a demonstration sport, New York City mayor Fiorello LaGuardia presented each player with a commemorative gold medal. With the American team's loss to West Ham, maybe silver medals would have been more appropriate.

What happened to the Olympians?

In 1937 Carson Thompson played in the London Major Baseball League for the Romford Wasps, and another member of that 1936 U.S. Olympic Team, Henry Wagnon, an outfielder and catcher, appeared over a three-year period for the University of Georgia baseball and football teams and was the captain of the Georgia baseball team in 1936. According to the University of Georgia's Web site, he was drafted three times—twice by the New York Yankees and once by the Detroit Tigers. For all this, Wagnon turned down professional offers to pursue a coaching career.

Herman Goldberg spent a short spell in spring training with the Detroit Tigers before playing for the Buffalo Bisons. But he quit baseball to return to school at Columbia University's Teachers College to take his master's degree in education of the deaf. He was a classroom teacher in New York from 1939 to 1948, and at the same time coached baseball at the New York School for the Deaf. He moved on to Rochester, New York, where he became coordinator of instruction, director of special education, and between 1963 and 1971, superintendent of schools.

In 1960, 1961 and 1963, the baseball Olympian went to Bologna, Italy, as a Fulbright professor and helped with that country's baseball development. Being fluent in Italian, Goldberg was able to teach the game and ran courses at the University of Bologna like a well-informed local. While he was in Rome, he visited the 1960 Olympics where he caught up with an old friend from twenty-four years earlier: Jessie Owens.

In 1971, Herman became the United States associate commissioner for elementary and secondary education for the Department of Health, Education, and Welfare (later the Department of Education). Goldberg was to remain a government employee for seventeen years, rising to the heady heights of assistant secretary of education, Office of Special Education and Rehabilitative Services. Herman worked at the Department of Education during the civil rights era and one of his assignments involved managing the funds for the desegregation of the segregated school systems in the United States, a massively challenging task and one that called for sensitivity and diplomacy, but also a firm and determined focus.

At the end of the 20th century Herm Goldberg lived, semi-retired, outside Washington, working as an educational consultant for ERGO Associates, Inc. He spent much of his time writing and reading textbooks for junior high and high school students, using a specialist process he had developed. He attended services at Temple Sinai in D.C.; he thought of himself as "an active Jew," and continued to be interested in learning more about Jewish issues and participated as a donor in Jewish fund-raising every year.

Following the Olympics, Les "Rabbit" McNeece, the speedy infielder who hit the game-winning home run in Berlin, turned down a basketball scholarship to Louisiana State University in order to play professional baseball.

He signed with the Brooklyn Dodgers, who sent him to their Louisville Colonels farm club. His salary: $350 a month. But McNeece fell on hard baseball times. Early in his first season, he was hit in the head by a pitch and sat out most of the season.

The following year, McNeece's contract was sold to the St. Louis

Cardinals. The move included a pay cut to $125 a month as he was assigned to Daytona Beach in the Florida State League. Alas, poor McNeece suffered another injury. He broke his leg and tore knee and ankle ligaments on a slide into second base. The injury ended his baseball career.

Never bitter, McNeece returned to his hometown of Fort Lauderdale, married his sweetheart, and ran the family dry cleaning business until his death in 1994.

When Dow Wilson returned to the U.S., he attended college at the University of Nebraska and set his sights on trying to get to, as he called it, "the big show." He had a workout in Boston and after discussions with some teams was poised to sign with the Cleveland Indians. But fate would not smile brightly on Wilson's major league aspirations: "On the day I got my contract offer from the Indians, I got a draft notice from the army. In one hand I had the contract, and in the other the draft notice. I had to go into the army."

Wilson would spend six years in the army and had a very successful military career, rising to the rank of lieutenant colonel. But the pay was not major league money. "I got $21 a month," he recollected. Wilson never went overseas to fight Hitler but after training, he commanded a battery of artillery guns on the Delaware shore. The guns guarded a port that was used to escort foreign neutral ships coming in from the high seas.

As for his run-in with Hitler, Wilson said it sometimes came up "in passing" with fellow soldiers. "I never tried to keep it a secret," he said. "But I didn't carry on too much conversation about it."

By the time Wilson was discharged, his playing days were over. Nevertheless, his baseball experience in Europe was always close to his heart. Following his time in the military, Dow relocated to Long Island, New York, and worked as a salesman in the textile industry. He would regularly commute into New York City where his office was, but he would also go down to the South often for work. For seventeen years after his stint in the military he would drive down from Long Island to visit his parents in Florida. On those trips, he would meet up with his old teammate Les McNeece and talk about their baseball times in England and Germany.

In 2005, at the age of 87, Wilson's European baseball journey remains at the forefront of his mind. To that end, he still keeps a detailed scrapbook of his adventures in England and Germany.

"That was a big time in my life," he remembers wistfully.

The West Ham bequest

As London's winter in 1936 sent professional baseball into hibernation, Britain's King Edward VIII abdicated following an eruption of a constitutional crisis over the king's plans to marry the American divorcee Mrs. Wallis Simpson. In the U.S. elections, America chose to re-elect Franklin Roosevelt as president, and in doing so probably saved the world from a much longer war than the one that was on its way. The year had also seen Charlie Chaplin's film *Modern Times* break a number of cinematic barriers, as well as the publication of Margaret Mitchell's classic novel *Gone with the Wind*.

With its victory over the Americans, West Ham had been triumphant in two battles. Not only had they taken the biggest baseball scalp in the country that year, but they also won the fight at the turnstiles as no team in the London Major Baseball League seemed to be able to draw the kind of attention that West Ham could command. Even more importantly, there were already signs that baseball was making a lasting impact on the West Ham sporting scene. As the first season of West Ham baseball ended on 6 September 1936 and the weather began to chill, one would have expected that those exposed to baseball in London's East End to immediately return to the area's first love—soccer. But the game had resonated with many of the children who had attended West Ham games. Custom House was not empty during the London Major Baseball League's off-months as groups of players used the stadium through autumn and right through the frigid winter. West Ham player Eric White-head recounted in his book:

> Every Sunday, rain, hail or snow saw a group of these budding ball players racing around the huge empty stadium in preparation for the coming summer season. To the experienced ball player, cold and rain are elements that simply do not mix with baseball and are much better left alone. But this eager group of youngsters seemed entirely oblivious to the terrible weather conditions in which they were learning. They had their hearts set on learning baseball by the time summer came along and were certain they were going to do it. We who went along to advise and coach used to wince inwardly as a hard, wet ball came into sharp contact with cold, stinging hands and fingers. Every time those youngsters caught or hit a ball it must have hurt. But they did not seem to care.
>
> Two teams especially, the West Ham Pioneers and the West Ham Boys, did what I thought no person, no matter how enthusiastic they might be, would ever do. They practiced right through a dismal winter in all weathers and emerged in the spring as teams that enjoyed baseball thoroughly, and understood and played it astonishingly well.

With East End children taking up the game with gusto and thousands of people going to the Hammers' games the future did appear very bright for the "Babes in Red."

The Canadian Babe

Roland Edouard Gladu was born in Montreal, Quebec, on 10 May 1911. From a young age, Gladu had confidence in his own abilities. Blessed with strong hands and the natural hand-eye coordination necessary to be a great hitter, he developed his skills on the sandlots of Montreal earning pocket money from his performances. Gladu started playing organized baseball at the age of 17 for Homer Cabana in Granby, Quebec, in a semi-professional league. The statistics of this time have disappeared, but Gladu played well enough to gain a strong local reputation. The short, stocky young man signed his first professional contract at Binghamton, New York. Then 18 years old, he lasted just three weeks before being released. It was not his athletic talent that betrayed him, but the fact that, like many young French-Canadians of his background at that time, he was unable to speak English. Undeterred, he signed with a pro team in Johnstown, Pennsylvania, within the week, but was again released for the same reason. Years later Gladu simply recalled that when he first arrived in the States, no one was able to understand him.

Nevertheless, the young Gladu didn't allow his American setbacks to derail the development of his baseball career. He returned to Canada, gaining valuable experience in the Provincial League with the Forrest Freres. His performance was impressive enough to earn him a spot with the Montreal Royals,[41] one of the greatest Canadian teams of that era. Beginning in 1939, the Royals of the prestigious International League were the top minor league affiliate for the Brooklyn Dodgers and had a loyal following. For any player in Quebec, the thought of playing for the Royals must have been as exciting as playing for a second-division major league team.

Showing a fearlessness that would mark him throughout his time in baseball, Gladu just showed up at a Montreal Royals open practice one day in 1930. He was just 19 years old but wowed the team's officials. The Royals signed him, but didn't have him play for the team in the International League until 1932. That year, he showed his prowess hitting a

142

game-winning, pinch-hit home run on the final day of the season. According to the Official Baseball Guide for 1932, he had four hits in 17 at-bats that year. For a player of his age to see action in what was a top minor league circuit was an impressive feat. Yet, Gladu failed to stick with the club in pre-season camp in 1933, and although he would eventually make it back to the Royals, he was released before the start of the season. Because of Gladu's hitting ability, the Royals did try hard to find a place for him. For example, Frank Shaughnessy, the Royals manager, attempted to convert Gladu into a catcher in an effort to compensate for his slowness on the basepaths and in the field. But Gladu ultimately returned to the outfield and was farmed to Richmond, where he batted .283. Despite the demotion, Gladu did not lose his self-confidence as a player and held his own

ROLAND GLADU.
Babe Ruth of Canadian Baseball,
and West Ham " star."

Roland Gladu (above) was sold as British baseball's biggest star. This picture ran in newspapers both in the London area and up north where West Ham toured. As far as the British fans could tell, Gladu lived up to his Ruthian billing. Moreover, he did make it to the majors thanks to a sweet swing from the left side of the plate. Photograph originally appeared in *The Express;* used here with permission of Archant.

in the Piedmont League. According to author William Brown in his book *Baseball's Fabulous Royals*: "Gladu was a serious man who seldom cracked a smile. He devoted most of his energy to hitting. He had tremendous discipline at the plate, rarely swinging at bad pitches, and he was hard on himself when he wasn't swinging the way he felt he should."

This seems to reflect how much Roland was a "made-player." His consummate professional focus made up for what he lacked in terms of natural athleticism. Although he was not born with the grace and physique of many great players, he was gifted with strength, concentration and intelligence; he made the most of these attributes and molded himself to the requirements of his sport.

Montreal Royals teammate Kermit Kitman was particularly impressed with Gladu's hitting ability. "He would hit everything where it was pitched," said Kitman in *Baseball's Fabulous Royals*. "If it was outside, he'd line it to left-centre. He had a beautiful swing." Mordecai Richler, who is considered one of Montreal's greatest writers, interviewed Kitman in 1978 for *From Gladu, through Kitman*. Kitman by that time was "a prospering partner" for a company in the garment industry. Even then, Kitman was still in awe of Gladu saying, "If I could hit pitchers like Gladu, I wouldn't be in the needle trade today."

Despite such high praise, Gladu was still grinding it out in the low minors by the mid–1930s. Gladu went back to Quebec in 1935, in the new Quebec Provincial League which had been established after 11 years of disordered competition. The Provincial League in Québec, at times an outlaw league, rustling outside the control of Major League Baseball, was a league with an impressive history. According to Peter Bjarkman, author of *Diamonds Around the Globe: The Encyclopedia of International Baseball*, the Provincial League was "[b]est known as a progressive champion of Native American and black players during its heyday as a preintergration rebel circuit." At times the league recruited U.S. college players (allegedly paying them, according to Bjarkman). The circuit also briefly had a team of native Mohawks from the Caughnawaga reservation.

During its history, the league also had at least one great hockey player in its midst. Much like England where hockey stars also took to the diamond, the Provincial League included Maurice "The Rocket" Richard, the Hall of Fame Montreal Canadians hockey player, who—for a time— used baseball as an off-season way to keep in shape. The star hockey player hit for considerable power, playing third base and the outfield, according to French-Canadian baseball expert Christian Trudeau.

Despite being in the comfort zone playing in a competitive league in his home province, Gladu, who proved that he either had an itinerant soul or, at the least, a willingness to go anywhere to make a living at the sport of baseball, received an interesting—if not strange—offer before the 1936 season. Gladu recalled:

> At the time it was a depression. It was hard to find a job and if you got a job, you were getting eight or ten dollars a week. I read in the papers that they were starting to play baseball in England, and about a week later somebody asked me if I would like to go to England, so I said "why not." I helped sign four or five Canadians and we built up the field and we had a pretty good time. I played in West Ham Stadium in London.

Parlez-vous Français?

Roland Gladu still spoke little English when he got to London. Nevertheless, he rapidly acquired an extensive acquaintance with the language and even developed a fondness for English literature. Although West Ham would be his team, L.D. Wood and, most likely, John Moores saw Gladu's self-made understanding of the game and employed him as a traveling coach. He would travel around England teaching baseball to British children.

Although Gladu restricted himself to participating in, promoting, and instructing baseball while in England, he was enterprising in his efforts to make money and spent time in the off-season playing hockey in Belgium. Undoubtedly, French speakers in Belgium probably made him feel far more comfortable than the cockney-accented English of West Ham.

Gladu was not one to complain. While he was willing to offer constructive criticism about his experiences in West Ham, he first emphasized that his experience in England was a good opportunity. In 1938, he reflected on his time with the Hammers. "I liked it fine," he told the *Montreal Gazette*. "The only drawbacks are the weather and lack of suitable stadiums. It is too chilly and damp. I wore two sweaters under my baseball shirt most of the time. At most fields, the spectators are too far away from the diamond."

For all this, he was well loved by the West Ham fans. A big question about Gladu's time in West Ham is whether he was the only player from his family to make the trip to England. Programs of the time reflect that an Eddie (also called Eric) Gladu, a first baseman, was also with West Ham about the same time as Roland (he would also play for the Hackney Royals in 1936). Although this player had the same surname as Roland, there's no evidence that they are related, according to Christian Trudeau. News accounts during that era indicate that Gladu did have at least two brothers, Roger and Rene, but there is no indication that there was another Gladu sibling by the name Eddie or Eric. Eddie could have been a cousin or some other sort of relative, but according to Trudeau the "other Gladu" might have been using a pseudonym. Certainly, there would have been many sportsmen in the East End who might have wanted to earn some extra cash by playing baseball.

While Gladu was a West Ham man through and through, he was not averse to picking up a game for a little extra money. In 1937, Gladu played at least one game for the Sheffield Dons in the Yorkshire League. By this point Gladu must have been a draw. After all, papers throughout England had dubbed him "the Babe Ruth of Canada." Teams were probably willing to give him a nice bonus to compete—if even for one night—for their squad. Still, Gladu appears to have remained loyal to Wood and the Hammers until his return to Canada.

One wonders whether Gladu's game was enhanced by his time in Britain. He'd already played at the top echelon of minor league baseball. At least one of his teammates was in awe of Gladu's ability. The Hammers' Eric Whitehead used Gladu as the ultimate example of how a hitter should approach the game in his book *Baseball for British Youth*:

> Perhaps the finest batter who has ever played for an English team, and certainly the possessor of as perfect a batting style as anyone in baseball was Roland Gladu [a left hander]. This was his religion and recipe for successful batting—be relaxed. Take a full, natural swing, making full use of your wrists, meeting the ball out in front of you. Glue your eyes to the ball from the moment it leaves the pitcher's hand. Those few simple points contain all the important fundamentals of batting.

While Gladu's hitting was probably already well-developed by the time he got to England, he did use his time with West Ham to add versatility to his defensive repertoire. At various times Gladu pitched, caught, played first, short, or in the outfield for West Ham. At the plate, the area where he excelled, he could not have found the British game too daunting. Not surprisingly, Gladu's stats in Great Britain from the 1937 season illustrated what a dominant hitter he was. The left-handed batter led the league in hitting, registering a gaudy .565 batting average.

After his two seasons in England, Gladu decided it was time to return to North America and try again to break into the major leagues. While the pitching he faced in England probably didn't help hone his hitting craft, his performance must have enhanced his confidence. Upon returning to Canada, he asked the Royals for another shot at the team and Montreal agreed. In the spring of 1938, he was again in camp with the top minor league club. In an interview with Montreal reporter J. L. McGowan, who was attending the Royals training camp in Lake Wales, Florida, Gladu said that if he did not make the Royals that year, he planned to look for a role as a player-manager. But McGowan was of the opinion that Gladu would "remain in organized Ball and that the Royals will have no great difficulty placing him in Class A or B company should he fail to make the grade with Montreal."

Gladu's time in England didn't appear to hurt his chances to make the Royals that spring. In fact, the team's management enjoyed ribbing the French-Canadian Gladu about his experience in London's East End. According to McGowan, when Gladu "dropped into the Royals' office, to talk things over. Guy Moreau, business manager of the club, remarked: 'First thing you know, we'll be having ball players with cockney accents'." It would seem that Roland had at least brought something back from the Docklands.

Even if England had not made Gladu a better ballplayer, it did help him become a more experienced and worldly individual. When Gladu met with Moreau, Gladu—who had suffered early in his career because of a lack of skill in the English language and still had little comprehension in the language when he arrived in West Ham—was carrying a book by George Bernard Shaw.

Regardless of Gladu's newfound maturity, Montreal reporter J. L. McGowan was sanguine about Gladu's prospects for cracking the Royals' 1938 roster because of Gladu's great talent hitting. "Baseball being a game of averages," McGowan wrote, "[Royals] Manager Rabbit Maranville may have a hard time keeping Gladu off the club."

But that type of optimism had to be tempered by the fact that Gladu remained a sub-standard fielder. Despite his versatility in England—and being noted for making a number of sterling plays at shortstop while a member of the Hammers—he would be expected to at least be an average fielder at one position in the States. Whether this would occur was questionable.

Montreal columnist Dink Carroll wrote snidely that when Gladu was in the outfield Maranville "was afraid Roland was going to be crowned [hit in the head] every time a ball was wafted in his direction."

Ever the realist, Gladu recognized his defensive deficiencies. He confessed,

> I wasn't worrying about my hitting. My fielding, though, on long run it gets on your nerves. In the outfield, I would have a lot of trouble yes; but at third base I could get along pretty good. I had a lot of courage there. I wasn't afraid to get in front of balls, things like that.

Royals manager Rabbit Maranville, a 23-year major league veteran who was inducted into the Baseball Hall of Fame in 1954, was openly concerned about Gladu's fielding but was willing to give him a shot as a hitter.

Gladu broke into the Royals' line-up in an exhibition game against Buffalo on March 30 and went a solid 1-for-2. Playing half the game in center field, he acquitted himself gracefully, and he helped Maranville's men maul the Bisons.

Despite the performance, Gladu couldn't stick with the club in 1938. Instead, over the next few years, Gladu marked time a little, kicking around the Provincial League,[42] which turned out to be a lucky turn of fate. While plying his trade with Quebec City, he met Del Bissonette, a former member of the Brooklyn Dodgers who served as Quebec's player-manager. Although Roland had been a teacher while in West Ham, he had never been exposed to great coaches himself. Bissonette was the first manager ever to truly help Gladu improve his craft. "I never had anybody to coach me; how to steal bases or anything," Gladu recalled. "I used to go to the movies and watch the news, and pick up a few things here and there. I liked Ted Williams and I tried to copy his style. The only one who ever taught me anything was Del Bissonette. I wish I had met him when I was younger."

Like many left-handed hitters, Gladu had difficulty hitting against left-handed pitchers. Bissonette worked with Gladu on improving his game against lefties, and also helped him work on hitting a curveball.

In 1940, Gladu finished with the third highest batting average in the Provincial League. However, the league failed. Still, Quebec and Gladu remained in baseball with the Canada-American League and he had two good seasons before the United States entered the Second World War.

In 1941, Gladu played for the Quebec Athletics (teaming up with his old mentor, Del Bissonette) in the Can-Am League and was named to the league's all-star team. When the 1941 season concluded, the United States was not yet involved in the worldwide conflict. But as the 1942 season approached, America had responded to the bombing of Pearl Harbor by declaring war on Japan and Germany. President Roosevelt wrote to the baseball commissioner, Judge Kenesaw Mountain Landis, on 15 January 1942, authorizing professional baseball to continue, as it was necessary for the morale of the country. Baseball would face many changes during the war, including the move north for spring training sites, in order to conserve the resources used in travel.[43]

The 1943 season remains a mystery in the career of Gladu, but the relationship he had created with Bissonette in Quebec proved to be the key to Gladu's big league opportunity in 1944. Following his years in Canada, Bissonette was recruited to work as a minor league manager in the Boston Braves organization. When Boston told Bissonette they were looking for wartime cover at third base, he knew he had the perfect man. Although not a strong fielder, Gladu had been a consistent .300 hitter during his years with Quebec and Bissonette knew Gladu would be able to hit at the major league level.

Gladu was keen to make the most of the opportunity and when he got to spring training he was eager to please. Although stocky at 185 pounds and 5 feet, 8.5 inches, the 33-year-old Gladu, who had told his new employers that he was actually 30, expressed a willingness to do anything to stick with the squad. Ultimately, that was his undoing. At spring training, Gladu agreed to throw batting practice. The exertion involved in the task led to strain and concluded in Gladu damaging his left arm. After a while, he was having trouble throwing the ball to first base, and it started to bother him when he swung the bat. This did not augur well for a third baseman who was going to be expected to get the ball across the diamond.

PARADE SPORTIVE
PAUL STUART
LE PREMIER PROGRAMME DU GENRE
Interviews des Célébrités de tous les Sports   Correspondance: 4314 St-André, Montreal, 34
SPORTez-vous bien !

Roland GLADU

Roland Gladu was West Ham's biggest star. The French-Canadian Gladu could boast having one of the most unique professional careers. After playing two pro seasons for West Ham, Gladu returned to North America and would eventually make it to the major leagues with the Boston Braves in 1944.

Nevertheless, Gladu broke pre-season camp with the Boston Braves. But it was apparent that he was having problems with the injury. Roland made five errors in 15 games at third base with the Braves (in total, he would play 22 games for the Boston team). His fielding percentage was .851, well below what was expected of a major league third baseman. However, as a hitter, he did show glimpses of what allowed him to make it to the pinnacle of baseball. In the season's opening game at the Polo Grounds against the New York Giants, Gladu connected for a triple which scored the Braves' only run in a 2–1 loss. "There was no doubt about it," Gladu said. "I could hit Big League pitching." But in the end, he was not given very long to show his potential. His record for the Braves shows that he played his first game on 18 April 1944, and his last on 24 May of the same year. He got only 66 at-bats and his batting average of .242 was not too impressive. As a result, he was demoted to the Braves' Eastern League club in Hartford, Connecticut, after only five weeks. When he joined Hartford his injury dictated that he could not play third base any more. But his shoulder healed, and he posted a .372 average.

As a reflection of the watered-down talent playing major league baseball during the Second World War, several of his Hartford teammates had seen immediate service in the big leagues. Among them were Vince Shupe, who played one year (1945) for the Braves, batting .269, and Steve Shemo, who played in 35 games for the Braves in 1944–45.

Gladu could have dropped his head at missing out on his big chance in the majors. Instead, he dominated at Hartford. He played 119 games for the Laurels and finished second in the race for the league's top hitter. Thanks in large part to Gladu's performance, Hartford was a dominant side that was later dubbed by baseball historians Bill Weiss and Marshall Wright as one of the top 100 teams in minor league baseball history. Granted, the standard of play in professional baseball was not at its highest at the time, but Hartford's ascendancy was notable. The team finished with 99 wins and just 38 loses. Hartford's best batters in 1944 were first baseman Shupe (.339, 109 RBI), Gladu (.372, 102 RBI) and Stan Wentzel (.323).

While with Hartford, Gladu achieved the notable feat of hitting three home runs in a double-header at Norfolk (in the Eastern League). He swatted two in the first game and ended Norfolk's 20-game winning streak at home. He walked four times during the afternoon.

Although Gladu shone in Hartford following his demotion from the Braves in 1944, the return of big league players from the war had a domino effect and the Braves no longer needed Gladu's services. The Royals jumped at the chance to get the sweet-swinging left-handed hitter back, and bought Gladu's contract from the Braves for $10,000. In the 1945 season, alongside the likes of Jean-Pierre Roy who pitched for the Brooklyn Dodgers briefly in 1946, Gladu was quick to make an impact, hitting a home run in his first at-bat of the campaign. He would go on to be one of the team's true stars. He played in every one of the Royals' 153 games and led the celebrated International League in hits (204), doubles (45) and triples (14). Kermit Kitman, a teammate of Gladu's that season, suggested that Roland could have also won the batting average title if he had not been influenced by a letter from a female fan. "[Gladu] showed me a letter one day from a girl who said she couldn't understand why he never hit any home runs," Kitman recalled. "Roland told me, 'I'm going to show you what happens when you try to hit home runs.'"

Gladu proceeded to hit nearly a half-dozen homers during the next seven or eight games, but his average dropped. He ended up finishing second in the batting title chase.

With Montreal that season, Gladu earned the elusive title he could not obtain in West Ham as the Royals won the regular season crown in the very competitive International League (95–58 .621). But it was during this period with the Royals that Gladu lost the person he had come to call his biggest fan. Gladu was devastated when his brother Roger died in a fire in Montreal in mid–September of 1945 while the Royals were battling to earn a spot in the finals of the Governor's Cup.[44]

The Royals had been beaten in the first game of a play-off series against the Baltimore Orioles in mid–September in front of 17,000 of their own supporters in DeLorimier Stadium. Montreal had leveled in the second game before the series moved to Baltimore, where, on Saturday, the third game would be played. Just a few hours prior to the game, Gladu was woken in his hotel room by the telephone call that informed him his brother Roger had been killed the previous day. He had to put the receiver down for a while and allow himself to take in the awful reality. He then returned the call to find out that the conflagration that took his younger sibling had started from an explosion in a factory on the street where Roger lived. He had been one of the four people who were killed and 50 more were injured, including 30 schoolchildren who were passing the factory at the point when the explosion happened. Despite the terrible news, Roland decided to play the first two games in Baltimore and then return to Montreal for the funeral. An emotional Gladu played a major role in the Royals' 8–1 win in Game 3, driving in three runs. The following day he went 3-for-4, but Baltimore had an easy 19–4 victory.

The best-of-seven-game series was squared at 2–2 and it seemed that Montreal would need to play the fifth game without Gladu. However, rain obliged a postponement of the series for 48 hours and Roland returned in time to join his teammates and score what might have been a vital seventh-inning run. Alas, there were no heroics that day as the Orioles ruined the compelling movie ending by dispatching the Royals. With his team facing elimination, Roland vowed before the next game to hit a home run in honor of his brother. He was not able to do that, but he took a leading part in his team's exciting 1–0 defeat of their foe.

A crowd in excess of 22,000 packed into the DeLorimier Stadium (and around 10,000 fans were turned away) on Sunday afternoon for what would be the deciding game. The Royals held on to a 2–1 lead into the eighth, when Roland fulfilled his vow, smashing a two-run hit high above the scoreboard to give the Royals a place in the final where the Newark Bears waited. This was a seminal moment for Gladu and he dedicated his play in the finals to the memory of his fallen brother.

Against Newark the bats went silent in the first three games. The Royals scored just five runs and stranded a dismal 31 base runners. The result: the Royals dropped all three games. However, they got back into the series by winning the fourth game 5–4 and the fifth game 7–2. On a freezing night, in front of 15,000 shivering DeLorimier faithful, the Royals had a chance to even the series. Going into the ninth Newark led 10–8 and it seemed that they were about to score one more run as Dick Baker led off with a double and attempted to advance to third on a fly ball. He arrived spikes first and high, slicing into Lee Hart, the third baseman. Baker was called out by the umpire. Hart leaped at Baker, which led to the benches clearing. With some fans joining the fracas, the police were summoned to the field to control the situation. However, it seems that the melee ruffled the visitors and the home side took the match 11–10 to force a seventh game.

For all this, apart from Gladu, who was 2-for-3, the Royals' bats froze in the deciding game and Montreal went down 5–1. It was a sad conclusion after the drama of the preceding game at which point the team had fought back from a nine-run deficit and 3–0 down in the series. For many who had thrilled and suffered with their team it was as if they had been robbed of a place in the 1945 Junior World Series.[45] But 397,517 had witnessed their efforts that season, nearly twice the number of fans who had attended games the previous season. The play-offs for the Governors' Cup had attracted 60,000 spectators. For a native son like Gladu the Montreal crowd resembled a family; to that extent they were not unlike those who supported the Hammers of West Ham. They rejoiced with their club in victory and suffered with them in defeat. Although Roland might be seen by some as having, in some ways, missed the boat in baseball, it has to be said that he was a player who knew how to pick his fans.

In the spring of 1945, as Montreal's leading hitter (although he knew his age and poor defensive ability was against him) Gladu became one of the first players to be signed with a new professional league; Gladu, agreed to jump to Jorge Pasquel's Mexican League. As Gladu had demonstrated his willingness to move to parts unknown a decade earlier with his adventures with West Ham, he once more showed he was ready to go to appreciable lengths for a good baseball job. But he was not alone. The new outlaw circuit attracted a number of major leaguers, including Brooklyn Dodgers catcher Mickey Owen, New York Giants pitcher Sal Maglie, and St. Louis pitcher Max Lanier, all of whom either had been or would become major league all-stars. But the decision turned out to be a bad one for Gladu. Pasquel, with the help of his brother Alfonso, was attempting to turn the Mexican League into a mirror image of its major league counterparts in the U.S. The Americans did not like the idea of competition from the Mexico and Major League Baseball commissioner Albert B. "Happy" Chandler slapped a lifetime ban on the players who had moved to the Mexican League; as far as professional baseball in the U.S. and Canada was concerned, Gladu and his migrating compatriots were denounced as renegades overnight.

Beyond the impact the outlaw circuit had on Gladu, the tale of the Mexican League is a fascinating one. Even before Jorge Pasquel made his bid to turn the Mexican League into a league on par with America's big leagues, he was a key player in the circuit's operations. Pasquel and Alfonso had a controlling interest in the Veracruz Blues and, according to author Peter Bjarkman, the siblings were also partial owners of a number of other clubs in the league.

Pasquel's motives for setting up the Mexican League are unknown to this day as the baseball mogul died in a plane crash in March 1955 before a reliable account of his purposes could be established. The man was certainly a baseball fan. According to Bjarkman's book, *Diamonds Around the Globe: The Encyclopedia of International Baseball,* Pasquel "had been a sandlot player as a youth and loved to take batting practice with the Veracruz club he directed. Like George Steinbrenner and dozens of modern big league club owners, Jorge Pasquel was apparently living out the fantasy of ball club ownership enjoyed by more than one wealthy businessman in possession of the ultimate grown boy's toy chest." But other undercurrents in Mexican politics at the time suggested another reason for Pasquel's efforts to lure major leaguers into the Mexican League. According to Bjarkman, the outlay for top talent was part of an elaborate plan to aid his business partner and childhood friend Miguel Aleman in his bid for the country's presidency.

"Aleman's election promised a windfall of preferential treatment for Pasquel's business interests, and any bolstering of big-time baseball by the Aleman-Pasquel camp could not fail to impress a baseball-crazed Mexican electorate," Bjarkman wrote.

Before the 1946 campaign, Jorge Pasquel became president of the eight-team Mexican League that consisted of Veracruz, Monterrey, Tampico, Torreon, Puebla, San Luis Potosi, Nuevo Laredo and Mexico City. Pasquel immediately began his efforts to attract experienced major league players south. But when Roland and the other North Americans got to Mexico for the 1946 season, they quickly found that the conditions were not good.

Many players complained about the fields and accommodations, but Roland took it all in stride, just as he had approached the conditions in England. "Playing in Mexico was all right for the money, compared to what they were paying in the National League," Gladu said. "The fields in some of the cities were not too good. The lights were terrible. When you had to face Maglie or Lanier under those lights, you could hardly see the ball. It was no joke."

The move to Mexico effectively ended any outside chance Gladu would ever have at returning to the major leagues. Although whether he could have made a return was questionable. Famed baseball executive Branch Rickey told the *New York Times* on 24 February 1946, about Gladu's Mexican move: "Gladu's decision was different from [Brooklyn Dodger prospect Luis] Olmo and [Jean Pierre] Roy. Gladu is not, nor will be a Major League player. He is 32 years old and the offer he received was very tempting. I don't blame him for accepting it." Still, Gladu's decision to leave the Royals also meant that he missed a brush with one of baseball's, and American culture's, biggest events. In 1946, when Gladu was playing in the Mexican League, the Montreal Royals, as the minor league affiliate for the Brooklyn Dodgers, added Jackie Robinson to its roster. Robinson quickly became a crowd favorite, leading the Royals to victory in the Junior World Series that same year.

Robinson would go on to break the major league's color barrier the following season. Baseball had been "white-only" throughout its 20th century professional history and Robinson's ascension to the big league marked a first monumental, albeit small, step in the move toward an integrated society in the USA. But before Robinson made history in the Major Leagues, he did so in Montreal.[46]

Roland did well in the Mexican League, hitting a robust .322 in his two seasons south of the American border. However, following the 1946 election, which Aleman won, the huge salaries promised by Pasquel were not being paid out. "Fabulous salaries tendered to imported players were cut by as much as half," according to Bjarkman. "The actual fact of the matter may only have been that Pasquel, for all his wealth, had largely overcommitted himself and was suddenly fresh out of pocket money to throw willy-nilly at baseball."

The Pasquel brothers' checks seemed to develop a rubber coating and as they bounced Roland was obliged to move on. In the winter of

1946, Gladu went to Cuba. Before the rise of Fidel Castro, players of all nationalities came to battle it out against some serious competition in this baseball hotbed. Roland played for one of Cuba's most distinguished clubs, Del Club Cienfuegos.

But for the prodigal players—particularly the best of the bunch—there was eventually forgiveness. Pitcher Max Lanier ended up being banned for only a single season and was back with the St. Louis Cardinals in 1949. Sal Magile returned to pitching in the majors in 1950 with the New York Giants and catcher Mickey Owen, who had played with the Brooklyn Dodgers before taking the money in Mexico, joined the Chicago Cubs in 1949.

It's unclear if Gladu would have received the same treatment or whether he was seriously considered for a spot on a big league roster. As for the Mexican League, Bjarkman reported that the league lost a total $400,000 over the period between 1947 and 1948; in 1948, the league had dwindled to four teams with all the circuit's games being played in Mexico City.

Throughout his journeying Gladu never let his professionalism slip away. Jean-Pierre Roy was a teammate of Gladu's in Cuba, Mexico, and Montreal. On most days while playing winter ball with Gladu in Cuba, Roy would meet Roland for breakfast. One morning following an uncharacteristic sub-par hitting performance by Gladu, Roy and others went to their normal breakfast spot to meet Gladu. But Roland was not there. When Roy reached the ballpark at noon, he found Gladu taking his swings, spraying balls all around the field as a kid he had brought along was furiously running around, collecting balls.

At the end of the 1947 season, Gladu was back in Quebec playing in the Provincial League. The Mexican deserters who were not among the elite players found that the Provincial League was their best option. Bobby Estalella, who registered a career .282 batting average over a nine-year career in the American League and played for St. Jean, St. Hyacinthe, recruited Mexican outcasts such as Roy Zimmerman and Danny Gardella, formerly a promising player with the Giants.[47]

Like those players, Gladu had become a league pirate, out of the network of affiliated baseball. He had a short spell with St. Hyacinthe but made good use of his time, playing his part in convincing league administrators to pardon the players who had gone to Mexico to be reinstated and take part in official baseball. He also backed the cause of the Provincial League in making peace with the authorities of baseball and regaining the status of official league.

Recalling his days with West Ham, Gladu went into player-management with Sherbrooke in 1948[48] and quickly called on his contacts to develop the team while continuing to play to a good standard.

Adrian Zabala—formerly of the New York Giants—joined the team, along with three Cubans that Gladu had met in the winter leagues—catcher Lauro Pascual, second baseman Jorge Torres and Claro Duany, whose power with the bat was renowned. Gladu and Sherbrooke dominated the league and won the championship in 1948. Gladu became a legend in Quebec as one of the best players in the league.[49]

During the following two seasons, Gladu stayed with Sherbrooke, bringing Sylvio Garcia onto the team. Garcia won the Triple Crown in 1950 and helped bring Sherbrooke to the championship in 1951.

During the night following this championship in 1951, the Sherbrooke stadium was destroyed by fire and as a consequence the club was forced to leave the league for the 1952 season. Gladu played ball in 1952, in the Laurentian League for Thetford Mines. As a player and manager, he had a .394–18–79 line.[50]

Gladu, then 41 years old, retired but became a scout for the Cleveland Indians and the Milwaukee Braves, where he was reunited with his mentor, Del Bissonette. Until 1963, he signed a number of outstanding players including Georges Maranda, Ron Piché, and Claude Raymond. Maranda played two seasons in the big leagues (1960 with the San Francisco Giants and 1962 with the Minnesota Twins); Piche logged six years in the majors between 1960 and 1966, playing for the Milwaukee Braves, the California Angels, and the St. Louis Cardinals; and Raymond, the most successful of the group, had a 12-year major league career (between 1959 and 1971) with the Chicago White Sox, the Milwaukee Braves, Houston Astros, Atlanta Braves, and Montreal Expos. In 1966, Raymond made the National League all-star team as a relief pitcher for the Astros.

Later in life, Gladu returned to work for the Boston Braves as a scout of young baseball talent. Canadian Baseball Hall of Famer Raymond recalled Roland's work (*Canadian Baseball News*, 1 March 1998):

> Other teams began coming back to make me offers. I went to the office of the Pirates—in St. Jean—one afternoon and they offered me a contract. Well, the original contract with the Dodgers was for $160 per month plus a $250 bonus for signing, so I kept that bonus. Roland Gladu, a former Boston Braves third baseman and a Canadian, came over to our house that night and my Dad was there. He said he was offering me $160 a month, $250 if I signed right then, $250 on 1 June and $500 on 1 August if I was still with the team they would send me to. Roland asked me if I would like to play professional ball and my dad looked at me and said, "Do you want to play for St. Jean (the Pirates team in the Quebec Provincial League) or do you want to play professional ball?" Well, I said I would like to play professional ball. So my father said to sign with the Braves because their team was in Quebec and I would be coming to St. Jean to play from time to time during the summer.

Gladu remained active in various organizations encouraging baseball in the Montreal area up to his last days. He was always grateful for his life in baseball. "I was treated very well and I loved the experience," he said. However, Gladu, who had experienced so much in his travels to West Ham and elsewhere, did wish he could have complemented his journeying with more education. Late in his life he expressed the wish, if he could do it over, that he would go to school longer, but saw himself as not really having the choice as he came from a big family. Seemingly with the resignation of age he related, "We were nine kids and I had to help my father a bit."

In keeping with his commitment on education, Roland Gladu instilled the importance of scholarship in his two children. One became an accountant and the other a doctor. He had remained active all his life, appearing for the Trois Rivières Lions Hockey team in Quebec during the mid–1950s. His life had been an amazing voyage of discovery. Roland Gladu, who died in 1994, was certainly an adventurous soul who could have delighted listeners if he had wanted to by explaining that he was the only player ever to play professional baseball in the USA, Canada, Great Britain, Mexico, and Cuba. The only problem is that people might not have believed him.

Custom House Days

On 26 April, just a week before London Major Baseball League games returned to Custom House for the 1937 season, the Basque town of Guernica in Spain was destroyed by Nazi bombers. A few days before, the near 800-foot, 110-ton German airship *Hindenburg* exploded in New Jersey, killing 35 of the 97 people on board and one ground crew member. As the first balls were being thrown and hit in the London league's second season, King George VI was being crowned king of Great Britain and its empire. About three weeks after that, on 28 May, Neville Chamberlain became prime minister. Just three days later, the German fleet bombarded the Spanish port of Almeria. By this time the development of Buchenwald, the first Nazi concentration camp, was well underway.

West Ham embarked on its second season as part of London's diminished professional baseball community. Only the Hammers, Catford, and Romford remained. In 1936, the North of England League decided to weed out weaker franchises and retrench with the strongest organizations financially. In its second season, the London Major Baseball League did the exact same thing. Each of the three surviving London clubs added second teams that would play autonomously at their venues. Along with the Hammers, West Ham Stadium became the home of the Pirates Baseball Club. Catford, which moved to the Nunhead Football Club Ground for the new campaign, was joined by the Nunhead Baseball Club. As for Romford, which continued to play at Romford Stadium, it shared the facility with the newly formed Corinthians. Despite the drastic changes, West Ham Baseball Club would prove to be the class of the league and the one team that would contend for the title in the two seasons of the London Major Baseball League.

While West Ham was financially flush with success from 1936, other teams in the league had not been as successful. The Streatham and Mitcham Giants had disbanded within the first month of the 1936 season. Even the league champion White City folded before the start of the 1937 campaign. Despite drawing crowds of as many as 5,000 and announcing plans to sign two English test (international) cricketers for the 1937 campaign, the cost of running the Citizens proved too great. With a fee of £70 per week to use the White City Stadium, the west Londoners failed to break even. The Harringay squad also left the league and the Hackney Royals decided to revert to amateur status.[51] As all three teams played at Greyhound Racing Association venues, it comes as no surprise that they all disbanded at the same time (it seems the GRA was not prepared to continue to sponsor the game).

In an effort to avoid the pitfalls that befell White City, Harringay, and Hackney, some of the remaining teams looked for innovative ways to increase financial stability. Nunhead and Catford, for example, became part of a new scheme called Economy Entertainment that tied baseball to a variety of other sports. Subscribers, who paid 2/6d (12.5p/20 cents), were entitled to two tickets for the price of one at a variety of sports stadiums and arenas. Along with the baseball field at Nunhead FC, the plan included Clapham Winter Gardens (a boxing venue before World War II), swimming at the Lido in Croydon, The Rink in Cricklewood for wrestling, Hendon Stadium for bicycle polo and Vale Hall in Kilburn for wrestling. Elsewhere in the league, prices remained reasonable. At Romford Stadium, where the Wasps and the Corinthians played, the cost for a ticket was 6d and 1/- for men, six pence and a shilling (or, in American money, seven cents) while women and children gained admittance for half-price.

At West Ham, L.D. Wood was also not averse to adding attention to his teams by making the experience at Custom House a little more "sexy." Baseball was hardly ever a game exclusive to one gender in England. According to Jim Appleby ("Past Times," *Bradford Telegraph and Argus* on 17 June 1998) women took part in the sport from the earliest part of its 20th century renaissance in Britain. "Baseball was becoming a major sporting event, and not just for the lads," Appleby said. "[Two northern teams, the] City Sox and English Electric, among others, fielded women's teams."

The West Ham Girls' softball team, which was coached by Bill Irvine, also played at Custom House. One wonders how highly contested the women's games were or whether they were more a sideshow attraction as the girls' games (at least in the first West Ham girls game against Romford on 27 June) was scheduled for one hour—much shorter than a normal contest. It seems likely that these games were more for spectacle than serious encounters. However, game reports in the local newspapers treated the games with respect. One such article in the *Echo* of 17 August 1937, entitled "Sport Gossip," reported:

Losing by 11 runs to 7 against the Romford Honey Bees at Romford last week casts no bad reflections on the West Ham Ladies' soft ball team. It was their first match against a side which has been in the field for some time and the fact that they held the home team until after the half-way stage gives them something to crow about. The Honey Bees are good, but with another week or so on the training ground, the home town ladies' should avenge this defeat. In Miss Steele as pitcher and Miss Hays at first base, are two hard workers, and with this mention must be paid to the team as a whole for their good work, not forgetting their coach, Mr. Bill Turner.

But there was a limit to the extent that Wood allowed himself to rely on sideshows. He used the realignment of the league as an opportunity to increase his stake in professional baseball in West Ham. Wood, who had showed tremendous marketing acumen in his 1936 efforts to convince East Enders that the West Ham Baseball Club was a viable and worthwhile commodity, went to work at selling the Pirates as well. His key strategy in this endeavor was differentiating the West Ham Baseball Club from the Pirates. While West Ham was the established "Babes in Red," the Pirates were sold as a swashbuckling, roguish team of lovable rascals. Their colors were all black with a white skull and crossbones and the team was referred to as the "Bold Bad Buccaneers." "Saucy" players were helpful to cultivate this image. Most notably, "Slim" Tyson, the team's shortstop, was dubbed "one of the most colorful players in the London Major League as well as one of the top hitters," according to the 11 July Pirates program. Keeping with the dangerous theme, the program implied that Tyson might not be as innocent as his 20-year-old age would suggest. It warned that "[p]eople don't believe he is that young." When asked how he was enjoying London, Tyson, a North American, replied that he was "beginning to like his stay in England a little better but don't ask him if it is [a] blonde, brunette or redhead," thus, adding to his rapscallion image.

The Pirates were also presented as confident and brash "gun-slingers," the complete opposite of the quiet sportsmanship that was emblematic of British sporting culture. In the same program that described Tyson's way with the women, new Pirates pitcher "Happy" Kasnoff said that he liked London and boldly promised that he was not going to lose very many games. It was a promise which the program said "the rest of the Pirates back him up in making." Alas, Kasnoff, who had played for the Hackney Royals in 1936, and his teammates were going to provide more bluster than wins. In fact, on the 4th of July, in Kasnoff's first game as a Pirate, the team lost to the Corinthians. As events were unfolding for the Pirates, history was also seeing memorable moments. In the same month Amelia Earhart, the U.S. aviator, vanished, and Japanese troops took Peking.

Along with Tyson and Kasnoff, the Pirates had a number of other solid players. L.D. Wood proved his eye for versatility by recruiting right-hand pitcher Jack Ward. The 185-pound, 22-year-old played the previous three seasons in Shanghai, China, and was chosen to pitch for that league's all-star amateur team. He was British-born but learned how to play baseball in the United States and Canada.

Frank Cadorette, a big-hitting speedy centerfielder, also joined the team. Along with his baseball exploits, Cadorette was a professional ice hockey player who competed for the Wembley Monarchs in the British National (Hockey) League. He would go on to great glory as a baseball player as a member of the English team that defeated the U.S. in 1938 (the first world amateur baseball championships). According to the 1938 U.S.-England program Frank was "[s]peedy between the bases" and "[o]ne of the big hitters on the team."

Like with Cadorette, the ice hockey ranks were becoming an increasingly popular place to recruit baseball players. Others included Maurice Gerth, who also played in the north with the Oldham Greyhounds in 1937; he was an ice hockey goalie for Streatham in the British National League. He traveled back to North America for the 1938–1939 hockey season, playing professionally for the Detroit McLean Pontiacs and then the Toledo Babcocks of the Michigan-Ontario Hockey Association. In 1945–46, Gerth appeared with the Hollywood Wolves of the Pacific Coast Hockey League. Jimmy Foster was another aficionado of the stick and

Front row—Tommy O'Rourke Leo Benson Charles Tate Lefty Schemer John McDermott Wendell Ringland. Back row—Lloyd Johnson Dean Graff Virgil Thompson Mizell Platt George Binger Ora Lindau Clyde Dean Clifford Cunningham. Panel—Leslie Mann(Director).

Hopwood,Photo,Liverpool,England.

U.S.A. "ALL-AMERICA" TEAM.

When England won what is today recognized as the first baseball world championships, they played a strong U.S. side. The team was formed by Leslie Mann, a former major leaguer who was at the forefront of developing baseball worldwide. The squad included two players who would go on to play in the major leagues: Lefty Schemer and Mizell Platt.

puck. He pitched (and played left field) briefly at the start of the season for the Pirates and plied his hockey skills in the British National League, turning out for the Richmond Hawks in 1935 before moving to the ice of the Harringay Greyhounds in 1936. Born in 1905 in Greenock, the 5-foot, 8-inch tall, 157-pound Scot was one of the best goaltenders outside the National Hockey League. Foster grew up in Winnipeg, Manitoba, Canada, and played for the University of Manitoba before taking up professional hockey with the Canadian Moncton Hawks from 1932–1935. In the fall of 1935, he was lured to England to play in the English National League. The following year, he led England to the Triple Crown, winning the World, European, and Olympic Championships.

Unfortunately for West Ham fans, Foster was acquired by the Romford Wasps in July. The 11 July 1937 Pirates program lamented the loss of the ice hockey legend, saying, "Jimmy's many friends are sorry to see him go but wish him the best of luck with his new team (except when they play the Pirates)."

In 1938, Foster carried on playing baseball, moving to the Romford Corinthians. His ice hockey career also continued with the Hackney Greyhounds until 1939 and he regularly represented Great Britain in hockey for three years staring in 1936. Foster returned to Canada in 1940, where he played professionally for the Glace Bay Miners and the Quebec Aces. He was chosen for the British Hockey Hall of Fame in 1950.

Front row—Frank Cadorette Danny Wright Larry Marsh Jack Ritchie Ken Robinson. Mascot. Back row—George McNeil(Capt.) Irvine Ruvinsky Sid Bissett Jerry Strong Sammy Hanna Doc Holden Ross Kendrick.
ENGLAND "ALL-STARS"—WINNERS JOHN MOORES CUP CHAMPIONSHIP.

When England won what is today recognized as the first baseball world championships, they played a strong U.S. side. The team was formed by Leslie Mann, a former major leaguer who was at the forefront of developing baseball worldwide. The squad included two players who would go on to play in the major leagues: Lefty Schemer and Mizell Platt.

Another impressive member of the Pirates was Sam Hanna, who was billed as a professional soccer player and played infield for the Pirates. He had been taught baseball in Canada but was of Irish descent (In fact, he'd been hoping "he [would] get a chance to visit his folks in Ireland" at the start of the 1937 season, according to the 11 July 1937 Pirates program.) Like his Pirates teammate Cadorette, Hanna also earned baseball glory playing for the England team that beat the U.S. in 1938. Hanna came in as a pinch hitter in game one of the world championships and hit a run-scoring double in Wavertree Stadium in Liverpool, watched by a crowd of 10,000. He scored a second run in the 3–0 victory in game three that clinched the world championships for England at the Shay in Halifax to the delight of the 5,000 northern spectators. Like Foster, Hanna's baseball playing life did not end in 1937. He was a member of the Halifax baseball club in 1938. The writers of the Pirates program boasted that Hanna was "acknowledged the finest short stop in the country."

While Wood was building up the Pirates squad, he did not forget his pride and joy—the West Ham side. The team's big three stars, Gladu, Strong, and Etheze, remained but Yvon, the veteran second baseman, returned to Canada. Among the players added was Butch Armstrong from Chicago.

As with the Pirates, West Ham mined other sports for potential players. Even with these new recruits, Gladu and Strong remained the team's biggest selling points. In fact, in May 1937, the two were featured in a magazine called *Supermen.* The article and pictorial was about "how baseball builds supermen," according to the 30 May West Ham Baseball Club program, which added: "Roland Gladu and Jerry Strong show off to swell effect. Girls better get their copies."

With both the Hammers and Pirates sharing West Ham Stadium, a healthy rivalry between the two teams quickly developed. The two clubs met early in the season in late May. The story in the *Echo* was probably too much for the established West Ham fans to bear:

Pirates Swing Back to Form and Punch Strong and Gladu Around the Park—Tyson's "Texas Leaguer" Paves The Way to a Six Run Barrage. Hammers Hammered to Tune of 15–5.

The inimitable "Homer," a pseudonym for the writer who wrote most of the game stories in the Echo, continued, showing that the competition was a serious business:

The Revitalized Pirates sank their cutlasses into Gladu's boys at West Ham on Sunday afternoon, and pumping hits all over the diamond with the regularity of a machine gun crossed the plate six times in the seventh inning to push their tally up to eleven runs. In notching the success, Happy Kasnoff yielded eight safe hits for 5 runs. Nothing could hold the Buccaneers and

Jerry Strong was flogged for eleven runs before Gladu came on the mound for the remaining two innings. Gladu could do little better, and was booted out for four runs on the Pirates' ninth.

Such was the position that all the Pirates with the exception of Sammy Hanna, had crossed the plate at the end of the seventh. Thompson and Mumma each notched a circuit drive.

Eddie Mumma made a grand come-back after his injury, scored three runs, and was responsible for some fine catching at centre field. One of his errors was costly and allowed Etheze to run the four bases on a long fly which should have been caught. Tyson came off the diamond with three runs to his credit but it was Vic Pope, who took the honours for batting and runs.

There seems to have been a lot of maneuvering within the two Custom House sides, seemingly looking to catch each other out or at least unprepared:

Changes were made in both teams. For West Ham, Charlie Stapleford took the first sack, Bill Irvin[e] went to his old position at third and Jerry Owen, acquired from the Nunhead contingent played in outfield.

Jack Ward, Jimmy Burden and Bill Davi[e]s were in the Pirates dug out, only Ward coming in the eighth for Thompson. Joe Carter, also from Nunhead, came in at second base to strengthen the infield and Eddie Mumma went to centre field.

Despite the on-field rivalry between the Pirates and the Hammers in 1937, the teams did not seem to have separate or distinct fan bases. During 1937, busloads of the Social Club members followed both the Hammers' and the Pirates' fortunes around London, but the application to be a member of the West Ham Supporters' Club was exactly the same in both the Pirates Baseball Club programs and the West Ham Baseball Club programs. (L.D. Wood must have thought that one robust club was better than two smaller associations.) West Ham aggressively marketed its supporters' club, regularly placing an application for membership in the back of its programs. West Ham was not the only organization to create such a club. For example, the Catford Saints and the Nunhead teams also had a club (the teams shared a field and, like the Hammers and the Pirates, seemed to pool its supporters as well, based on its members application).

The membership fee for the "West Ham Baseball Supporters' Club" was one shilling (5p—about £5 or $8.50 today). That covered the cost of a supporters badge and subscription for the season.

Presumably, West Ham offered more than just a badge and a subscription for the "bob" price tag. According to a 1937 Nunhead Baseball Club program, the Catford–Nunhead club not only gave a subscription and a "distinctive white and red enamel badge"[52] but also made arrangements for members who were interested to learn baseball on the field under the "expert guidance" of various members of the Saints and

Nunhead sides. The clubs also promised assistance in organizing junior clubs in their own localities and in helping "obtain proper equipment at reasonable prices."

Maybe because of the shared West Ham-Pirates supporters club, the biggest rivalry in the London league in 1937 was between the Hammers and Romford Wasps. Showman Archer Leggett's squad left a lot to be desired in 1936. On opening day that season, in front of its "celebrity" crowd, the Wasps were victorious 25–7, but, ultimately, the team would consistently be at the bottom of the standings. By early July, the Wasps were mired in last place with a 2–8 record. Not surprisingly, a late 1936 season Romford program didn't even include league standings.

Despite his team's poor performance, Leggett was undeterred going into the 1937 campaign. Of course, he increased his commitment to baseball in the second season of the London league, adding the Corinthians to the Romford stable. As with the Wasps' squad, Leggett used his tried and true marketing tactics with his new team. The Corinthian players would be dubbed with various colorful nicknames. They included "Sudds" Sutherst, "Bunt" Roberts and "Nip" Nishikawa (the latter nickname for the team's Japanese pitcher is disturbingly racist by today's standards).

On the field the Corinthians struggled, but the Wasps had a tremendous season in 1937. Leggett undertook a serious recruitment drive for the Wasps' second campaign. His top player Merrick "Slugger" Cranstoun, returned and took firm charge of the team. By season's end Leggett and Cranstoun had put together a formidable offensive machine composed of top Canadian and American athletes.

The Wasps' top hitter was Tallie Ellis, an American catcher who led the London league in home runs in 1937. Carson Thompson, who had earned the win in the 1936 Olympic baseball demonstration contest in Berlin, and "Poison" Absell, who had appeared for West Ham in 1936, were also now Wasps.

In addition to the Americans, there was a host of Canadians, many of whom were also accomplished ice hockey players. Most notably Romford nabbed Jimmy Foster from the Pirates in mid-season to roam the outfield for the Wasps. Another gold medal-winning Olympic ice hockey player, Jimmy Chappell, played third base, while fellow Canadians "Swifty" Peterson (a Toronto native who played first base), Gib Hutchinson (a left-handed-hitting second-baseman who was also an ice hockey star) and Art Childs (a defensive stalwart in centerfield) were starters as well.

The success of the team turned the Wasps into a force with a legitimate British following. Moreover, those in attendance were appreciating baseball for the show of athleticism and did not mind that they were watching foreigners play the game. The team was simply worthy of civic pride in Romford. According to Ellis Harvey, "My recollection is that practically all the fans were British.... The friends I went with [to Romford Wasps games] were not bothered about most of the players being American or Canadian; in fact I believe we rather expected that they would be."

Although the Wasps would be a top team, Leggett must not have had too much energy or time—beyond giving the players nicknames—for his second squad, the Corinthians. The team did have Nishikawa, who was among the league's top pitchers and was once described by the West Ham paper, *The Echo*, as a pitcher who could throw "really 'hot' curves down the alley." But the team had difficulty competing with the likes of West Ham. For example, in one visit to East London the *Echo* trumpeted that the "Corinthians Quake Before Strong's Pitching—Gladu Slams Nishikawa's Offerings for Two Triples."

The other new center of the league would be in Nunhead. Located in southeast London, the population, although predominantly working class, was probably, as a whole, slightly better off financially than residents of West Ham. It probably should not have been a surprise that the Mormon missionaries, the Catford Saints, would have moved on from the greyhound stadium after the 1936 season. Together with the apparent withdrawal of support of the GRA, perhaps a massive "gambling den" was not a place where they felt terribly comfortable. Their new home, not too far from Catford, was Brown's Ground (more generally it was referred to as the Nunhead Sports Ground) which had been the home of the Nunhead Football Club since 1907. For over thirty years Nunhead had been playing at the top level of amateur soccer.

Brown's had been well known even before Nunhead's occupancy. When he was prince of Wales, King Edward VII regularly turned up there for shooting (with a gun rather than a boot) just after the First World War and the immortal W.G. Grace, considered by many to be the Babe Ruth of cricket, was also reputed to have often played cricket there in the late nineteenth century.

The ground was an enclosure within a larger sports ground with the northern extremity forming one of the boundaries with the rest of the sporting area. This side had a quarter length grandstand which was erected by the club in 1908–09. A railway embankment ran alongside the eastern boundary and therefore may have provided a natural graded grass area behind that goal. A covered standing area was later built behind the goal at the opposite Ivydale Road end, and changing rooms were located opposite the stand. At the front of the changing rooms, there would eventually be the only concrete terracing at Brown's Ground, just six steps and around 20 meters long. Narrow embankments were to be introduced later in the ground's history along most other sections around the pitch. In due course, the ground was sandwiched by rugby pitches to the north and south.

The stadium had been through a lot just before Catford and its new sister team Nunhead begun playing baseball there. On 24 January 1936, the stand was destroyed by fire. The cost of rebuilding the stand was £700, and was met personally by club treasurer Mr. E.G. "Eddie" Mash. Possibly, the stadium's owners took on the baseball teams in the hope that they would help defray the cost of the unforeseen expenses.

Nunhead's soccer team continued playing at Brown's Ground after war broke out and it completed its South-Eastern Combination fixtures there in the 1939–40 season. They may also have started the 1940–41 season, but it was not long before their inability to pay the rent meant that they became dependent on sharing Dulwich Hamlet's Champion Hill ground. Not long after the Nunhead FC left Brown's Ground the War Department requisitioned the ground and it was subsequently used for American forces baseball games.

After the war the ground was used as a sports field by Aske's School and was later transformed into a rugby pitch. By 1987 the enclosure fences, stand, and embankments had disappeared although the dilapidated dressing rooms and terracing were still standing. Now even those few remnants of the home of one of England's top amateur soccer clubs have also gone.

Whether Catford and Nunhead were sister teams in the same way that West Ham and the Pirates were both owned by L.D. Wood, and the Wasps and the Corinthians were Leggett's clubs is unclear. Regardless, neither team was a top competitor for the league crown in 1937, although the Saints would briefly feature "Lefty" Wilson, whom Gladu would later dub the greatest pitcher he faced in England.

Still, with White City out of the picture, the Romford Wasps quickly emerged as the team West Ham would have to beat. In 1937, the pitching of the "Men of Essex" was bolstered by the American Olympic pitcher Thompson, and Cranstoun, who was referred to as the grand old man of baseball in Romford by *The Romford Recorder*, anchored the lineup. The Wasps won their first three games, while West Ham started with an unimpressive 1–2 record. But when the teams met at West Ham Stadium on 30 May, it was clear that this would be a closer race than the clubs' early season records would indicate. Behind the play of Jerry Strong, who not only was the team's pitcher in the game but also its leading hitter, smacking a home run, West Ham defeated the front-running Wasps and were still in the hunt in third with a 4–3 record. In addition, West Ham, which had been embarrassed earlier in the season by its sister team, the Pirates, refused to be upstaged again. On 20 June, Wood's two squads squared off at West Ham Stadium. Although the Pirates took their first matchup earlier in the season 4–3, the Hammers scored six runs in the second inning en route to an 8–1 win. The Chicagoan "Butch" Armstrong was the hero, hitting a home run and Strong struck out 10 Pirates batters.

As the season reached its midpoint, the Pirates began to fade, while West Ham made its move for the top spot. The big problem for the Pirates was their team captain, Eddie Mumma. He was an exceptional utility player, filling in at various positions as needed, but in May he tore muscles in his back. At one point, doctors finally ordered Mumma to stop playing until his back had healed, but he refused to take a long trip to the disabled list. Instead, he took only a small break to recuperate, and was back in the lineup on 11 July. There's little doubt that the injury hindered Mumma's performance. While Mumma battled through the pain that season, at least one other Pirate was lost before the season was out; catcher Ron Rumpal decided to go on a tour of Germany and other European countries before returning home to Springfield (Mass.) College. Early in the season, the Pirates had led the league in home runs. Mumma had slugged two, while Tyson, Rumpal and Hanna had one each (they all trailed Tallie Ellis, the Romford catcher, who topped the home run charts with three.) But with the injury to Mumma and Rumpal's departure, the slugging Pirates were no more.

Things got so bad, that at one point toward the conclusion of the season the Pirates had to appeal for players. In a story in the *Echo* Pirates supporters were told that the Custom House Buccaneers

> could only field a scratch team, two of the regular players having left, and Bert Rawlings who came in on first base to help Mumma's crowd, dislocated an ankle in the forth inning.
> Features of the game was the fine fielding by Jimmy Burdon at right field, and the play of Tommy Durling who had a perfect day at bat, stole five bases and battled three runs in.
> No ball club can go out on the diamond and expect to win games when they do not get a work out. For the last couple of weeks there has been little done in this line, and unless this is remedied, the Pirates in the London Major League are going to be like the Pirates of the old days—a thing of the past.

This said, throughout the season the Buccaneers could still put on a show when they took on the hapless Corinthians on the Essex lads' own field. Under the banner Seven in the Last Two Innings—Pirates beat Corinthians 9–7 After being Five Runs Down, it was reported in the Echo that,

> Charlie Muirehead has often said that anything can happen in a ball game while a team are still at bat.
> This was proved on Sunday evening at the Romford Stadium, when the Pirates defeated the Corinthians after being five runs down.

Eddie Mumma, short stop and newly elected captain, put the finishing touches to the slowly developing headache that was attacking the Corinthians when with bases loaded and one out, he punched one of sou' paw Galbraith's swingers over the fence for three bases and drove in Davies, Hanna, and Rumpal.

Corinthians had the first touch of dizziness when in the Pirates eighth Hanna hit a home run. A couple of errors showed the Romford contingent to be truly rattled and Mumma and Tyson quick to take advantage of any slip, made the home plate to reduce the deficit to two.

Mumma Cleans 'em In

Brilliant infield work made short work of the Corinthians in their eighth, only one man getting into a bag.

In the Pirates last visit, Foster opened and was struck out. Davies, batting for Burden made first and was advanced by Hanna. Rumpal placed a ball over the short stop for a single and Mumma in with a full house.

Corinthians were in a spot and they knew it. Their little talk and plan of campaign hatched in the centre of the field was of no use. Mumma looked a couple over carefully and then did his "clean-up" stuff. Tyson hit hard past pitcher Galbraith and the play was made on Mumma at the plate, but a big lead off and clever slide added the fourth run to the tally for the inning.

Tail end of the Corinthians failed to wag, smart fielding seeing both Pitt and Sirota dying at the first bag. Peebles created a little excitement with his safe two base hit, but Foster turned the screws on Roberts and struck him out.

As luck would have it, the Pirates' setbacks occurred just when other teams in the middle of the pack were heating up. The Catford Saints brought in "Lefty" Wilson who would prove to be one of the best pitchers in England at the time, striking out between 17 and 20 batters in each of his first few outings contest.[53] The Pirates' bravado from the early season, when their program was claiming they would be hard to stop, was becoming far more muted as the season wore on.

At the top of the league, West Ham had a lot to be excited about. On 3 July, the Hammers finally pulled even with the Wasps at 6–3 when they beat Romford 8–4. At the same time, the Pirates had faded to third place with a 4–6 record. But West Ham began to slip thereafter. On 4 July they jumped out to a 3–0 lead against Nunhead thanks to a Strong home run but ultimately fell apart, losing 6–3. On 18 July, Romford visited West Ham Stadium for what would be one of the pivotal matches of the season. West Ham was now 7–4, holding on to a slender lead in the standings with the Wasps sporting a 7–5 record. A win might have propelled the Hammers to a championship, but instead, the game served as a death knell for the Docklands boys; Romford took a 5–0 lead and despite West Ham's best efforts in the final three innings, the "Babes in Red" fell 5–2.

For all this, West Ham kept battling and stayed in the race up until the final weekend of the season, but it was Romford who was to win the league championship. Perhaps part of the Hammers' inability to drive home the potential they had shown was the loss of "Butch" Armstrong. He was to return to his home town at the end of June. The program of 18 July said that "Butch" would be "missed by his many friends and according to word from him, would like to be back. He reached his home last week after a quick trip on the Queen Mary."

Losing the league title was not the most disappointing element of the season for the men at Custom House. It was becoming clear that London had lost its position as the place for the best of British baseball.

This transition was exemplified by Romford's efforts in 1937 to keep the national championship trophy, won by White City the season before, in London. In the nationwide National Baseball Association Challenge Cup tournament, which was open to all British teams and would decide the national champion, the Wasps cruised through the opening rounds, scoring no fewer than nine runs in any match to earn a spot in the finals against the Hull Baseball Club.

The final against Hull, played at Hull's Craven Park, is considered one of the most memorable in British baseball history. Hull sent the dominating "Lefty" Wilson to the mound against the potent Wasps' lineup, which had scored 51 runs in its previous four tournament games. Wilson was a close friend of the Wasps' Tallie Ellis and had first made a name for himself with the Saints in the London league but ultimately migrated to the north of England. Wilson's legacy is remembered to this day by Hull residents. Wilson was an icon in the Hull baseball community. On his arrival in the city the *Hull Daily Mail* of 10 May 1937 described him as a "pitching genius." According to Alf Spendlow, an amateur player in Hull at the time, Wilson was a dominating figure. In 2003, Spendlow told *The Mail* in Hull:

> We once played a friendly against the Hull Major team—Lefty Wilson was their pitcher and Don Adams their catcher. With Lefty Wilson you never knew if it would be an inswerve [slider], outswerve [screwball], drop ball [curveball] or a straight and fast. I managed to connect once but it was a foul ball. I never managed it again as he was very good.

The Challenge Cup Final was highly anticipated by locals in Hull. In the United States, baseball's first fan base came from the working class, so it is perhaps congruent that Hull, a city built on the hard, proletarian fishing industry, quickly took to the game. At the same time, Hull's connections with the sea made it a relatively cosmopolitan place, and the presence of Canadians and Americans around the port areas would not have been unusual. Hull has something of a tradition for supporting unconventional sporting ventures; for instance, it gave birth to two major Rugby League (a variation on the more well-known Rugby

Union) clubs. As such, the city's industrial, sporting and cultural heritage has made it one of Britain's hotbeds of baseball up to the current era; Hull hosted the European (Qualification Pool) Baseball Championships in 1996.

Thus, the Wasps might have been a little surprised when they entered Hull's Craven Park to the "welcome" of some 11,000 enthusiastic fans. Although as many as 4,000 or so fans might come to a contest at Romford Stadium, and a game against West Ham at Custom House could attract twice that number, the size of the Hull crowd was probably something the Wasps were not very accustomed to. This may have been the reason why Romford appeared to play a very nervous game in the field, making errors early on. It also did not help that Wilson was on his game. The left-handed pitcher dominated, striking out 14 batters. For the Wasps, only Wilson's friend Ellis could do anything against the Hull pitcher, delivering three hits for the losers. In fact, the Wasps could muster only a lone run, which they scored in the final inning as Hull prevailed 5–1.

The defeat must have been a huge disappointment to Leggett, who had appeared to have finally put together a winning squad. Despite Leggett's larger-than-life approach with his sporting spectacles, his true feelings about his Wasps' demise may never be known. His daughter Carolyn Baker told the *Financial Times* in 2004 that: "My father never discussed the stadium in the house.... He felt that it was not the sort of environment that we women should be attending."

One thing was for certain: the fan support and excitement in Hull indicated a shift in the balance of power. A season before, West Ham had traveled to Yorkshire and destroyed the competition. Now Hull, a team the Hammers defeated in 1936, was the champion.

Part of the reason for the quick transformation was the way in which people in Yorkshire were taking to baseball. Alf Spendlow was emblematic of this northern affinity for the game. In 1936, Spendlow and his friends, who had seen baseball for the first time with the Hull professionals, decided to try baseball but had a bit of difficulty finding equipment. Although proper gloves, bats and balls were not immediately available when Spendlow and eight others tried the sport for the first time, the group was undeterred. They found a plot of "waste ground" in East Hull and took a swing at the game. Spendlow told *The Mail* in Hull in 2003:

> We only had one baseball bat and two baseballs and a pair of gauntlet gloves. As I was the catcher I used the gloves. Each of the lads took it in turn to see who would make the best pitcher and it was Tom McCormick who got the job. He and I made a good team and improved all the time.... Our home base was just a piece of rough cut wood; other bases were makeshift.

With an immediate zest for baseball, Spendlow and his cohorts organized quickly. A local office worker named G. Dalton organized "Penny Doubles" (a low-cost form of group gambling, a bit like a sweepstakes) to help the teenagers earn money to buy equipment. The squad was named Ranks Green Sox, named after a team organizer Joseph Ranks, and purchased proper uniforms and gear.

In what could be seen as a testament to the abilities of British athletes, Spendlow and his team won the Hull Amateur League's Championship Trophy in 1938—just two years after taking their first try at the sport.

Back in London, the amateur game was developing as well to a certain degree. Amateur teams in London like the Ilford Nomads, the Ilford No-Varys and Gross Sherwood and Heald were competing in the East London League.[54] The local paper, *The Echo*, was publishing huge amount of baseball results each week, demonstrating the enthusiasm for baseball in the area. It seems that there was also a side that used the West Ham United ground, the Boleyn Greys (the Boleyn Ground, or Boleyn Castle are other titles used at the time for Upton Park, the home of the West Ham United Football Club). In the early part of the season they were advertising for players:

Boleyn Greys Need Players

Boleyn Greys (headquarters, Boleyn Castle Social and Sports Club) require a few more members for their team, preferably with some experience, especially on the pitching side of the game.

The Club was formed last May and has some seven or eight fixtures to fulfil before the season ends.

An application for membership of the East London Amateur League next season will be made, and cups, etc., will be entered for. The Club is affiliated to the N.B.A.

Particulars of membership can be obtained from the Baseball Secretary, Boleyn Castle Social and Sports Club, Green-street, E13.

Around the same time a small article appeared in the local press: "Baseball for Schools?—Members of the LCC to Attend Game at Hackney Marshes." Readers were informed:

An important match is being staged at Hackney Marshes on Saturday afternoon, pitch-off 3.30, when members of the London County Council are to attend the game between boys teams, Pioneers and Grafton, with a view to considering whether the game should be included in the school games.

Despite the spike in amateur play, the talent drain of players had become obvious. "Lefty" Wilson was a prime example of this. He had left the London league after a short stint and headed up north. Even Roland Gladu moonlighted in 1937 for the Sheffield Dons of the Yorkshire league. The loss of good players was so obvious that by way of the Pirates'

6 June program the team was looking for new recruits—and they were not alone. "Each team in the league is supposed to have a player list of twelve men," the program explained. "If you know anybody that would like to try out for the teams, get in touch with the baseball office or contact the manager of the teams. At present time few of the teams have their full quotas."

By the end of the season, the departure of top talent to the north would prove too much for the London Major Baseball League. Despite the enthusiasm that Wood had shown for the professional game, it became apparent that 1937 would be the final year for baseball in West Ham. On 3 September *The Recorder* in Romford reported, "the London Major League has closed." Although "attendances were definitely good," the paper blamed the failure of the league on stadium owners who "have at some time or another tinkered with baseball and have since fought shy, with the result that there are not enough promoters willing to finance a full league." While it is possible that West Ham and L.D. Wood might have been willing to persevere if a league could have remained intact, the fortunes for the "Babes in Red" and the "Bad Bold Buccaneers" seemed to have taken a turn for the worst. "Even at West Ham," wrote *The Recorder*, "the gates have shown an evident falling off and the enthusiasm of '36 has been conspicuous by its absence."

Although West Ham had no trophies to show for its efforts, few would disagree that the Hammers had been the class of the league. West Ham had competed for the league championship for two straight seasons just to fall short in each campaign's waning days. They had beaten the best team to play in the country during those years, the U.S. Olympic team, and had employed some of the best players ever to compete on British soil. Most importantly, the team had brought fans to the game, having consistently drawn the biggest crowds.

As West Ham's diamond faded in the rains of the East End winter, the Spanish government removed to Barcelona and Shanghai fell to the Japanese. East London's huge Irish population, many of whom had come to West Ham to work the docks just a decade before, wondered about the future of their homeland as the Irish Free State became Eire in the last days of the year. In 1937, *The Hobbit* by J.R.R. Tolkien was published as was Ernest Hemingway's *To Have and Have Not*. Despite the waning success of the professional circuit in London, Wood tried until the very end to use his marketing skills to sell the pro game. Late in the season, the league touted that it had "something new in English Sport" when it announced in 1937 that it planned "play-offs." Although common today in all sports, the idea of pitting the top four finishers in the league against each other at the end of the season appeared to be, or at least it was claimed to be by London Major Baseball League organizers, novel in Britain. The league gushed that this "new idea" was already being used in the United States, Japan, Mexico and Australia. Now Britain via baseball would get some of this sporting innovation. Alas, it was an idea whose time had not come.

Aftermath of Apotheosis: From Anticlimax to Accession

When the London league disbanded at the end of the 1937 season, one couldn't have blamed Wasps owner Archer Leggett if he had put an end to his baseball experiment. After all, even L.D. Wood, who adored the game of baseball, scuttled the West Ham club when the London Major Baseball League folded. But by that time, it seems that Leggett had given his heart to baseball, because in 1938 Leggett kept both his teams going; against huge odds the Wasps and the Corinthians lived on.

With the London Major Baseball League disbanded, the Wasps and the Corinthians continued to compete in the amateur ranks. It appears that even after the departure of professional baseball from Romford Stadium, support hardly wavered and the team continued to draw a loyal following of enthusiasts. Ellis Harvey did not notice "any significant reduction in their number after 1937."

Gone were the big marketing ploys that L.D. Wood had used to lure fans to greyhound stadiums the two previous years. Now, according to *The Recorder*, Romford had "the only stadium in the London area where the game is played as a public spectacle." But there were still some loyal baseball fans in Britain's capital. In early May 1938, an exhibition match between the Wasps and the Corinthians drew about 300 fans despite very cold weather, and the fact that game was not advertised. *The* (Romford) *Recorder* noted on 6 May that this decent-sized turnout "even surprised Wasps ownership." However, without adequate financing, it is not surprising that the Wasps and Corinthians were generally hit by a "gate slump," as *The Recorder* put it. The local press blamed the National Baseball Association in Liverpool for "completely overlook[ing] the needs of the London Clubs."

For William Morgan, the London Major Baseball League failed because "Greyhound racing in the 1930s was a goldmine.... When baseball wasn't a big money spinner after the first season the backers who were involved with Greyhound racing pulled out. It wasn't a money spinner and the Greyhound people were business people." But, according to Morgan, the general feeling about the professional game in the London Major Baseball League was that "people who knew something of baseball weren't really impressed ... people here didn't know" so for them it was a spectacle and as such would be missed.

As such, a non-professional league was organized to serve the capital and its environs; the London Senior Amateur League was formed and included the Romford Wasps and the Corinthians. The stars that had graced West Ham Stadium, men like Gladu and Strong, had moved on. Even Merrick Cranstoun, described as "the GOM [Grand Old Man] of baseball in Romford" by *The* (Romford) *Recorder*, had forsaken the stage and left the London game. But Romford did profit from the disbanding of West Ham, picking up three former Hammers, Eric and Sam Whitehead and Art Dunning. The Pirates' most reliable pitcher, Vic Pope, and the team's catcher, Jack Robbins, went to the Corinthians and another pitcher who played briefly for the "Bold Bad Buccaneers," ice hockey star Jimmy Foster, also joined the Corinthians. Unlike the Wasps and Corinthians, most of the teams in the new league did not need much in the way of support as they were affiliated with major companies. The De Havilland Comets were sponsored by the airplane manufacturer of that name and Fords and Briggs Brigands were affiliated with the car companies who gave their names to the teams.

Now that the stars were gone, fans of baseball in London became concerned about the development of British-born players. An editorial in *The Recorder* on 20 May 1938 complained that, "after 'stars' are forgotten, it will be English boys who will keep baseball alive." The writer was in favor of the new amateur structure because it meant more English players getting a chance to improve their skills. The amateur incarnation of the game, the writer concluded, was "in the interests of [British] baseball that they be given a chance, even at the expense of sacrificing one or two Canadians or Americans." Nevertheless, even with the new amateur league, foreigners were still dominant figures. For example, the Wasps grabbed the former Corinthian, Japanese pitcher Nishikawa, who was nearly unstoppable, striking out as many as 16 batters in a game.

Although not professional, London's Senior Amateur League with the De Havilland Comets, Fords, Briggs Brigands and the Old Josephians was still quite competitive. The Corinthians spent most of the season battling just to stay afloat as the team had difficulty putting together a competitive squad on a number of occasions. But the Wasps continued to shine.

When the regular season was completed, the Wasps found themselves in a deadlock for first place with the De Havilland Comets. A one-game playoff was set up in Uxbridge to decide the champion and the Wasps prevailed 7-4.

As late as 1939, some in the London baseball community remained optimistic about British baseball's future. Eric Whitehead, who had played two seasons for West Ham and then had moved over to play for the Romford Wasps in 1938, put a wholly positive gloss on baseball in his 1939 book *Baseball for British Youth*. He pointed out that more than 600 teams were registered with the National Baseball Association and said that even in 1939, "[c]apacity crowds of well over ten thousand fans have become commonplace in certain sections of the country." But Whitehead said the most promising development was that the sport was on the cusp of being ingrained into everyday British culture. "[B]aseball is being investigated by education authorities with the probability of installing it as a major sport in the nation's school."

In terms of development in London, Whitehead must have been merely trying to sell the game. As the Second World War loomed the accompanying demand for labor power (and shift work) meant that attendances of baseball games at Romford plummeted; as Ellis Harvey recalled, "By that time my employment and the fact that war appeared inevitable meant that I was developing other interests so that I was not attending so regularly."

While imminent conflict ended the Wasps' reign, the team's performances in 1937 and 1938 cemented its place as one of London's best sides of the time. The Wasps and Corinthians faded into history as World War II dominated the hearts and minds of the people of Romford, who existed on the destructive fringe of the devastation of the Blitz, but Leggett continued to lend his stadium to the game. During the war, the track was a popular spot for American soldiers who continued the tradition of playing baseball in Romford. However, the eventual departure of baseball from the Romford sporting horizon was a loss for the district. This left a small but significant void in the life of Ellis Harvey:

> After returning from France and a spell in the Orkney Islands I was married before embarking for North Africa and on my eventual demob[ilization I] lived with my wife's parents in Wimbledon before we were finally able to obtain accommodation back in Romford. By that time the Major League appeared to have ceased to operate.

While no baseball has been played at Romford Stadium for many years, the track still exists today as the vibrant home of greyhound racing for native Essexians and the large number of "ex-pat" East Enders that populate the area.

Happening Hull

Although excitement for baseball diminished with the departure of professional baseball in London, the war did seem to be the only deterrent for further growth of the game in northern towns like Hull. Evidence of Hull's civic support for baseball was clear in the Hull Amateur Baseball League's 1939 Official Handbook. The publication was peppered with advertising from all corners of the town's business community. The Hull Savings Bank had a full-page advertisement, while Brooks' Band, which dubbed itself "the Finest Professional Combination in Yorkshire," also took a whole page.

Some advertisers pitched themselves directly to the baseball market. For example, "Merthene," which claimed to be "[t]he wonder lotion for all aches and pains (for external use only)," advised that "Sports Enthusiasts should never be without a Bottle." The cost: 1/9 per bottle (something less than 9p or 15 cents). Even Joe Kirk's Orchestra, which saw itself to be "Hull's Most Versatile Dance Musicians," aimed its act directly at ballplayers. The group's promotion told readers, "Keep Fit for the BALL GAME by DANCING TO JOE KIRK'S ORCHESTRA."

Other northern towns had equally supportive communities. While West Ham programs included advertising for only the stadium's greyhound racing, the Greenfield Giants, a top team in the Yorkshire League which played in the greyhound race venue Greenfield Stadium (opened in 1927 at Dudley Hill, Bradford), had numerous advertisers from a cross-section of businesses. Among them: Taylor and Parsons, which sold lawn mowers; Watson & Widd, a menswear store; Smith & Hardcastle, Ltd., a general and furnishing ironmongers; Barracloughs, which sold port wines; and The Creamery Cafes, which boasted "pleasant & efficient service" and "extremely moderate prices."

Likewise, the Sheffield Dons also had broad-based support that included a sporting goods company, a milk producer, a radio "amplifying specialist," the local newspaper and a brewery taking ads in the team's program.

According to Ian Smyth, who has written extensively about baseball in the north of England, baseball in Hull and the surrounding Yorkshire County benefited tremendously from the tireless energy of one man during this era, an Australian named Alf Grogan. Smyth has interviewed many individuals who were active in the game in the northeast of England in the late 1930s and found that Grogan, who was the Yorkshire area secretary of the National Baseball Association, was the "lynchpin" of the sport's success in Yorkshire. It seems Grogan was a man of many talents who umpired professional games as well as managed and commented on matches at various times. Equally as important, he devoted a huge amount time working on grassroots efforts, developing a schools program, dispensing equipment, and coaching.

Like teams in the London, the professional squads in the North also had financial backers, but Smyth suggests that those financially supporting individual teams "were not seeking profit, rather baseball was a hobby." It seems that the philanthropic attitude displayed in England's largest and (as Yorkshire natives might have it) most independently minded county was a marked difference from some London owners, like those at White City, Harringay, and Hackney, who tired of baseball after just one season, seemingly because they did not get immediate returns on their investments.

Along with their "hobby" disposition, organizers in Yorkshire also took a different approach to marketing the game than the likes of West Ham's Wood. A diehard baseball fan, Wood calculated that spectators would want to see the best players he could put out on the field. As a result, his team was made up almost exclusively of North Americans. In contrast, in 1936, the teams in the Yorkshire League focused on getting star athletes from other established sports to take on baseball. So while the Yorkshire teams would have a sprinkling of foreigners, the emphasis on getting British athletes, most notably Rugby stars, appeared to legitimize the game for the media. For example the Leeds Oaks included both Eric Harris, a top player in the Leeds Rugby League side, and Dick Auty, who played for Headingley and was an England Rugby Union[55] player. When the two took to baseball, the press automatically heralded them as stars. For Smyth it was unclear whether or not this was an intentional ploy by the administrators of baseball. It may have been that calling on such sporting celebrities was no more than a blatant attempt to promote the game, but it is certain that the likes of Auty and Harris were superb athletes in their day and they drew public attention.

Most importantly, the press in Yorkshire were strong supporters of baseball. On 20 June 1936, a writer for the *Scarborough Evening News* recounted:

> It is probable that the reason why the game is becoming popular in England is that the spectators can "root" to their hearts content and when all is said and done, there is nothing the average Englishman likes better than to say what he likes without fear of reprimand.

Elsewhere there had been other sanguine responses with regard to the prospects of baseball; on 25 March 1936, the *Leeds Mercury* commented, "Before long, baseball will find a permanent place in Yorkshire summer sport programme."

The *Sheffield Telegram* also was impressed with how baseball was being received in Yorkshire. In its 25 May 1936 edition, it wrote about a tight game between the Sheffield Dons and the Hull Baseball Club: "Hull people do not quickly take to fresh pastimes, but it is safe to say that Sheffield's visit has done an inestimable amount of good in the way of popularizing the game along the Humberside," the paper commented.

As in the South, the top teams in Yorkshire quickly emerged. From the beginning of the 1936 season, the Dons' games were considered to be something of an event in the industrial city of Sheffield, as the *Scarborough Evening Post* testified following the team's opening day, which attracted 6,000 spectators:

> Among those present were Mr. A Ferris, the resident American Consul and Mr. Ayrds, vice-president of the Sheffield Baseball Club, the Lord Mayor and Lady Mayoress of Sheffield, Mr. James Bamford, chairman of the Scarborough Football Club, and Mr. Gleeson, President of Owlerton Stadium....
> The game was opened by the Lord Mayor of Sheffield, who pitched the first ball. He was presented with a bar of Scarborough Rock made in the form of a baseball stick by Mr. Bamford, who was given a Sheffield pen knife.

As well as attracting the attention of their respective communities, Sheffield and Hull were quite profitable. In contrast, a well-attended game for the Scarborough Seagulls, which would fold in August of the 1937 season due to a financial deficit of £2 7s 9d, was around 500 fans. Another team in the league—Leeds—averaged 1,000 at the gate in 1936. However, it is an accomplishment worth noting that some baseball games attracted more spectators than "Club Cricket" matches in Yorkshire during this time, according to British baseball writer Daniel Bloyce.

Despite the mixed results, only one team, the Dewsbury Royals, did not return for the 1937 season (they were replaced by the York Maroons). With the domination of West Ham and other London teams like White City in 1936, it is perhaps not surprising that the proud organizers of baseball in Yorkshire were keen on turning the tables on their southern counterparts in 1937. According to Smyth:

> 1937 saw the game develop into a more serious sport. Yorkshire League teams were now importing Americans and Canadians to strengthen their squads.... By recruiting these players, the clubs hoped for a successful team which, in turn would attract large crowds. This seriousness of involvement was highlighted by the complexion of the teams. Gone were the rugby players and in came the experienced foreign players.

Unfortunately, the results were often not exciting offensive games that would attract fans, but pitching duels with the likes of star pitchers like "Lefty" Wilson dominating hitters. The *Hull Daily Mail* wrote on 24 May 1937 about a game between Hull and the York Maroons, a newcomer to the league that season: "The pitchers were on top all the time and it is no great fun to English baseball crowds to see little else than an almost unending progression of batsmen swiping thin air to earn immediate dismissal."

For all this, the sport continued to thrive in the north of England, with (according to Smyth) attendance remaining steady in the 1937 season. However, in 1938, John Moores and other National Baseball Association organizers decided to make a change. With the London Major Baseball League no more, the Yorkshire League was folded and a ten-club Yorkshire-Lancashire league was created in its place. The new league would include the strongest ten clubs from the Yorkshire and the North of England League in Lancashire. It was a strategy professional baseball in England had employed following both the 1935 season in the North of England League and after the 1936 season in London. The teams that remained were those that had the most solid footing in their respective communities: Leeds, Hull, Sheffield, York, Greenfield, Oldham, Rochdale, Liverpool, Bolton, and Halifax.

Unlike the purely professional ventures of the London Major Baseball League, this new circuit was semi-professional. Each team would have only two pros and the rest of the athletes were British. The purpose was to emphasize home-grown talent. Along with trying to improve the British plight on the field, Moores' National Baseball Association was also very keen to help the paying public get a better grasp of the finer points of the game. For the 1938 season, all games featured expert commentators who described the intricacies of the baseball action. In addition, instead of leaving promotion to each team, endorsement of the game was managed centrally.

In a sense, this new approach demonstrated the shrewd awareness of Moores and his cohorts. For the game of baseball to take long-term root in England, there had to be a seed-bed of skilled British players. The reorganization of the game in 1938 was designed to meet this goal. However, although the league continued into 1939, the war prevented the experiment of the Yorkshire-Lancashire league to be given any chance of showing fruit.

Alf Spendlow, the young Hull lad who had taken up baseball just before World War II, decades later in the *Hull Daily Mail* told of the impact the war had made both on the sport of baseball and those who had taken up the game:

> The war spoilt everything and some of the lads in [a] photograph [of the Ranks Green Sox] never saw the end of it.... Although my parents' house was badly damaged during the blitz my mother kept all the cuttings, cup etc. ... for me, and gave them to me when I returned home after the war after being a prisoner in German Prisoner of War camps for five years.

West Ham Baseball's Legacy

Although the West Ham Baseball Club and their Custom House compatriots the Pirates disbanded at the end of the 1937 season, a number of players from those teams did go on to make notable impacts on the game of baseball above and beyond their performances at West Ham Stadium and made a positive impact in the name of England.

After the 1937 season, with Roland Gladu returning to Canada, former Hammer Jerry Strong went north to play for Hull. Buccaneers Sam Hanna and Frank Cadorette also migrated up the country to compete for Halifax. All three players were among the professionals in the newly created semi-pro Yorkshire-Lancashire League. While a league title eluded West Ham, these three former Docklands heroes helped lead England to one of its most unlikely of sporting achievements—the first Baseball World Championship.

England—World Champions

On 11 August 1938, the U.S. Olympic baseball team returned to England, arriving in Plymouth for a five-game "Test Series" with an English select team. At the time, there was no talk of a world championship. The U.S. squad was preparing for the Games that were planned for Tokyo in 1940.[56] Leslie Mann, who had led the American baseball Olympians to Berlin in 1936 and to defeat against West Ham that same year, was once again at the helm of a United States representative squad. His team was a combination of high school and college players picked the month before at the USA national amateur baseball trials held in Lincoln, Nebraska. The squad was formidable, including in its ranks two future major league players. Mike "Lefty" Schemer went on to play two seasons for the New York Giants and Mizell Platt was a big leaguer for five seasons with the Chicago White Sox, Chicago Cubs and St. Louis Browns.

The English team was made up almost entirely of players born in Canada. Perhaps England's best player was Ross Kendrick, who was described in a game program as a "pitcher with a very clean style of hooks, speed, and endurance." Kendrick would become a legendary fixture in British baseball, playing well into his middle age in England; one eyewitness claimed seeing the 60-year-old-plus Kendrick pitching a game many years after the world championship triumph.

The five-game US vs. England series in Liverpool, Hull, Rochdale, Halifax, and Leeds attracted large crowds. The first match drew 10,000 people to Wavertree Stadium in Liverpool. They watched England soundly defeat the Americans 3–0. The ex–Pirate Hanna was a hitting star, coming off the bench as a pinch hitter and delivering a run scoring double. In game two at Craven Park, home of the Hull Kingston Rovers Rugby League Club, one-time Hammer Jerry Strong took center stage in front of a crowd of 5,000. The pitcher struck out 12 batters, giving up only two runs through the first six innings. He did eventually give way to fatigue, but England won again 8–6. Hanna hit a two-run home run for England during a five-run outburst in the game's fifth inning and Cadorette contributed a run. The Americans took the next game 5–0 in Rochdale, but the laudable (if honorary) Limeys clinched the series at The Shay in Halifax with a 4–0 victory. Both Hanna and Cadorette scored runs for England in front of 5,000 celebrating spectators. England also won the final game 5–3 in Leeds to complete a four-games-to-one beating of the Americans.

In retrospect, the defeats were not the biggest setback that history had in store for the U.S. squad; the outbreak of war led to the cancellation of the 1940 Olympics. Time smiled more favorably on the winning England side. Following the results of the series, the International Baseball Federation decided to designate the contest as the first World Championships and named England the inaugural World Amateur Champions. To this day, that bureaucratic decision may be England's greatest baseball victory.

Thus, just as West Ham United players Bobby Moore, Geoff Hurst, and Martin Peters were to win the soccer World Cup for England in 1966, Strong, Hanna, and Cadorette brought part of the credit for the World Championship victory to the baseball played at West Ham Stadium.

Baseball in Britain during World War II

From the beginning of hostilities, the British Army was clear that sports were going to be a big part of war. To that end, the Army Sport Control Board, War Office, published "Games and Sports in the Army,"

The 1966 Soccer World Cup Final (just before kick-off). West Ham was always a home of champion players. Three baseball players who played for either the West Ham Baseball Club or the Pirates went on to win the first recognized world baseball cup. On a bigger stage, three members of the local soccer team, West Ham United, led England to its only soccer World Cup triumph. The World Champion Hammers: Martin Peters (second from right) next to him Geoff Hurst, and captain Bobby Moore (his arms in the air).

which provided explanations of sports, including baseball, that the Army should and could organize during the war. The cost of the book was 4 shillings (20p).[57]

Games and Sports in the Army opens with a history of sport in the military: "Sport entered into the profession of arms many years ago, but, perhaps, it was not until 1914 that its spirit was subjected fully to the acid test of war."

The book then points out that personal fitness is a key to military success and that sport is a means to that end. "No efficient Army, of course, ever underrated the value of personal fitness."

But sport, the book continues, does more than just serve as a way to increase heart rate and burn calories. "Team and individual games enable us to do rather than to learn things and they provide splendid opportunities to apply bodily strength and mental alertness, to take a chance, to be constructive and bold, and to receive hard knocks without flinching."

In 1918 Great Britain formed the Army Sport Control Board and similar organizations were set up after that by the Royal Navy, Royal Marines, and the Royal Air Force. These boards saw that sport was a way to keep the soldiers' morale high.

The secret of command rests on gaining the trust and affection of all those under their respective commanders. That trust is best gained by working with and for every member of the team. Trust is gained by team work. Team work, in peace time, requires grounds for the teams to play on.

Although war is certainly hell, the British Army was unwilling to deviate from the standards of comportment in the sporting world that the empire had conformed to for so long. *Games and Sports in the Army* insisted that, even in the military, soldiers must be sportsmen. The book quoted the late General Sir Charles Harrington,[58] who was the first president of the Army Sport Control Board, on this matter:

> Our definition of a Sportsman is one who–
> 1. Plays the game for the game's sake.
> 2. Plays for his side and not for himself.
> 3. Is a good winner and a good loser, i.e., modest in victory and generous in defeat.
> 4. Accepts all decisions in a proper spirit.
> 5. Is chivalrous towards a defeated opponent
> 6. Is unselfish and always ready to help others to become proficient.
> Service games are modeled on the above. If we keep these six points always before use, we shall not go far wrong.

To this end, *Games and Sports in the Army* listed some 30 different sports plus detailed general physical fitness regimes, how to set up fields, and taught general refereeing and umpiring skills. Some of these sports, not necessarily having the appeal of athletics or soccer, were listed in a section on "small side games," which were "small side" versions of better-known national pastimes and also rules of various other games, the majority of which can be organized under all conditions.

While baseball did not get a place in the larger section of sports, it was represented in the "small side team games" with five pages of the book's 628 pages. The section included a diagram of a baseball field, and the "Canadian Rules" of the sport. In proper military fashion, the description of the sport is spartan and provides just the bare nuts and bolts.

In 1939, the Army Sport Control Board spent £2,419, 13s. 3d. on sports, including £25 each for the Army Basket Ball Association, the Modern Pentathlon Association and the Army Fencing Union. More popular sports like soccer (in excess of £237) and athletics and cross country (£360) received even greater amounts for clerical and general purposes. Baseball appeared to get nothing.

Nevertheless, while baseball did not get the attention of other sports by the British Army *per se*, people all over Britain and thousands of soldiers throughout the theaters of war would play baseball vigorously over the war years and probably did their best to live up to the sportsman's credo suggested by General Harrington.

In 1940, Canadian soldiers began arriving in Britain. While Canadians in England's professional baseball leagues had already made their mark for baseball in the United Kingdom over the previous half-decade, the influx of "Canuck" soldiers caused a huge increase in baseball participation in the British Isles.

According to Gary Bedingfield, author of *Baseball in World War II Europe*, the Canadians who first arrived in England were too spread out to create cohesive leagues of Canadian-only teams. As a result many joined in with British sides. This was probably quite easy since most British teams were already accustomed to the foreign influence.

In London, clubs like the DeHavilland Comets and Ford Motor Company, which had played against the likes of the Romford Wasps since 1938, were quick to take on players. For example, DeHavilland, as an aviation company, had numerous Canadian employees before and during the war. Its team actually won the British baseball championship in 1939.

But when the United States forces began arriving in 1942, baseball competition reached a new high and big crowds came out to see the North Americans play each other. The first such contest occurred on 4 July 1942 at Selhurst Park in London (home of the Crystal Palace Football Club). In that game, a Canadian all-star team lost 19–17 to a United States Air Force squad. Later that summer, the Canadians got their revenge. On 3 August, 6,000 spectators watched the Canadian Army Headquarters defeat the U.S. Army Headquarters 5–3 in a charity match at Wembley Stadium, and the game raised $3,800 for the British Red Cross. These events proved to be effective fundraisers as evidenced by a game between Canadian and American servicemen at North London's Finchley Football Club that raised more than $1,000, thanks to a crowd of 4,000. The proceeds in that event went to purchase a mobile x-ray unit as part of "Aid to Russia" week. The Americans were the winners in that game 9–5.

These games were also great displays of baseball. On 7 August 1943, 21,500 spectators watched as Sergeant Bill Brech of Secaucus, New Jersey, threw a no-hitter for the U.S. Air Force against the U.S. Ground Force in an "All-professional game" at the Empire Stadium, Wembley Stadium. Brech overpowered a team of professionals that included former Washington Senators pitcher Lou Thuman, striking out six batters and allowing just three balls hit out of the infield. For good measure he also drove in the game's only run in the 1–0 victory.

Bedingfield described the right-handed Brech as "arguably the best pitcher to serve with the Air Force in England during the war." As a member of the 988th Military Police, Brech pitched for three seasons winning more than 20 games and throwing another no-hitter against the 1st BADA Bearcats in the 1944 Air Service Command Championships.

By 1943, 750,000 troops were stationed in Great Britain. With so many soldiers, individual games and smaller leagues gave way to some highly competitive circuits. Most notable was the London International Baseball League. The eight-team league "attracted the most talented players in the London area," according to Bedingfield. Many games in the league were played at Stamford Bridge, the famed home of the Chelsea Football Club. This league gave birth to one of the top all-star teams of the war years, the CBS (Central Base Station) Clowns. Led by Charles Eisenmann, a former pitcher in the Pacific Coast League, the Clowns traveled throughout the British Isles in 1943 taking on all comers. Their record that summer was 43–4 as they played games not only in London but also in Blackpool, Liverpool, and Scotland. With very few stadiums sporting a mound, the team's leader Eisenmann even created a traveling mound that he brought with his team from game to game. Just after D-Day, the team moved to France and continued playing until the end of 1945.

As for the British playing baseball during the war, there were very few teams that lasted. The most notable was the Hornsey Red Sox. The Red Sox were established in 1935 by Doug Cowling and battled for British pride against numerous American and Canadian service teams. For example, on 4 July 1943, the Red Sox fell to a U.S. Army team 8–3 in Muswell Hill, in Northern London. The game was held to aid the Duke of Gloucester's Red Cross & St. John Fund.

The great escape

As Tim Wolter explained in his book *POW Baseball in World War II: The National Pastime Behind Barbed Wire*, the history of British baseball continued to be written even in the hostile atmosphere of Axis prisoner of war camps: "The YMCA was active in collecting Baseball and softball equipment, which was then transported, stored, and distributed to the camps by the International Red Cross, which had a protective role for prisoners of war of most nations during the Second World War."

During 1940 and 1941, soccer and cricket were the main sports at many of the prison camps as the U.S. had not entered the war and most prisoners were British. By 1943, Americans were beginning to enter these camps and during 1944 their numbers had swelled. With the mix of Americans and the British, Wolter said that there were some British converts to the game of diamonds. Wolter quotes American colonel John Vietor, who wrote in *American Airmen in Stalag Luft I:* "One of the unexpected reversals of the war occurred when we beat the British at rugby and they promptly turned around and beat us at baseball."

Clearly, not all the British POWs had seen a game at West Ham Stadium. An RAF officer named A.E. Bullock wrote in a wartime log,

> Strange games they play with sticks and balls
> Sometimes they utter curious calls
> Of 'Huba-Huba, let's get two'
> We don't know what they mean, do you?

Stalag Luft III, which was located near the city of Sagan some 100 miles southeast of Berlin, was the prison camp that was the inspiration for *The Great Escape.* By 1944, 200 teams were actively playing baseball in six compounds. Wolter estimates that softball began being played in the summer of 1942 at Luft III alongside cricket.

The British were also involved with baseball in Luft III. According to a Canadian officer, Harold Garland, who recounted an intercompound game:

> The Canadian pitcher was Bill Paton, and he had pitched in the Beaches League in Toronto. And the umpire was Larry Wray, our Senior British Officer. And Larry Wray had to go to Bill about inning number five or six and say "Please let them hit, Bill." They hadn't touched the ball all that game!

Throughout the Stalag system, the Americans and the Canadians played a role in selling baseball to their fellow British POWs. One British prisoner of war was quoted in the October 1943 edition of the Red Cross *Prisoner of War Bulletin*: "We have now 37 of your [American] compatriots here from Tunis. They all seem fit and cheerful and are very popular. They and the Canadians are making us baseball minded."

While the British continued to play cricket, more than a few were proselytized by American "baseball missionaries." According to Major Charles Page, upon being repatriated from a POW camp: "The English officers played softball ... and were enthusiastic about it and played well."

Impact

The wartime baseball had an impact on British youth. Goff Phillips, who was born in 1928 and was an evacuee from London during the war, recounted to Bedingfield his first interaction with baseball.

> The American Air Force began playing baseball at the Bedford rugby ground ... I used to go along to watch but I didn't understand the rules. Then one day, while cycling to school, I noticed a book in the window of a sports shop. The book was called "Baseball For the British Youth" and it cost me one crown (5 shillings, 25p) which was a great deal of money in those days. I studied the book every moment I could and soon learned the rules and fell in love with the game.

The volume Goff picked up for "five bob" was likely West Ham player Eric Whitehead's book. Phillips returned to London to become a baseball player and his active career went on for more than a half a century. He played for some of the area's top amateur sides including Thames Board Mills (that played just a few miles from West Ham Stadium) and the Hornsey Athletics, winning league championships with both clubs and being named an all-star on four occasions. He also represented Great Britain at the 1967 European Baseball Championships in Belgium, helping his country reach the final and take the silver medal.

Through it all, the echoes of the London Major Baseball League could still be heard. White City was the location for many military baseball games and Romford also hosted matches.

Could baseball have made a comeback in West Ham? Would English kids in London have developed as top baseball players? Both greyhound racing and speedway stopped at Custom House during World War II and managed a renaissance when peace came, so the coming of hostilities cannot be used to explain why the foundations of baseball were not built on in East London, although there are those who insist that British baseball, by the last part of the 20th century, might have been able to compete with America and Canada if World War II had not caused the end of the Yorkshire-Lancashire League, since players of all nationalities went off to fight. Understandably, during the years of war, whatever little sway baseball had on the sporting consciousness was eliminated by the clear and present danger facing the British people. The interests of John Moores were taken up with guiding his wider investments through the half decade of conflict and perhaps the same distractions drew L.D. Wood away from the game he had put so much into over the previous two years. For all this, most sport continued in one way or another and soccer teams like West Ham United were able to take advantage of being at the crossroads of Britain's war effort and close to places where forces were stationed. During the war, with allied soldiers organizing recreational baseball, the London International Baseball League became a highly competitive eight-team circuit, contested by American and Canadian military personnel in front of large crowds of mainly allied soldiers.

But as Jim Appleby suggests ("Past Times"—*Bradford Telegraph and Argus* on 17 June 1998) the coming of conflict nipped the national development of baseball in the bud:

> Sadly, just as baseball was taking off, so were Hitler's Luftwaffe. The Second World War came along and somehow, afterwards, the enthusiasm seemed to have waned.
> Hull maintained its liking for the game and still has a handful of teams. But Bradford, Scarborough, Whitby, Oldham, Bury, and the like let it drop.

Post-War

After the Second World War baseball attempted to reclaim its place in British sport. With a huge number of American and Canadian soldiers stationed in the United Kingdom, the game had enough experienced players to gain minor prominence. In London, baseball received some solid coverage in local newspapers, while in the north some very capable baseball teams were developing, most notably in Hull and in Stretford near Manchester. But the quality of the leagues depended on foreigners. Andy Parkes, who played for the Stretford Saints in the post-war era, recalled that the team leaders would run over to local factories and firms whenever they heard that an American or a Canadian had joined their workforce. One of the Saints' (and Northern England's) top players in this period, Wally O'Neil, was recruited by this brand of approach. O'Neil, a Canadian, had come to England to work as an electric control engineer but he was swiftly enlisted to play baseball. He went on to lead the Saints to numerous championships.

Baseball of the 1930s could have had some impact on the politics of sport in England during the late 1940s. A short time before his final illness, in the spring of 1939, Babe Ruth visited Britain. There was no doubt as to the universality of Ruth's popularity and influence; as with Muhammad Ali years later, Ruth's appeal knew no borders or boundaries. Former star Middlesbrough striker and England soccer international Wilf Mannion was greatly influenced by the words and thoughts of Ruth, so much so that a decade after the Babe's visit Wilf as good as went on strike for higher wages.

In 1996, in an interview with Richard Whitehead, Mannion recalled how "The Babe" "had never seen such a big crowd.... He said: 'Gee, how much are the 22 players on?' All on the maximum wage of £8, he was told. 'Jeez, are they bloody idiots or something?' he said. We were, too, weren't we?" A good soccer player's income was not a bad sum for a workingman, but it was nothing to compare to the salaries that equivalent sporting champions were earning in the U.S. Ruth, during his earlier heyday, would not have gotten out of bed for that kind of money and many of Ruth's fellow big leaguers could have easily taken home an amount ten times greater than a top British soccer star at any time during Ruth's career.

By the conclusion of the 1947–48 season, Mannion had become frustrated with his lot. He turned down a new contract and made a formal request to be transferred to another club. He refused to train and was dropped from the Middlesbrough team. After eight months, Mannion was almost ready to take his case to Parliament and the House of Lords, the highest court of justice in Britain. A verdict in his favor might have changed the shape of industrial relations within professional sport in the

United Kingdom, with undoubted consequences not only for soccer but also for international tennis, rugby and cricket and those who had made big profits from these essentially (in the British context) amateur-led sports. But following complications in the later stages of Mannion's wife's first pregnancy, Wilf could fight on no longer. He signed for Middlesbrough and helped the club avoid relegation.

After much turbulence between players and the establishment elite of soccer, the maximum wage was abolished at the start of the 1960s. By that time Mannion had been retired for near half a decade. Marked out as a troublemaker, he was never given the opportunity to manage a club, the destiny of many international players, and after his playing career was over, the great Wilf Mannion was obliged to work in unskilled employment. He passed away in April 2000, having lived to see footballers,

Babe Ruth had an impact on both sides of the Atlantic. In a chance meeting with star soccer player Wilf Mannion, the great home run slugger questioned the fairness of wages for soccer players. Years later, the Babe's comments spurred Mannion in a failed attempt to increase salaries.

with far lesser skills than he had commanded, become millionaires. However, Mannion might be seen a pioneer of "player power"; he certainly was an early precursor of the movement that created a fairer deal for sports people in Britain, but the fact that he had been motivated by a star from American baseball might in itself be seen as telling in terms of the failure of baseball to re-establish itself after the Second World War.

Baseball in the United States clearly had to reward its best exponents to a level much closer to their worth, in terms of public enthusiasm and interest than was the case in British soccer or sport in general. This "tradition" was not something that sporting entrepreneurs in the United Kingdom would have been keen to inherit; the import of baseball was a comparatively unattractive option financially. In short it would have meant that a relatively cheap and controlled workforce would have placed alongside it more expensive, organized and liberated labor. As such, there was a danger that baseball would not just be a straightforward competitor for soccer and cricket, but a serious threat to the labor relations that pertained in British sport at the time. Wilf Mannion's response and experience was an exemplar of the dissatisfaction and strife that might have become much more general had baseball been supported and nurtured in Britain post–1945.

Although baseball continued to be played throughout London, equipment was hard to find and there is little doubt that it had lost ground during the war. Most sources said that it became very difficult to find equipment. Before the war, in 1939, baseball bats cost between five shillings and £1–16 shillings, baseballs from 1s.9d to 7s. 6d and catchers masks cost 14s.6d to 27s.6d, about the same as good quality cricket equipment. Prices must have been much higher than that following the hostilities. The British championship would not be contested until 1948. However, the Hornsey Red Sox remained one of the top teams in the country winning national championships in 1949 and runners-up in 1950.

Doug Cowling, who had become a fan of the sport in 1935, kept the team going for all those years. In 1935, as a fifteen-year-old, Cowling decided that he would start a baseball team and name it the Red Sox— after Boston's storied major league franchise. He figured he would write to the Red Sox' owner, Tom Yawkey, and tell him his team's new nickname. At the same time, he asked if Yawkey had any unwanted equipment that the Hornsey boys could use to start up their team. Amazingly, Cowling received a letter back from Yawkey and the team's manager, Joe Cronin, with a suitcase full of big league gloves, bats, balls, and catcher's equipment.

Although the team had lasted through the war, they were struggling by the late 1940s. The Red Sox were averaging about 100 to 150 spectators at their home games in Barnet (on the north London–Hertfordshire border). But for big games, there were still fans of baseball. In 1949, a crowd of 20,000—a number that would have made even the Hammers of baseball jealous—came out to see the Red Sox beat the Birmingham Beavers in the semi-finals of the British baseball Challenge Cup (the equivalent of the national championship). Then, more than 10,000 witnessed the Red Sox defeat the Liverpool Cubs in the 14 August finals at

White City Stadium, according to Cowling, who recounted the glory of his team in the August 1990 issue of *Baseball UK* magazine.

> Our games were dominated more by the pitcher ... there were far fewer hits per game and fewer errors. Most of the teams I've seen recently [in the UK in the late 1980s and early 1990s] are not as well drilled in the fundamentals of defense as we were. We worked hard on defense, cut-offs, and relays and it paid off.

As the 1950s dawned, the players of one of the last continuously running British teams since the sport's golden age in England drifted apart. Maybe it was the fact that by the 1950s, the players were in their late 30s and early 40s and were tired of fundraising to keep the team going. These aging men would buy ice cream at tuppence (2d, about .5p) and sell it for six-pence (2.5p) during their home games to raise money. In any event, the players turned their attention to family responsibility and the Hornsey Red Sox, once partially supported by Tom Yawkey himself, were no more.

With the 1950s hitting full stride, North Americans were more and more choosing to run their own sides rather than join British teams.

Up north, the Stretford Saints (based near Manchester) developed into one of the best post-World War II clubs. When a British team like Stretford faced off against Americans there were generally good crowds. Here, the mainly British Saints take on the American powerhouse military team, the Burtonwood Bees. Stretford's George Livsley (batting) looks for a good pitch. Used with permission of George Livsley.

The Burtonwood Bees, for example, was a squad from an American Air Force base that was all-conquering in the 1950s. But financial support and general interest from Britons was limited. George Livsley, an organizer of the Stretford Saints, recollected that by the end of the war there was very little equipment available for British teams and that the cost of what baseball paraphernalia could be purchased was often prohibitive. However, it appears the sport continued to have a place in the British consciousness and was associated with fun and the future. For example, Chuck Cole, a player from that era, recounted how baseball was included at the Festival of Britain exhibition in London in 1951. The game was demonstrated for four to five weeks during the summer and drew some inquisitive spectators; Chuck remembered only "one or two inquiries" about playing.

Although the status of the sport was nowhere near what it had been in its glory days of the late 1930s, some maintained optimism about the prospects of the British game. Scoutmaster Fred Lewis, who handmade his own equipment at the start of the 20th century and traveled throughout England teaching baseball to young scouts, worked to develop the game in his hometown of Chipping Norton in Oxfordshire. His activity exemplified the enthusiasm that the British could have for baseball. Lewis also injected some British optimism about the staying power of the sport in England. In 1950, at age 71, more than four decades after he had discovered the game, Lewis continued to hold out hope for baseball's continued place in the British sporting prospect:

> Still the good old game goes on. Sons of our first players are now back from the Services and have taken on where father left off. Maybe I shall live to see the third lot knocking one or two out, for quite a number of small "pitchers" follow around with their smart young mothers on Sunday afternoons, saying: Go on Dad, it's the seventh. Give 'em all you've got.

But baseball's main attraction in the country at this time came from U.S. and Canadian military games, which could still draw substantial crowds. However the spectators were mainly other soldiers; audiences for British contests were much smaller. For example, a game in 1954 between the U.S.A.F. Cowboys and R.C.A.F. Langar attracted more than 4,000 while in contrast Leeds, which could easily draw 1,000 spectators to a game before the war, got only 300 to watch them lose to the Kingston Diamonds.

Many leagues included a combination of North American and British teams, for example, a six-team baseball league that operated in Essex and Kent during the early 1950s. Two of the six teams seem to have been based at Fords in Dagenham while the Aylesham Magpies from Kent came about because the manager of the Snowdown Welfare Football Club, a soccer team from the English county of Kent (the cross–Thames neighbor of Essex) also coached a soccer team at a nearby US air base at Manston,

ALL AMERICAN BASEBALL

by teams specially selected from the

U.S. AIR FORCE

A T

WHITE CITY STADIUM

AUGUST 6th, 1954

IN AID OF

THE ROYAL LONDON SOCIETY FOR THE BLIND

(Registered in accordance with the National Assistance Act, 1948)

OFFICIAL PROGRAMME 1/–

Even after the demise of the London Major Baseball League, the stadiums that housed the circuit were occasionally used for baseball events. White City, which was home to the Citizens in 1936, hosted numerous baseball games following World War II, including this charity matchup in 1954 between U.S. Air Force squads.

near Canterbury. The Snowdown coach saw the virtue of baseball as a way to keep his players in shape during the summer. In fact, the team put on an exhibition of baseball prior to a big cricket match in Canterbury in 1955, according to British journalist David Mankelow.

The fact that British baseball's modest success in the 1950s was largely due to foreign players was not lost on British baseball pundits. In the 16 July 1953 issue of *Baseball News*, the newsletter of the South Eastern Baseball League, an editorial ran revealing the concerns about non-British involvement:

> The scarcity of "home-produced" players has led to an increasing demand for the services of visitors to this country who are "ready-made" ballplayers. Whilst U.S. Servicemen are in England it is natural that there will be a large number of them competing in British baseball, ... [but] there will naturally be a difference should there be a future decline in the numbers of "guest stars" available. It is for this fact alone that all teams should concentrate on building up "local talent" side by side with the experienced men.

Concerns about foreign influence were not limited to the specialty newspapers. Parkes of the Stretford Saints told a newspaper reporter in the mid–'60s that the "Americanism" of baseball was inevitably hindering the game's growth. What had been such a novelty in the days of Roland Gladu was now a distraction. "I think it's bound to put some people off.... But the game is American," Parkes said. "All the terms are American. There aren't English words for them."

In an article in the Manchester area's *Evening News & Chronicle*, 29 June 1964, writer Jack McNamara echoed the words of the prince of Wales some 75 years previously: "Cricket is so deeply entrenched in the affections of thousands of red-blooded supporters that baseball has not a chance."

For all this, a team from Essex, Thames Board Mills, represented the South well, earning back-to-back national titles in 1959 and 1960. But baseball's brief run as a professional sport seemed to have made more of an impact in the Merseyside and Yorkshire areas. The consequences of this were a major contributing factor to baseball's uncertain future; the sport was becoming regionally fragmented between the North and the South. To some extent there had always been a divide—maybe it was started with West Ham's all-conquering northern crusade—but signs that the split was becoming more profound appeared just a few years after the Second World War. On 27 June 1952, an England squad traveled to the Netherlands to play in what the *Evening News*, which covered the London area, described as "the important" Dutch Jubilee Celebration. Although the England side lost both its matches, the games were close. However, the *Evening News* criticized the English organizers for having a bias toward players from the North. According to the newspaper, the

Sutton Beavers, which was a particularly strong team in the London area, sent the names of its three top players, but they were rejected. In the end, only one player from the South was selected to represent the nation.

In response to the situation the leagues in the South formed their own squad to play an international game. On 26 July a team representing England took on a squad from the Canadian military. The English side was essentially an all-star squad from the Western League, but was given the England title to help publicize the contest. It worked. The game, which was played in Surrey, attracted a sizeable audience, according to Norman Adams, who played for England in the contest.

The North and South did reunite in September to play in a tournament against a U.S. Air Force side from Lakenheath in Suffolk and a squad representing Spain. Although England had eight players from the South and seven from the North, the results were not great: England lost 8–2 to the U.S. and 4–2 to Spain.

Fear of the future

However, those who organized British baseball were not ready to give up. While some companies offered sponsorship (for instance, the Ford Motor Company), gone were the days of substantial financial support from the likes of A.G. Spalding or John Moores. But in 1963, a National Baseball League was formed with teams from all areas of the country: Stretford, Hull, Nottingham, Coventry, Manchester, Birmingham, and London. The league aimed to start competition at the end of the association football season and play until soccer began again in the late fall. The league survived until 1972, but the game was strictly amateur and any hopes of reclaiming a place in the panorama of British sport was never likely at a time when even the traditional summer game of cricket was struggling to hold its position.

By the late 1960s baseball was purely an amateur phenomenon, with the best of its competition being played in pockets north of London in places like Liverpool, Hull, and Nottingham. Organizers in the North (centered in Hull) and the South (with teams mainly in London and the surrounding "home counties") appeared to be focusing on their own areas. Despite winning the silver medal at the 1967 European Championships in Belgium, the country had difficulty in assembling a consistent, cohesive, national squad. International play in 1969 was emblematic of the factional nature of the baseball in that period. Representative teams from both South Africa and Zambia traveled to Great Britain to play in separate series. Instead of British baseball's governing body forming a single squad, various regions organized all-star teams to face the foreign

Since the professional game in England disappeared with the start of World War II, it has become difficult to find proper baseball diamonds. Here's a photo of a typical all-grass field in England from the 1960s. Used with permission of George Livsley.

competition. The Zambia team played all-star sides from the Midlands, the Northeast and the Northwest, and also competed against various individual clubs. The South Africans met the National League Southern all-stars in London and then played the National League Northern all-stars in Hull. This situation did not improve throughout the 1970s. At times throughout this era, the Great Britain national team reflected this situation, seemingly being chosen exclusively from particular areas of the country; the choice of favored regions was apparently dependent on who was doing the selecting.

In 1975, Mr. Myron Ferentz, who had formed a baseball equipment company, "took the initiative in calling a meeting aimed at getting the warring factions in British baseball to sit around a table and attempt to sink their differences," according to the leading British baseball publication of the time, *Baseball Mercury*. Since 1969, representatives from the main baseball-playing areas—the Southeast, Midlands, Merseyside and Humberside—had not all met once at the same time face to face. The meeting must have been some kind of a success as a number of issues, including matters relating to England's national team, were decided.

It wasn't until 1977 when a London-based team, the Golders Green Sox, won a national championship again. It should be said that sheer practicality played a role in the split. Although some regional competition (most notably all-star games and cup competitions) did continue, a lack of adequate funding made it difficult for teams and players to travel up and down the country every week. But there were also periodic disagreements on the direction of the game's development. Mike Carlson, who was Major League Baseball's representative in Great Britain between 1990 and 1994, believed these distinct power bases ultimately hurt the overall growth of the game. "To a certain extent, the problem [in Great Britain] is the club structure," Carlson said. "You can't get to a wider area; you can't disseminate the sport beyond small areas. There were a lot of little fiefdoms. People liked running their small program. They'd rather be a big fish in a small pond."

The contemporary situation

The cyclical moments of optimism and bouts of despair about the future of British baseball have continued up to the present era. In 1987, the Scottish Amicable Life Assurance Society, a British-based insurance company, agreed to sponsor British baseball. The value of the three-year deal was said to be about £300,000. With the funding, the British Baseball Federation formed the Scottish Amicable National League. The new league was created, according to a 1987 issue of *Touching Base*, the organization's official newsletter, "to provide British Baseball its 'Shop-window' that gives [the] sport credibility by staging games for the sporting public to the best possible standards."

Many involved with baseball at the time argued that the game appeared to be gaining ground on other sports. It also helped that Major League Baseball was being televised by a number of outlets during this period including, the national network Channel 4, and later the cable channels Screensport (now defunct) and Sky Sports. British baseball leaders staged several high-profile events to draw attention to the game. The British National Team took on The Legends of Baseball side, a traveling all-star team of ex-major leaguers including Hall-of-Famers Bob Feller, Willie Stargell and Billy Williams, at Old Trafford cricket ground, the grand and historic home of the powerful Lancashire Cricket Club.

But by 1990, the 100th anniversary of organized baseball in Great Britain, Scottish Amicable ended its financial support of the game. The reasons for the withdrawal of funding were unclear. Some suggested that funding was misappropriated. Others insist that the sponsorship just ran its course. Whatever the case, future sponsors of Great Britain's National League, Coors and then Rawlings, were generous, but not to the same degree as Scottish Amicable. British baseball was also marred by another controversy. In 1991, an entrepreneur, Malcolm Needs, organized the new National League. It was intended to make use of large stadiums and hopefully attract British fans back to baseball. But a disagreement between Needs and British Baseball Federation president Mike Harrold resulted in the National League breaking away from the British Baseball Federation. Its players, which were among the country's best, were banned from playing for any BBF-related organizations, including the national team. In 1994, baseball's governing body in Europe got involved and Needs left the British game and the formally banned players were welcomed back into the BBF fold.

British baseball was also held back by a foreign player limit put into place in 1988. According to Alan Smith, a longtime British player and organizer, the restriction, which followed a long history of fear that non-British players would dominate the domestic game, seriously curtailed participation. More specifically, the limit on foreigners caused the demise of the Surrey Baseball Association and the dismantling of three major adult teams: the Oxshott Orioles, the Woking White Sox and, most importantly, the Cobham Yankees, which was founded six years earlier and had won the All-England club championship four times. "It caused David Brown, the man responsible for the Surrey Association, to lose interest in the sport here and affected the future of the six junior teams that he had created," said Smith.

But through all this, a hard core of interest was sustained and a level of potential in terms of curiosity about baseball continued Richard Weekes reported about a meeting of New York Mets and Boston Red Sox minor leaguers in 1993 from one of the centers of English cricket, The Oval, in Kennington, southwest London, the almost sacred ground on which innumerable international matches have taken place down the years, home of the Surrey County Cricket Club, one of the mighty powers of England's summer game: "But for the gasholders and the spires of Parliament, the 5,190 gathered here yesterday might have thought they had parachuted into downtown Cincinnati or St Louis...."

It seems that the crowd was a little perplexed by the rites of baseball, but the presence of Alec Stewart, Graham Thorpe and Syd Lawrence[59] in the pre-game home-run derby created a deal of interest. Weekes recounted the events:

> Lawrence showed up his England colleagues by clearing the fence more often than they did. "It's not hard to make contact," he said. "In cricket we practice with a narrow bat to get used to hitting it off the middle." He then strode off, grabbed the hand of a Mets official and demanded, "Where's the contract?"
>
> Stewart's failure drew criticism from some of the fans. "His stance is all wrong," said Andrew Boyd, one of a group of players from the Crawley Comets. "He's swinging it like a cricket bat."

Raymond Seitz, the American ambassador, took in the game from the sponsor's lounge, but took time out to talk to Weekes about the European sales pitch being made by Major League Baseball, making the point that a country could play only a certain number of sports, but that baseball ought to suit the British temperament, as it was, not a violent game and not played against the clock.

As to the central drama on the field, the Mets' first baseman, Alan Zinter, with four home runs was the only player to beat Lawrence's three in the home run derby. In the actual game Zinter came up in the eighth with the score tied 3–3 and the bases loaded. It was not another big swing but a modest, trickling bunt that caused an error at third and provided the winning runs as the Mets went on to defeat the Red Sox 8–3.

Zinter's comments after the last spectators left the grand old English setting of the Oval seemed to sum up the appeal of baseball: "There's nothing like the unexpected.... That's the game."

Despite the enthusiasm created by the game at the Oval, between the end of the Scottish Amicable deal, the National League tumult and the foreign restrictions, the number of people playing baseball continued to diminish into the mid–1990s. Since then, Major League Baseball

In the 21st century, baseball in Britain continues to have a small but dedicated group involved. A hitter from the Brighton Buccaneers squares off against the Bracknell Blazers at the British Baseball Final 4 Championships in Brighton in 2002. Brighton would go on to win the national championship that season. Photograph from Josh Chetwynd's collection.

has given considerable support to the British game in an effort to help the sport regain some stature in England. Starting with just Mike Carlson and a single assistant in 1990, MLB's operation in London, which is now run by Clive Russell, a former aide to British prime minister Tony Blair, has grown quickly. In 2005, a dedicated group of full-time employees and a host of part-timers and interns work in MLB's London branch. This office is responsible for game development including TV and merchandise licensing for MLB in all of Europe, the Middle East and Africa. For British baseball, there have also been signs of growing support. In 2002, Frubes, a children's yogurt dessert made by Yoplait, became the first title sponsor of MLB and BaseballSoftballUK's "Play Ball!" program, which gave young people a chance to play baseball and softball both in and outside of school (that deal ran its course by 2005.) In addition, in 2000, the BBF joined with the Baseball Softball Federation under the umbrella BaseballSoftballUK banner in an effort to consolidate financial and political muscle. BaseballSoftballUK has a paid professional staff to undertake developmental work that in the past was done by unpaid part-timers. In 2005, Sport England raised its support of baseball and softball in the UK from £41,000 a year to £300,000 per annum. The hope is that a handful of full-time employees will increase both baseball and softball's profile in the United Kingdom.

Alas, 2005 did see a devastating setback for British baseball. On 6 July, all those involved with the sport in Great Britain rejoiced when London won its bid for the 2012 Olympic Games. For those in the small British baseball and softball communities the news could not have been better. As the host country, Britain would automatically get its national teams into the baseball and softball Olympic tournaments. The London Olympics also meant that a permanent baseball and softball field of an international quality would have to be built. A "legacy" baseball facility was earmarked for the Lea Valley in Essex (outside of London). This would represent the first top-rate baseball facility in the country in as long as anyone could remember. In addition, money would have to pumped into baseball in preparation for the games.

Two days later the fates conspired against a baseball regrowth. The International Olympic Committee announced that both baseball and softball would be taken off the Olympic program for the 2012 Games. While the IOC told baseball organizers that they could reapply for Olympic status after the London Olympics, it was little solace for those hoping to help baseball along in Great Britain. The type of backing that came from the likes of Spalding and Moores was in British baseball organizers' grasp one day and 48 hours later had disappeared.

New Dawn

Despite the setback, the question still remains: Is baseball finally ready for sustained growth in Britain? It's hard to tell. While the numbers involved with baseball in Great Britain are small, their passion is huge. It is infectious. Despite a lack of fields of any quality, the players of Britain try not to complain. Some of the best athletes have started to travel to America to play at U.S. universities. One British pitcher even turned out for two seasons in the Frontier League, an independent minor league in the Midwest.

One of British baseball's longest observers is pessimistic about baseball's chances. William Morgan, who was born in 1923 and has watched British baseball's ebbs and flows for nearly seven decades, believes that the current landscape of British sports leaves little room for baseball. "Baseball is up against premiership football, which is a tremendous draw," Morgan says. "It is almost an impossibility for baseball [to get big] because you'd need a tremendous amount of money."

It is true that baseball in Britain needs benefactors—especially after the sport has lost its Olympic status. People like John Moores, L.D. Wood or A.G. Spalding must come to the fore. When a sport's rich history is not widely known it requires true believers to push it forward. One would hope that there is a critical mass of those types currently involved with baseball in the UK. Perhaps more than ever, English culture appears very concerned about protecting traditional English sports (in contrast, the Scottish sports attitude appears more open to baseball). A popular anti-baseball chant among detractors is that the game is "glorified rounders," a child's game that bears a resemblance to baseball. This comparison has not changed in more than 100 years. On the plus side, other problems that plagued British baseball like regionalism are no longer major concerns.

In 1891, Newton Crane, the former U.S. consul in Manchester and a British baseball organizer, asked, "Will baseball 'take' in this country?" He was worried that too many people believed "it will prove a hostile rival to cricket." But he pointed out that baseball had taken hold in countries like Japan and Australia and was cautiously optimistic. Crane said of the game of baseball: "It requires nerve, pluck, daring, control of temper, ready wit, supple muscles, unity in team work ... and ability not only to bat well, but to field expertly, and to run the bases fleetly and with judgment."

British baseball players continue to wait for many of their fellow Britons to fully understand and appreciate these words.

Post-war, baseball has never returned to West Ham. Today, there is a sprinkling of teams in the London area and amateur slow-pitch softball (a sister game of baseball) is popular among professionals in London. Games are often played throughout the summer in Regent's Park. The best of London baseball was played by the London Warriors, which over the past quarter of a century competed at such diverse venues as Regent's Park, Tufnell Park, Richmond Athletic Ground, Barns Elm Playing Fields in Barnes and Finsbury Park. Alas, that team, which had been crowned national champions five times folded after the 2005 season. The Croydon Pirates, which are located in a London suburb, did win back-to-back national titles in 2004 and 2005 and the southwest London Richmond Flames took the championship in 2006.

Although baseball is broadcast now on both terrestrial network television on Five (TV) and on satellite on the North American Sports Network (NASN), the game has not caught the interest of the public like it did for that short period in the late 1930s. While there are dedicated people involved with baseball in the country, the sport in Britain lacks people who have the combination of vision and funding to take a crack at the big leagues of British sports.

For those who love the game of baseball and believe it has something to add to British culture, the hope is another Wood is out there ready to give a West Ham of today new baseball glory. Comfort can be taken from the fact that there have been the shoots of life, that a vibrant and promising professional league lasted two seasons, during a period much less affluent than the current era. The thrill of the diamonds did catch the imagination of Londoners and found a way of capturing hearts and minds. The game generated enough magic to draw thousands, sometimes tens of thousands of fans to its encounters. The former West Ham United and England soccer star Sir Geoff Hurst once said that "Football is a game of tomorrows." It is up to us, those who have tasted the heady wine of the "freedom game," to make sure that it is not a sport of yesterdays, for it is the yesterdays that prove there can be tomorrows.

Appendix 1: People

The following lists the known players who appeared for the home sides that turned out at West Ham Stadium between 1936 and 1937. The number to the left of the player's name is his number. In some cases we were unable to locate a player's number.

The Custom House Rosters

West Ham—1936

7 Jerry Strong, P
8 George Etheze, C
12 Bill Turner, 1B
5 Pam "Peter" Yvon, 2B
3 Bill Irvine, 2B, 1B
15 Roland Gladu, 3B, OF, P, C, SS (captain)
14 Jack Durant, LF (also spelled "Jack Durrant")
11 Bert Rawlings, RF, CF
6 Eric Whitehead, RF (in 1936), 2B (in 1937). Wrote *Baseball for British Youth* in 1939.
1 Bill Cutler
  Jimmy Blackwell. Released and went to Hackney Royals mid–1936 season.
  "Poison" Absell, P, SS: played for Romford in 1937.
  Bill Cumberland
4 Art Dunning, LF
16 Harry "Hank" Simpson, CF
4 Ron Cameron, 1B
9 Eddie (also called Eric) Gladu, 3B, RF
  Ellis Lydiatt. Served as team secre-tary. Also a top player up north for the Hull Baseball Club in 1937. According to a Hull newspaper he was a former West Ham player, although it is unclear how many times he played for West Ham.

West Ham—1937

7 Jerry Strong, Two-year player
8 George Etheze, Two-year player
15 Roland Gladu, Two-year player (Captain)
3 Bill Irvine, Two-year player
4 Art Dunning, Two-year player
6 Eric Whitehead, Two-year player
5 Maurice Gerth, 1B, 3B.
16 Hank Wilson, RF, LF
12 Sam Whitehead, LF, RF—brother of 1936-37 player Eric Whitehead. He went to the Romford Wasps with Eric Whitehead in 1938.
10 Charlie Stapleford, CF
9 Sid West, P, CF
11 Hank Yeandle, outfielder, trans-ferred from West Ham to Nunhead in mid–June 1937.
14 "Butch" Armstrong, 1B:
  Jerry Owen, acquired from Nunhead in May 1937.

Pirates—1937

5 Jack Ward, CF/RF/P
1 Jack Robbins, C
7 Sam Hanna, 3B
11 "Slim" Tyson, SS
3 Eddie Mumma, Util. (captain)
8 Bill Davies, RF
6 "Red" Thomson, 2B/CF
4 "Happy" Kasnoff, P
10 Vic Pope, LF/P
9 Alf Taylor, 1B
2 Jimmy Foster, P/LF
12 Jimmy Burden, LF
1 Frank Cadorette, CF
5 Ron Rumpal, C
  Joe Carter, 2B acquired from Nunhead in May 1937.
  Bert Rawlings, OF played for West Ham in 1936 and played, at least briefly, for the Pirates in 1937.
  Tommy Durling

The organization of baseball at West Ham Stadium by 1937 was relatively elaborate. Listed below are some of the details of the people involved.

West Ham Baseball Club—1937

Board
L.D. Wood, chairman
Roland Gladu, team manager
W.S. Waters, commentator
Ellis Lydiatt, secretary
Eddie Mumma, publicity manager. Also played for Pirates in 1937.
G. Semon, scorekeeper

Pirates—1937

Board
L.D. Wood, chairman
W.S. Waters, commentator
Eddie Mumma, secretary and team manager
G. Semon, scorer

Appendix 2:
Explanations of the Game

The following are two tables of contents for and a lengthy quotation from three British publications instructing the public on the rules and procedures of baseball. First, a look at the table of contents of West Ham owner L.D. Wood's *Baseball for Boys and Beginners* demonstrates his thoroughness and consideration of what novices might need to know to play and appreciate the sport.

Second, owner Wood was not the only member of the West Ham baseball family to write a book on how to play baseball. Eric Whitehead, a two-year player with the team, penned *Baseball for British Youth* in 1939. The table of contents for his book is also presented.

And third, while baseball had been around in England since 1874, many fans who entered West Ham Stadium between 1936 and 1937 to watch the game played professionally knew very little about the sport. Organizers, faced with the challenge of explaining the complex rules, peppered their game programs with various tutorials on how the game is played. In a 15-page program as many as nine pages were dedicated to rules. The "Canadian and N.B.A. Rules" show word for word how baseball was explained to Hammers fans during those years. The explanation of the rules is precise and an excellent overview of the sport. The only incorrect statement is that British baseball organizers claimed that a pitcher could throw the ball at 120 miles per hour. The fastest clocked pitch is about 19 miles per hour slower than that.

Baseball according to L.D. Wood

CONTENTS

Baseball according to Eric Whitehead

1. A GAME RETURNS TO ITS HOME (Origins of the game, Doubleday and "English rounders in a slightly changed form")
2. HOW TO ORGANISE AND COACH AN INEXPERIENCED TEAM
3. THE ART OF BATTING
4. THE BATTERY—PITCHING AND CATCHING
5. FIELDING—INFIELDERS AND OUTFIELDERS
6. BASE RUNNING
7. THE UMPIRES AND COACHES
8. EXPLAINING THE BATTING ORDER
9. BASEBALL "SLANGUAGE"
10. MISCELLANEOUS ADVICE

The rules of baseball explained to West Ham fans in 1936–1937

Canadian and N.B.A.
[Britain's National Baseball Association] Rules

The number of innings in Baseball ranges from 7 to 9, but 5 innings can constitute a game. Each side is allowed three outs to an inning. Players may bat in consecutive order throughout the game. Although three outs puts the side out for one inning, this does not mean that the batsmen have been put out in consecutive order.

There are four Bases, the fourth Base near which batsman stands being known as "Home Plate." The Batsman tries to hit the ball thrown by the Pitcher, and if he does, he runs to 1st Base, thence if possible to 2nd Base, etc., in an effort to complete the circuit around the four Bases. If he is able during the innings to ultimately arrive at "Home Plate," he has scored a run. The fielders try to prevent him from advancing from Base to Base. The batsman becomes known as a "Baserunner" or "Runner" as soon as he is eligible to go to 1st Base. A Baserunner may stay on any Base he has attained (unless forced off base by a succeeding baserunner), but, as his advanced position is of value for the inning only, he tries to score at Home Plate before three outs have been declared against his side. The team scoring the most runs wins the game.

After reading the following pages of rules and the various methods by which a baserunner may be out, it will be realized how difficult it is for a baserunner to score if the opposing fielders are able to throw the ball to one another with great accuracy and speed.

Fair and Foul Balls. A batted ball is either "fair" or "foul" (except a "foul tip"). A batsman cannot run on a foul ball. A "fly" batted beyond 1st or 3rd Base is fair if it lands on fair ground and foul if it lands on foul ground. Between Home Plate and either 1st or 3rd Bases, a fair or foul ball is determined by the ground into which it rolls. A ball landing on or bounding over 1st or 3rd Base is a fair ball.

Left fielder, centre fielder and right fielder are known as "outfielders." The others are known as "in-fielders."

Bases are 90 feet apart.

There are many ways to put the batting side out. The more common "outs" are as follows:

RULE:—STRIKING OUT. Three strikes puts the batsman out (unless catcher drops the third strike under certain conditions, whereupon the batsman becomes a baserunner). There are various kinds of strikes.

RULE:—STRIKES. It counts a strike if batsman hits an uncaught foul ball. A foul is applicable to the first and second strikes only. After two strikes, uncaught fouls count neither for nor against batsman. (Note: An attempt to "bunt" after two strikes, which results in a foul is a strike, and batter is out). An uncaught foul puts ball out of play and batsman and base-runners cannot advance. Ball is not considered in play again until it is held by the pitcher standing in his position and the umpire calls "Play."

It counts a strike if a pitched ball goes over the Home Plate at a height between the batsman's knees and shoulder, even though the batsman does not strike at it.

It counts a strike if batsman strikes at a pitched ball and does not touch it with his bat, whether the ball goes over the Home Plate or not.

It counts a strike if batsman makes a "foul-tip." A foul-tip is a pitched ball at which batsman strikes; his bat touches it, but not sufficient to deflect it much, if any, from its course and the catcher catches it. It goes sharp and direct into catcher's hands. It is the only batted ball, caught by a fielder, that does not put a man out, unless it acts as his third strike, when he is considered struck out. A foul tip can act as the first, second, or third strike.

RULE:—"BALLS" & "WALKS." If a pitched ball does not result in a strike, a foul, or a fair hit, it is called a "ball." If four "balls" are registered for the batsman before three strikes are registered against him, or before he makes a hit, he acquires the right to occupy the 1st Base. Should the pitched ball strike the batsman while in his batting position, he likewise acquires the right to occupy 1st Base (unless he has struck at the ball, and in this case he would be out if it were his third strike and could not become a baserunner if catcher failed to catch ball) Should a runner be occupying 1st Base at these times of free bases (called "walks"), this runner moves on to 2nd Base without liability of being put out in doing so.

RULE:—BASERUNNER OUT AT 1ST BASE. After hitting an uncaught fair ball, the batsman (now called baserunner) runs to 1st Base. If he arrives there before the ball, he is "safe" and entitled to occupy the Base. But if the ball arrives before the runner, the runner is out.

RULE:—FORCED OUT. If a baserunner is occupying 1st Base at the time an uncaught fair ball is hit, he is no longer entitled to occupy that Base. He must vacate it for the baserunner who made the hit. If he fails to arrive at 2nd Base before the ball he is out. Likewise if there are runners on 1st and 2nd Bases and this hit is made, the runner from 2nd Base can be forced out at 3rd Base. If the three Bases are occupied at time of hit, the runner from 3rd Base can be forced out at Home Plate. In the latter instance a fielder could have effected an out on any of the four bases. The fielder must have the ball firmly in his hand and some part of his person in contact with the Bases to effect his out. The runners may not over-run 2nd and 3rd Bases.

RULE:—DOUBLE-FORCED OUTS. Two or even three outs may be effected by a forced play. If a runner is occupying 1st Base at the time an uncaught fair ball is hit,, he can be forced out at 2nd Base, as described above; if the 2nd baseman can then throw the ball to 1st Base to beat the runner who made the hit there would be another out If the first act of the fielders was to put the runner out who made the hit (by a throw to 1st Base) the runner coming from 1st Base to 2nd Base cannot be forced out, as 1st base is no longer occupied. But he can be "touched out." Similarly, if 1st and 2nd Bases are occupied when a hit is made, three outs may be effected by a throw to 3rd Base, thence to 2nd Base, and thence to 1st Base, each throw beating the runners to their legal bases, the ball traveling backwards around the Bases.

RULE:—CAUGHT OUT. A batsman is out if he makes a foul that is caught. A baserunner is out if, while batsman, his fair hit ball is caught.

RULE:—DOUBLE-PLAY ON CAUGHT BALL. If a fair or foul hit ball is caught and there is a runner occupying a Base at the time the runner must touch his Base after the ball is caught before he tries to advance to the next Base. If, in returning to touch his Base, he does not touch it before the Ball gets to that Base, he is out. If he touches his base after the ball is caught, he may advance immediately whether the ball be caught on fair or foul ground. If any fielder touch runner with ball while returning to touch his Base and runner is not in contact with his Base, runner is out. This Rule does not apply to a foul tip; that is, runner may advance as on any other strike (except foul strike).

RULE:—TOUCHED OUT. Any fielder having the ball firmly in his hand may put out a baserunner by touching him with the ball at any time the runner is not in contact with his Base. This is not applicable to baserunners who are allowed free bases as in the case of "walks" and "balks" until they have reached the free base, nor is it applicable when the ball is out of play.

There are several other ways outs are made, such as interference with fielder or ball, batter stepping out of his box, etc.—mostly of a disciplinary nature.

RULE:—IF CATCHER DROPS THIRD STRIKE the batsman becomes a baserunner provided 1st Base is not already occupied. The catcher picks up the ball and either tries to touch out the runner or throws to 1st Base to beat the runner. If 1st Base was allowed to be occupied the catcher would throw to 2nd base forcing out the man coming from 1st. The ball could then be thrown to 1st in time to make the two outs, which would encourage the catcher to play bad baseball, that is, drop the ball. If there are already two outs, however, 1st Base may be occupied. The catcher would naturally throw to 1st Base as the distance is shorter than to 2nd Base, thus acquiring the third out.

RULE:—A RUN DOES NOT COUNT if it is made on or during a play in which the third man be forced out or be put out before reaching 1st Base.

RULE:—"INFIELD FLY." This is the hardest rule in baseball to understand, and an attempt is made here to make it easier to remember. At first glance the rule seems unnecessary but examine a situation on the Bases:—1st and 2nd Bases are occupied and the batsman hits an easy fly in the 3rd baseman's hands. The fly would perhaps travel slow enough so that the 3rd Baseman could see out of the corner of his eye whether baserunners are advancing or not. Supposing the rule did not exist. The fielding side would be practically certain of two or even three outs, either on a double-force play or a double-play on a caught ball. If the runners advanced in an effort to avoid being forced out, the 3rd baseman could decide to catch the ball (retiring the man who made the hit), he could then get the ball to 2nd Base before, the advanced runner from that base could get back, and no doubt the second baseman could then perhaps get it to 1st before the runner from that base could get back. If, on the other hand, the runners held their bases, the 3rd baseman could feint to catch the ball drop it, pick it up, touch 3rd Base, throw it to 2nd Base, and the 2nd baseman could then perhaps get to 1st before the man who made the hit reached 1st—thus making 3 forced outs by an exhibition of bad catching, while no amount of skill on the part of the runners would be able to extricate them from their perilous position.

The rule therefore states that sometimes the batter is out immediately a fly is hit that can be handled by an infielder, whether the fly is caught or not, thus allowing the runners already on bases to hold their Bases. It is a concession to the bating side when 1st and 2nd Bases, or 1st, 2nd and 3rd Bases are occupied, but as a concession to the fielding side, the rule does not apply when 1st Base only is occupied.

As the official rule requires remembering too much at once, it is perhaps easier to take it in two lessons.

The first lesson is this: The rule does not apply to line-drives nor to bunted hits.

The second lesson can be memorized, as follows: If there are no outs or only one out and 1st and 3rd Bases are occupied, the batter becomes an out if he hits an infield fly.

Appendix 3: Terminology

Along with providing rules, baseball organizers also included explanations of some of the nuances of baseball in the West Ham and Pirates programs. The following are some of the ways in which West Ham fans were taught advanced elements of the sport.

It should be noted that an article highlighting the various pitches that the pitcher throws to the batter uses terms that are no longer used today. The "upshoot" would be called a "rising fastball" today; the "inshoot" would most likely be the equivalent of a "screwball"; the "outcurve" is now a "slider"; the drop is a "curveball" or a "12-6 curveball" (because it drops straight down in a direction like the 12-hand to the six-hand on a clock); the "outdrop" is a "slurve" (a combination of a curve and a slider); and the "slow ball" is now a "changeup."

Base Stealing and Team Work

The bases are ninety feet apart. This does not look a great distance unless you are close to the diamond. Measure ninety feet on the ground. Stand at one end of it and look toward the other end. Then throw a ball so that it lands within a foot of the other end. You will then appreciate better the difficulties of both the base stealer and the infielder's throwing arm. From the catcher's position to 2nd base is approximately 131 feet. These distances make the ball appear to be traveling comparatively slow. Actually the balls travel across the diamond from 70 to 90 miles per hour, which is considerably faster than most of us have traveled in motor cars and trains. Tests have been taken on this, and it has been shown that a baseball has been thrown at the rate of 120 miles per hour.

The catcher, perhaps more than any other member of the team, prevents a runner from stealing a base. Upon the accuracy of his aim and the speed of his thrown ball depends whether or not a base is stolen on a pitched ball. Just as important as these two factors, however, is the agility he displayed in getting the ball away once he has received it from the pitcher.

Once a runner is on base, the responsibility of the pitcher and catcher increases immensely. They must keep the runner "froze" to the base. The pitcher knows that the ninety foot distance from 1st to 2nd is just right to make a race of it. The runner has an even chance of reaching that base on a pitched ball, for the ball must travel from the pitcher to the catcher then to 2nd base. Should the runner get to 2nd he is in a scoring position in the event of a clean hit being made.

The pitcher tries to maintain this distance by sudden throws to 1st, keeping the runner near the base. A part of the art of baserunning is to diminish this distance by every inch possible, so a good base runner will take as large a "lead off" as possible. He must also be fleet of foot, but more important still, know the exact moment when to make the dash to the next base.

Believe it or not, when there is a runner on base the efficiency of the pitcher deteriorates. He must divide his attention between the baserunner and the batsman. A part of his job is to know the batsman's weaknesses. He remembers these from seeing him bat before. High balls strikes out some, low balls others, some "bite" at "outcurves," others at "drops." A runner on base gives a batsman an advantage. This will often account for some "freak" scores during an inning.

The "Squeeze Play"

When the pitchers are in good form and the play is close, a game may go five or six innings without a run being scored. One run becomes a matter of great importance certainly more important for the batting side than having one of their men put out.

If, at this stage of the game, the batting side are fortunate enough to get a runner on 3rd base and they have only one or no outs against them, they are apt to try to "squeeze' the runner on 3rd into "home."

The coach gives the "squeeze" signal to both the runner and the batsman. This means that the batsman must hit the next pitched ball. The batsman invariably "bunts"* the next pitched ball because he is more sure of bunting it than swinging at it. The runner's part of this play is to start running at full speed for home as soon as the pitcher starts his delivery to the batsman. Thus we have both the runner and the ball traveling towards home plate at the same time. The ball is then bunted into fair territory away from home plate, allowing the runner to score, while the man who was at bat runs to first base, hoping that he gets there before the ball, but seldom does.

The fielding side are aware that the "squeeze" play is apt to take place when the proper conditions arise. So they have to be prepared to run in for the bunt but at the same time cover their usual territory, in case the batsman drives a "place"† hit.

Pitched Balls

The art of pitching is to deceive the batsman. There are scores of ways of doing this, but in this article only the various types of pitched balls are considered— all of which have for their purpose this deception. A good pitcher may be a wizard in the delivery of curves, "slow balls," etc., but if the batsman knows the type of curve about to be delivered the pitcher is at a great disadvantage, as the batsman has time to set himself for that particularly delivery. A game of bluff is carried out by the pitcher and the batsman.

---

*A "bunt" is a fairly batted ball not swung at, but met with by the bat and tapped slowly within the diamond by the batsman.

†A "place" hit is a fairly hit ball that is deliberately hit to a place where the fielders cannot field it.

The pitcher "winds up" for his delivery, the batsman meanwhile trying to discover what kind of ball the pitcher is about to throw by watching the hand holding the ball. The pitcher tries to conceal this by holding the ball in the same manner for each pitch. In throwing the ball, however, the efficient pitcher makes alterations or effects "spins" by unnatural twists of the arms, wrists and hand at the moment the ball actually leaves the hand.

Any ball held and thrown normally spins slightly whilst in flight, but not sufficient to change the direction of flight. For "curves" the pitcher increases that spin to such an extent that a greater air resistance (or friction) is created on one side of the ball than the other. One side of the ball travels with intense speed against the air, and the surface of the opposite side meets with none at all, as it is traveling in the same direction as the air that goes past the ball. The momentum of the ball passing through space remains the same as though no spin were put on it, but the spin makes the ball slide off and away from the heavy air resistance much the same as though it were more solid matter than air.

THE UPSHOOT. The ball rises in the air, and is usually thrown overhand. The ball is held and delivered normally with the exception that the pressure of the thumb on the ball is lessened. The ball leaves the hand by rolling in the normal manner off the tips of the index and second finger. Great speed is necessary.

THE INSHOOT. This is generally delivered by right hand pitchers in the same manner as an upshot with the exception that they will use a side arm delivery. Some right hand pitchers are able, however, to deliver much more effective inshoots by an overhand delivery by contorting their hand, making control and speed more difficult but deception greater.

THE OUTCURVE. Opposite to an inshoot. The ball, as a rule, is held in the normal way, but some pitchers get more effective results by having the index and second finger grip the ball very tightly. The ball leaves the hand by rolling off the side of the index finger. This is the easiest curve to throw for a right hand pitcher and it breaks the most. It may be thrown overhand or sidearm, but in both cases the index finger is vertical when the ball leaves the hand. Sometimes it is thrown with a sweeping side arm motion with no twist of the wrist though much more effective results are obtained when the wrist snaps as the ball leaves the hand. Slow wide breaking outcurves are called ROUNDHOUSES and are derided by good pitchers. Fast breaking outcurves do not break until they get near the batsman; they are thrown so fast that the air resistance has no effect in changing their course until they have slowed down a bit, which is generally a few feet in front of the batsman.

THE DROP. Thrown overhand after the manner of the outcurve but the index finger is in a horizontal position. Some pitchers get much more effect by an overhand motion in which their hands twist so much that the palm is facing upwards and the ball gets its spin by leaving the hand off the tips of the index and second fingers, and this is perhaps the most trying on the muscles of the hand, arm and elbow.

THE OUTDROP. A combination of the outcurve and drop ball.

THE SLOW BALL. The purpose of this is to put the batsman's timing out of order. The pitcher holds the ball in the normal way, goes through all the motions of throwing a fast ball, and in doing so, the ball drops to the palm of the hand where it is pushed to the batsman. It does not spin at all, which adds to the batsman's difficulties because the lack of spin is apt to make the ball "float" even though the batsman is prepared for a fast ball. He can count the stitches on the ball as it comes towards him, but he can't hit it.

KNUCKLE BALL. This is held between the thumb and third finger with the nails of the index and second fingers on top. Like the "slow ball" this is pushed towards the batsman without revolving, but at great speed. It floats through the air in an uncanny way, bouncing off air spots of heavy density and making at least two breaks in flight.

SPIT BALL. This delivery acts in the air the same as the knuckle ball except at high speed. It is held in the hand in the usual manner of throwing a ball, but instead of leaving the fingers last, it leaves the thumb last or at the same time that it leaves the fingers. This is made possible by wetting or greasing the fingers to make them slippery. The "spit" ball is forbidden in the United States as it is too effective against batsmen.

THE FADEAWAY. This ball travels slowly through the air and not only drops because of gravity but the dropping is accentuated by intense top spin. It is a very difficult delivery and few pitchers ever master it.

Appendix 4:
Decoding Baseball

In 1935, the year that professional baseball came to England and a year before the London Major Baseball League was formed, baseball was listed in the *Comprehensive Encyclopedia of Sports Games and Pastimes,* a book published at the Fleetway House in London. The 772-compendium included some 1,250 illustrations and dedicated five pages and one full-page "art plate" to baseball. The book was billed as "The History, Principles of All Outdoor and Indoor Sports and Pastimes, with Rules and Regulations, and their Up-to-date Records alphabetically arranged for Ready Reference."

The editor of the encyclopedia wrote in his "Editor's note" that "all the articles on the different sports and pastimes information had been acquired from experts only."

Here is an excerpt from the baseball article that gives insight into how baseball was explained to the masses by those other than British baseball organizers like John Moores, L.D. Wood and Archer Leggett on the eve of professional baseball in the country.

Baseball: America's National Game
Simple in Theory, it Gives Opportunity for Great Skill

"Here in a brief space are given all the necessary facts both for the follower and the player of baseball. Popularly known as the "ball game" it demands a rapid mind and a quick eye, and is as well suited for amateurs as for professionals.

Cricket, traced to its earliest phase, may be found to be a variety of the older game of rounders; to this ancient English game of ball, too, does American baseball owe its origin. But the latter, which has become the national game of the United States of America, differs materially from the English game of rounders. True, both are played on a diamond-shaped field and with a round bat and ball; but there is a great difference between the manly game of baseball, as played by the American professionals, and the English schoolboy game of rounders, as much so, indeed, as between draughts and chess, both of the latter games being played upon a chequered board. In fact, to enter upon a contest for the palm of superiority in the American game, and to display the skill in pitching, batting, and fielding which baseball requires, needs men of pluck, nerve, and presence of mind—courageous and intelligent fellows, who have their wits about them; for the game, when played up to its highest mark, is anything but a boys' game in any respect, as the amount of fatigue involved, and the injuries frequently sustained, fully prove.

Nevertheless, baseball can be played and enjoyed by boys as well as men, for its theory is simple, and when played by amateurs the demand for those qualifications which make a player excel in professional contests is of course not so great.

The theory of baseball in brief is as follows: A space of ground being marked out on a level field in the form of a diamond, with equal sides bases are placed on the four corners thereof. The contestants include nine players on each side—one side takes the field and the other goes to the bat. When the field side take their positions the pitcher delivers the ball to the batsman, who endeavours to send it out of the reach of the fielders, and far enough out on the field to enable him to run round the bases, and if he reaches the home base—his starting point—without being put out, he scores a run. He is followed in rotation by the others of his side until three of the batting party are put out, when the field side come in and take their turn at the bat. This goes on until nine innings have been played to a close, and then the side scoring the most runs wins the game.

It will readily be seen that the theory of the game is simple enough, and it is this simplicity of construction which forms one of the chief attractions for the masses; and yet to excel in the game as a noted expert requires not only the possession of the physical attributes of endurance, agility, strength, good throwing and running powers, together with plenty of courage, pluck, and nerve, but also the mental powers of sound judgment, quick perception, thorough control of temper, and the presence of mind to act promptly in critical emergencies.

Appendix 5: British Champions

1890 Preston North End
1892 Middlesborough
1893 Thespian London
1894 Thespian London
1895 Derby
1896 Wallsend-On-Tyne
1897 Derby
1898 Derby
1899 Nottingham Forest
1906 Tottenham Hotspur
1907 Clapton Orient
1908 Tottenham Hotspur
1909 Clapton Orient
1910 Brentford
1911 Leyton
1934 Hatfield Liverpool
1935 New Briton London
1936 White City London
1937 Hull
1938 Rochdale Greys
1939 Halifax
1948 Liverpool Robins
1949 Hornsey Red Sox
1950 Burtonwood Bees

1951 Burtonwood Bees
1959 Thames Board Mills
1960 Thames Board Mills
1961 Liverpool Tigers
1962 Liverpool Tigers
1963 East Hull Aces
1964 Hull Aces
1965 Hull Aces
1966 Stetford Saints
1967 Liverpool Yankees
1968 Hull Aces
1969 Watford—Sun Rockets
1970 Hull Royals
1971 Liverpool Tigers
1972 Hull Aces
1973 Burtonwood Yanks
1974 Nottingham Lions
1975 Liverpool Tigers
1976 Liverpool Trojans
1977 Golders Green Sox
1978 Liverpool Trojans
1979 Golders Green Sox
1980 Liverpool Trojans
1981 London Warriors
1982 London Warriors

1983 Cobham Yankees
1984 Croydon Blue Jays
1985 Hull Mets
1986 Cobham Yankees
1987 Cobham Yankees
1988 Cobham Yankees
1989 London Warriors
1990 Enfield Spartans
1991 Enfield Spartans
1992 Leeds City Royals
1993 Humberside Mets
1994 Humberside Mets
1995 Humberside Mets
1996 Menwith Hill Patriots
1997 London Warriors
1998 Menwith Hill Patriots
1999 Brighton Buccaneers
2000 London Warriors
2001 Brighton Buccaneers
2002 Brighton Buccaneers
2003 Windsor Bears
2004 Croydon Pirates
2005 Croydon Pirates
2006 Richmond Flames

Appendix 6:
British Baseball Year-by-Year Standings and Records, 1890–2005

The following is a compendium of standings from some of Great Britain's top leagues as well as national winners, the name of the sport's governing body at the time and top hitters and pitchers (as available). This should be described as a "living document." There are certainly gaps in the information provided. Some years are incomplete and not all statistics and standings could be found. There are also undoubtedly other top leagues that competed during these years that are not represented. Alas, there are most likely some standings and records lost in history. Special thanks goes to William Morgan for his previous work on this historical data and Alan Smith for his assistance in putting this material together.

1890   Baseball Association of Great Britain & Ireland

National League of Professional Base Ball Clubs of Great Britain* (professional)

Team	Wins	Losses	GB
Aston Villa (Birmingham)	20	9	-
Preston North End	17	11	2½
Stoke	5	22	14

*Derby also competed in the league but was disqualified.

LEAGUE CHAMPION: Aston Villa. NATIONAL CHAMPIONS: Preston North End. RUNNERS UP: Birmingham Amateurs. SCORES: 42–15, 42–7 (best of three).

League Leaders

Batting Average

Jack Devey (Aston Villa)	.428
Simon (Aston Villa)	.425
Hendry (Preston North End)	.406
Livesey (Preston North End)	.389
P. Prior (Stoke)	.376

1892   National Baseball Association. NATIONAL CHAMPIONS: Middlesborough. RUNNERS UP: St. Thomas's (Derby). SCORE: 26–16.

1893   National Baseball Association. NATIONAL CHAMPIONS: Thespians (London). RUNNERS UP: Darlington St. Augustine's. SCORE: 33–6.

1894   National Baseball Association. NATIONAL CHAMPIONS: Thespians (London). RUNNERS UP: Stockton-on-Tees. SCORE: 38–14

1895   National Baseball Association. NATIONAL CHAMPIONS: Derby. RUNNERS UP: Fullers (London). SCORE: 20–16.

1896   National Baseball Association. NATIONAL CHAMPIONS: Wallsend-on-Tyne. RUNNERS UP: Remingtons (London). SCORE: 16–10.

1897   National Baseball Association. NATIONAL CHAMPIONS: Derby. RUNNERS UP: Middlesborough. SCORE: 30–7.

1899   National Baseball Association. NATIONAL CHAMPIONS: Derby. RUNNERS UP: Nottingham Forest. SCORE: 14–3.

1900   National Baseball Association. NATIONAL CHAMPIONS: Nottingham Forest. RUNNERS UP: Derby. SCORE: 17–16.

1906   British Baseball Association. NATIONAL CHAMPIONS: Tottenham Hotspur. RUNNERS UP: Nondescripts. SCORE: 16–5.

1907   British Baseball Association. NATIONAL CHAMPIONS: Clapton Orient. RUNNERS UP: Fulham. SCORE: 8–7.

1908   British Baseball Association. NATIONAL CHAMPIONS: Tottenham Hotspur. RUNNERS UP: Leyton. SCORE: 6–5.

1909   British Baseball Association. NATIONAL CHAMPIONS: Clapton Orient. RUNNERS UP: Leyton. SCORE: 6–4.

1910   British Baseball Association. NATIONAL CHAMPIONS: Brentford. RUNNERS UP: West Ham. SCORE: 20–5.

1911   British Baseball Association. NATIONAL CHAMPIONSHIP: Leyton. RUNNERS UP: Crystal Palace. SCORE: 6–5.

1934   National Baseball Association (II). CHAMPIONS: Hatfield (Liverpool). RUNNERS UP: Albion (Liverpool). SCORE: 13–12.

1935   National Baseball Association (II).

North of England Baseball League (professional)

Team	Wins	Losses	Ties	Points
Oldham Greyhounds	12	1	1	25
Bradford Northern	10	2	2	22
Rochdale Greys	8	4	2	18
Salford Reds	6	6	2	14
Manchester N. End Blue Sox	5	7	2	12

Team	Wins	Losses	Ties	Points
Belle Vue Tigers	5	8	1	11
Hurst Hawks	3	11	0	6
Hyde Grasshoppers	2	12	0	4

LEAGUE CHAMPION: Oldham Greyhounds. NATIONAL CHAMPIONS: New London [aka New Briton]. RUNNERS UP: Rochdale Greys. SCORE: 7–1.

1936   National Baseball Association (II). LONDON MAJOR BASEBALL LEAGUE (CHAMPIONS): White City Citizens. NORTH OF ENGLAND LEAGUE (CHAMPIONS): Oldham Greyhounds. YORKSHIRE BASEBALL LEAGUE (CHAMPIONS): Greenfield Giants. NATIONAL CHAMPIONS: White City (London). RUNNERS UP: Catford Saints. SCORE: 9–5.

1937   National Baseball Association (II). NATIONAL CHAMPIONS: Hull Baseball Club. RUNNERS UP: Romford Wasps. SCORE: 5–1.

1938   National Baseball Association (II). CHAMPIONS: Rochdale Greys. RUNNERS UP: Oldham Greyhounds. SCORE: 1–0.

1939   National Baseball Association (II). CHAMPIONS: Halifax. RUNNERS UP: Rochdale Greys. SCORE: 9–5.

1948   Baseball Association Ltd. CHAMPIONS: Liverpool Robins. RUNNERS UP: Thames Board Mills. SCORE: 13–0.

1949   Baseball Association Ltd. CHAMPIONS: Hornsey Red Sox. RUNNERS UP: Liverpool Cubs. SCORE: 10–5.

1950   Baseball Association Ltd.

Western Amateur Baseball League

Team	Wins	Losses	GB
West London Pioneers	12	0	-
Pirates	6	6	6
Tigers	6	6	6
Mitcham Royals	0	12	12

South Eastern Baseball League

Team	Wins	Losses	GB
Dodgers	12	2	-
Thames Board Mills	12	2	-
Essex Nationals	9	5	3
Hornsey Red Sox	8	5	3½
Enfield Cardinals	6	8	6
Briggs Brigands	5	8	6½
Paragon	3	11	9
Ford Sports	0	14	12

NATIONAL CHAMPIONS: Burtonwood Bees. RUNNERS UP: Hornsey Red Sox. SCORE: 23–2.

1951   Baseball Association Ltd. NATIONAL CHAMPIONS: Burtonwood Bees. RUNNERS UP: Ruislip Rockets. SCORE: 9–2.

1954*

Northeast Counties—Hull League—Division A

Team	Wins	Losses	GB
Giants	9	1	-

*According to official records, no national champion was crowned in 1954.

Team	Wins	Losses	GB
Hull Royals	6	3	2½
East Hull Aces	6	4	3
Pirates	4	6	5
Priestman Panthers	3	6	6½
Eagles	0	9	8½

LEAGUE CHAMPION: East Hull Aces (Hull District Cup.

Midland Counties—Birmingham League—Division I

Team	Wins	Losses	GB
Wellingborough USAF	7	1	-
Valor	7	1	-
Allens Cross	4	4	3
Dunlop Tigers	4	4	3
Beavers	0	8	7

LEAGUE CHAMPION: Wellingborough.

Nottingham League

Team	Wins	Losses	GB
RCAF North Luffenham	11	1	-
Dodgers	11	1	-
RCAF Langar	7	5	4
Athletics	6	6	5
Braves	3	9	8
Senators	2	10	9
Leicester	2	10	9

LEAGUE CHAMPION: RCAF North Luffenham.

Western Counties—Western League

Team	Wins	Losses	GB
Sutton Beavers	13	2	-
Epsom Lions	12	3	1
Tigers (Mitcham)	10	5	3
Mitcham Royals	5	9	7½
Wokingham Monarchs	3	10	10½
Dulwich Blue Jays	1	13	11½

LEAGUE CHAMPION: Wokingham Monarchs (Western Counties Cup and Noakes Cup).

South Eastern Counties—Senior Division

Team	Wins	Losses	GB
Briggs Brigands	12	2	-
Essex Nationals	11	3	1
Thames Board Mills	10	4	2
Kodak	9	5	3
Hornsey Athletics	6	8	6
Dagenham Royals	4	10	8
Ford Sports	4	10	8
Aveley Cubs	0	10	10

LEAGUE CHAMPION: Briggs Brigands (South Eastern Counties Cup and S.E. League Senior Cup).

1957* Southern League

Eastern Section

Team	Wins	Losses	GB
Thames Board Mills	9	1	-
Briggs Brigands	8	2	1
Essex Nationals	7	3	2
Ford Sports	4	6	5
Esso Tigers	2	8	7
Briggs Tigers	0	10	9

Western Section

Team	Wins	Losses	GB
Queens Park Aces	10	2	-
Hornsey Athletics	9	3	1
United States Navy	8	4	2
Leatherhead Maple Leafs	7	5	3
Sutton Beavers	5	7	5
Epsom Lions	2	10	8
Kodak	1	11	9

League Champion: Queens Park Aces.

1959 British Baseball Federation (I). NATIONAL CHAMPIONS: Thames Board Mills. RUNNERS UP: East Hull Aces. SCORE: 12–4.

1960 British Baseball Federation (I). NATIONAL CHAMPIONS: Thames Board Mills. RUNNERS UP: Liverpool Tigers. SCORE: 6–1.

1962 British Baseball Federation (I). NATIONAL CHAMPIONS: Liverpool Tigers. RUNNERS UP: East Hull Aces. SCORE: 8–3

1963 British Baseball Federation (I). NATIONAL CHAMPIONS: East Hull Aces. RUNNERS UP: Garrington's (Bromsgrove). SCORE: 8–6.

1964† NATIONAL CHAMPIONS: Hull Aces.

1965 British Baseball Association (II). NATIONAL CHAMPIONS: Hull (Kingston) Aces. RUNNERS UP: Stretford Saints (Manchester). SCORE: 4–2.

1966 National Baseball League (UK). NATIONAL CUP CHAMPIONS: Stretford Saints (Manchester). RUNNERS UP: Liverpool Aces. SCORE: 3–1. LEAGUE LEADERS: SOUTHERN MAJOR LEAGUE BATTING CHAMPION: J. Read, Beckenham Bluejays B.C. NORTHERN MAJOR LEAGUE BATTING CHAMPION: A Parkes, Stretford Saints B.C. SOUTHERN MAJOR LEAGUE HOME RUN CHAMPION: Blakely, Middlesex Athletic. NORTHERN MAJOR LEAGUE HOME RUN CHAMPION: Wally O'Neil, Stretford Saints B.C. SOUTHERN MAJOR LEAGUE PITCHING AWARD: J. Campbell, Thames Board Mills (Essex). NORTHERN MAJOR LEAGUE PITCHING AWARD: Alan Asquith, Hull Aces B.C.

1967 National Baseball League (UK). NATIONAL CHAMPIONS: Liverpool Yankees. RUNNERS UP: Beckenham Blue Jays. SCORE: 4–2.

**According to official records, no national champion was crowned in 1957.*

  †*Official records list the Hull Aces as the national champions in 1964, but it's unclear what organization was the governing body at the time and who the Aces beat for the title.*

1968   National Baseball League (UK). NATIONAL CHAMPIONS: Hull Aces. RUN-NERS UP: Hull Royals. SCORE: 4–1.

1969   National Baseball League (UK). NATIONAL CHAMPIONS: Watford Sun-Rockets. RUNNERS UP: Liverpool Trojans. SCORE: 8–7 (11 innings).

1970   National Baseball League (UK). NATIONAL CHAMPIONS: Hull Royals. RUN-NERS UP: Hull Aces. SCORE: 3–1.

1971   National Baseball League (UK). NATIONAL CHAMPIONS: Liverpool NALGO Tigers. RUNNERS UP: Hull Aces. SCORE: 8–3.

1972   National Baseball League (UK). NATIONAL CHAMPIONS: Hull Aces. RUN-NERS UP: Hull Royals. SCORE: 6–4.

1973   British Amateur Baseball Federation. NATIONAL CHAMPIONS: Burtonwood Yanks. RUNNERS UP: Hull Aces. SCORE: 23–2.

1974   British Amateur Baseball Federation. NATIONAL CHAMPIONS: Nottingham Lions. RUNNERS UP: Hull Royals. SCORE: 5–3.

1975   British Amateur Baseball Federation. NATIONAL CHAMPIONS: Liverpool NALGO Tigers. RUNNERS UP: Nottingham Lions. SCORE: 5–3.

1976   British Amateur Baseball Federation. NATIONAL CHAMPIONS: Liverpool Trojans. RUNNERS UP: Kensington Spirit of '76 (London). SCORE: 5–4.

1977   British Amateur Baseball Federation. NATIONAL CHAMPIONS: Golders Green Sox. RUNNERS UP: Hull Aces. SCORE: 9–5.

1978   British Amateur Baseball and Softball Federation. NATIONAL CHAMPIONS: Liverpool Trojans. RUNNERS UP: Crawley Giants. SCORE: 14–12.

1979   British Amateur Baseball and Softball Federation. NATIONAL CHAMPIONS: Golders Green Sox. RUNNERS UP: Hull Aces. SCORE: 9–7 (11 innings).

1980   British Amateur Baseball and Softball Federation

Southern Baseball League

Team	Wins	Losses	%	GB
London Warriors	14	2	.857	-
Croydon Bluejays	12	3	.800	1½
Crawley Giants	12	4	.750	2
TBM Raiders	10	5	.667	3½
Regents Park Eagles	8	7	.533	5½
Golders Green Sox	3	10	.231	9½
Wokingham Monarchs	3	10	.231	9½
Sutton Braves	3	11	.214	10
Rochester Dodgers	1	14	.067	12½

NATIONAL CHAMPIONS: Liverpool Trojans. RUNNERS UP: Hull Aces. Score: 12–1

1981   British Amateur Baseball and Softball Federation

Southern England Baseball Association (Group A)

Team	Wins	Losses	%	GB
London Warriors	15	2	.882	-
Crawley Giants	14	3	.824	1

Team	Wins	Losses	%	GB
Croydon Bluejays	11	5	.688	3½
TBM Raiders	11	5	.688	3½
Regents Park Eagles	8	8	.500	6½
Golders Green Sox	0	15	.000	14

Southern England Baseball Association (Group B)

Team	Wins	Losses	%	GB
Sutton Braves	12	4	.750	-
Wokingham Monarchs	9	7	.563	3
Croydon Borough Pirates	5	11	.313	7
Enfield Deerheads	5	11	.313	7
Ashford Hawks	4	12	.250	8
Rochester City Dodgers	2	13	.133	9½

NATIONAL CHAMPIONS: London Warriors. RUNNERS UP: Hull Aces. SCORE: 23–3.

1982   British Amateur Baseball and Softball Federation. NATIONAL CHAMPIONS: London Warriors. RUNNERS UP: Liverpool Trojans. SCORE: 16–7.

1983   British Amateur Baseball and Softball Federation. NATIONAL CHAMPIONS: Cobham Yankees. RUNNERS UP: Hull Mets. SCORE: 10–3.

1984   British Amateur Baseball and Softball Federation. NATIONAL CHAMPIONS: Croydon Blue Jays. RUNNERS UP: Hull Mets. SCORE: 9–8.

1985   British Amateur Baseball and Softball Federation. NATIONAL CHAMPIONS: Hull Mets. RUNNERS UP: London Warriors. SCORE: 10–8.

1986   British Amateur Baseball and Softball Federation.

Southern England Baseball Association

Team	Wins	Losses	%	GB
Cobham Yankees	12	3	.800	-
Sutton Braves	11	4	.733	1
Crawley Giants	10	5	.667	2
Croydon Bluejays	9	6	.600	3
Enfield Spartans	6	8	.429	5½
Barnes Stormers	5	9	.357	6½
Golders Green Sox	3	11	.214	8½
Basildon Raiders	2	12	.143	9½

NATIONAL CHAMPIONS: Cobham Yankees. RUNNERS UP: Hull Mets. SCORE: 12–0.

1987*   British Baseball Federation (II)

East Midlands League

Team	Wins	Losses	%	GB
Southglade Hornets	9	0	1.000	-
Nottingham Pirates	9	1	.900	½
Arnold Astros	7	3	.700	2½
Leicester Green Sox	4	3	.571	4

In 1987, the Scottish Amicable National League consisted of essentially the country's best players; but today, the BBF club champions from that season are officially designated that national champions. NOTE: The players in the National League also played for BBF club teams.

Team	Wins	Losses	%	GB
Nottingham Imperials	4	7	.364	6
Newark Giants	3	6	.333	6
Nottingham Bulldogs	2	7	.222	7
Mansfield Marvels	0	10	.000	9½

Humberside League

Team	Wins	Losses	%	GB
Hull Mets	7	0	1.000	-
Hull Warriors	5	3	.625	2½
Hull Royals	4	3	.571	3
Hull Mariners	2	4	.333	4½
Hull Giants	0	8	.000	7½

North Western League

Team	Wins	Losses	%	GB
Skelmersdale Tigers	8	2	.800	-
Southport Trojans	7	3	.700	1
Liverpool Tornadoes	6	3	.667	1½
Burtonwood Braves	6	4	.600	2
Skelmersdale Giants	1	8	.111	6½
Skelmersdale Mets	1	9	.100	7

Southern League

Team	Wins	Losses	%	GB
Enfield Spartans	12	1	.923	-
Sutton Braves	9	3	.750	2½
Cobham Yankees	10	4	.714	2½
Croydon Bluejays	8	6	.571	4½
Crawley Giants	5	7	.417	6½
Barnes Stormers	4	9	.308	8
Golders Green Sox	4	10	.286	8½
Gillingham Dodgers	1	13	.071	11½

Tyneside League

Team	Wins	Losses	%	GB
Blackadders	7	0	1.000	-
Gosforth Lasers	3	3	.500	3
Sunderland Monkeys	0	7	.000	7

NATIONAL CHAMPIONS: Cobham Yankees. RUNNERS UP: Southglade Hornets. SCORE: 6–0.

Scottish Amicable National League

Team	Wins	Losses	%	GB
Lancashire Red Sox	7	3	.700	-
London Warriors	6	4	.600	1
Nottingham Knights	5	5	.500	2
Southern Tigers	5	5	.500	2
Humberside County Bears	4	6	.400	3
Mersey Mariners	3	7	.300	4

LEAGUE CHAMPIONS: Lancashire Red Sox.

Scottish Amicable National League Leaders

Batting	At Bats	Hits	HR	RBI	Batting Average
Alan Bloomfield (Tigers)	38	22	4	13	.579
Steve Nero (Mariners)	21	11	1	9	.524
D. Kyles (Red Sox)	24	11	2	8	.458

Pitching	G	W	L	IP	H	BB	SO	ERA
Ed Fischer (Red Sox)	7	NA	NA	62.00	64	28	47	2.61
Mike Saur (Warriors)	5	3	1	29.66	24	11	35	2.73
Steve Frost (Knights)	6	NA	NA	28.33	35	21	30	3.81

1988*   British Baseball Federation (II)

BBF—South

Team	Wins	Losses	%	GB
Cobham Yankees	19	5	.792	-
Barnes Stormers	17	7	.708	2
Croydon Bluejays	16	8	.667	3
Sutton Braves	16	9	.640	3½
Enfield Spartans	15	10	.600	4½
Crawley Giants	7	17	.292	12
Waltham Abbey Arrows	6	18	.250	13
Golders Green Sox	1	23	.042	18

NATIONAL CHAMPIONS: Cobham Yankees. RUNNERS UP: Burtonwood Braves. SCORE: 16–1.

Scottish Amicable National League

Team	Wins	Losses	%	GB
London Warriors	9	1	.900	-
Lancashire Red Sox	7	3	.700	2
Humberside Bears	6	4	.600	3
Mersey Mariners	4	6	.400	5
Southern Tigers	4	6	.400	5
Nottingham Knights	0	10	.000	9

LEAGUE CHAMPIONS: London Warriors.

Scottish Amicable National League Leaders

Batting	At Bats	Hits	HR	RBI	Average
Julian Dodwell (Tigers)	51	27	3	15	.529
Lee Pierce (Warriors)	35	17	4	12	.486
Alan Bloomfield (Tigers)	42	18	3	11	.429

Pitching	G	W	L	IP	H	BB	SO	ERA
Dave Taylor (Red Sox)	3	3	0	31.00	36	10	6	2.61
Tony Kuramitsu (Warriors)	8	7	1	68.67	66	21	131	2.88
Steve Nero (Mariners)	8	3	2	55.67	44	93	93	3.56

*In 1988, the Scottish Amicable National League consisted of essentially the country's best players; but today, the BBF club champions from that season are officially designated that national champions. NOTE: The players in the National League also played for BBF club teams.

1989* British Baseball Federation (II).

British Baseball Federation (South)

Team	Wins	Losses	%	GB
Enfield Spartans	19	5	.792	-
Sutton Braves	17	7	.708	2
Croydon Bluejays	16	8	.667	3
Barnes Stormers	16	8	.667	3
Reading Royals	12	12	.500	7
Crawley Giants	8	15	.348	10½
Hemel Red Sox	7	16	.304	11½
Gillingham Dodgers	0	24	.000	19

NATIONAL CHAMPIONS: Enfield Spartans. RUNNERS UP: Sutton Braves. SCORE: 15–9.

Scottish Amicable National League

Scottish Amicable National League (Southern Conference)

Team	Wins	Losses	%	GB
Southern Tigers	7	2	.778	-
London Warriors	5	4	.555	2
Bedford Dukes	3	6	.333	4
Nottingham Knights	3	6	.333	4

Scottish Amicable National League (Northern Conference)

Team	Wins	Losses	%	GB
Humberside Bears	8	1	.889	-
Lancashire Red Sox	4	5	.444	4
Mersey Mariners	4	5	.444	4
Yorkshire Yankees	2	7	.222	6

LEAGUE CHAMPIONS: Southern Tigers. RUNNERS-UP: Humberside Bears. SCORE: 8–7.

1990 British Baseball Federation (II).

North West League

Team	Wins	Losses	GB
Liverpool Tigers	9	1	-
Burtonwood Braves	8	2	1
Liverpool Trojans	6	4	3
Preston Bobcats	4	6	5
Skelmersdale Tigers	3	7	6
Stretford A's	0	10	9

LEAGUE CHAMPION: Liverpool Tigers.

*In 1989, the Scottish Amicable National League consisted of essentially the country's best players; but today, the BBF club champions from that season are officially designated that national champions. NOTE: The players in the National League also played for BBF club teams.

South West League

Team	Wins	Losses	GB
Wedmore Brewers	14	2	-
Bristol Black Sox	8	8	6
Torbay Tigers	4	14	12

LEAGUE CHAMPION: Wedmore.

Scotland

Team	Wins	Losses	GB
Kilcardy Warriors	7	3	-
Clydesdale Kestrals	6	4	1
Dundee Dodgers	6	4	1
Edinburgh Reivers	5	5	2
Glasgow Diamonds	4	6	3
West Lothian Wildcats	0	10	7

LEAGUE CHAMPION: Kilcardy Warriors.

South—Division I

Team	Wins	Losses	GB
Enfield Spartans	20	1	-
Sutton Braves	16	5	4
Reading Royals	14	7	6
Waltham Abbey Arrows	8	13	12
Barnestormers	7	14	13
Croydon Blue Jays	7	14	13
Crawley Giants	5	16	15
Arun Panthers	2	19	18

LEAGUE CHAMPION: Enfield Spartans.

Yorkshire League

Team	Wins	Losses	GB
Menwith Hill	10	0	-
Harrogate Redwings	8	2	2
Leeds City Royals	6	4	4
Barnsley Old Town	4	6	6
Sheffield Bladerunners	2	8	8
Huddersfield	0	10	10

LEAGUE CHAMPION: Menwith Hill.

Humberside League—Senior

Team	Wins	Losses	GB
Hull Mets	6	0	-
Hull Giants	3	3	3
Hull Royals	2	4	4
Hull Warriors	1	5	5

LEAGUE CHAMPION: Hull Mets.

East Midlands—Division I

Team	Wins	Losses	GB
Southglade Hornets	11	0	-
Nottingham Pirates	8	3	3
Nottingham Imperials	5	6	6
Birmingham Braves	5	6	6

LEAGUE CHAMPION: Southglade Hornets. NATIONAL CHAMPIONS: Enfield Spartans, RUNNERS UP: Hull Mets. SCORE: 22–3.

1991 British Baseball Federation (II).

National League

Team	Wins	Losses	%	GB
London Athletics	17	4	.810	-
Enfield Spartans	16	5	.762	1
Nottingham Hornets	16	5	.762	1
Humberside Mets	10	11	.476	7
Cambridge Royals	8	13	.350	9
Essex Arrows	6	15	.286	11
Liverpool Tigers	6	15	.286	11
Nottingham Pirates	5	16	.238	12

NATIONAL CHAMPIONS: Enfield Spartans. RUNNERS UP: London Warriors.

1992* British Baseball Federation (II)

National Premier League[†]

Team	Wins	Losses	GB
Humberside Mets	16	2	-
Bury Saints	13	5	3
Leeds City Royals	12	5	3½
Chicksands Raiders	9	6	5
Nottingham Hornets	10	9	6½
Liverpool Tigers	3	11	11
Essex Arrows	4	15	12½
Ainsdale Trojans	2	19	15½

NATIONAL CHAMPIONS: Leeds City Royals.

National League

Team	Wins	Losses	%	GB
London Warriors	22	4	.846	-
Enfield Spartans	20	6	.769	2
Cambridge Knights	16	8	.667	4
Birmingham Devils	11	13	.458	9
Newham Jays	9	15	.375	11

*In 1992, the National League was an outlaw organization outside of the British Baseball Federation. Teams in its league were not eligible for the national title.

†The National Premier League standings are through 14 September 1992. A couple of final games may not be included.

Team	Wins	Losses	%	GB
Essex Eagles	6	18	.250	14
ANC Bulldogs (Reading)	2	22	.083	18

LEAGUE CHAMPIONS: London Warriors, Runners Up: Enfield Spartans

1993* British Baseball Federation (II).

National Premier League (North)

Team	Wins	Losses	GB
Humberside Mets	10	2	-
Leeds City Royals	6	6	4
Nottingham Hornets	5	7	5
Humberside Warriors	3	9	7

National Premier League—South

Team	Wins	Losses	GB
Bedford Chicksands Indians	15	5	-
Brighton Buccaneers	11	9	4
Milton Keynes Truckers	10	10	5
Essex Arrows	10	10	5
Hounslow Rangers	9	11	6
Crawley Comets	5	15	10

NATIONAL CHAMPIONS: Humberside Mets.

National League

Team	Wins	Losses	%	GB
London Warriors	19	2	.905	-
Bury Saints	14	7	.667	5
Enfield Spartans	12	8	.600	6½
Birmingham Brewers	11	9	.550	7½
Essex Eagles	10	11	.476	9
Cambridge Knights	7	14	.333	12
Waltham Forest Angels	5	15	.250	13½
Croydon Bluejays	4	16	.200	14½

LEAGUE CHAMPIONS: London Warriors

1994† British Baseball Federation (II).

National Premier League (North)

Team	Wins	Losses	GB
Humberside Mets	16	4	-
Nottingham Hornets	15	5	1
Leeds City Royals	9	11	7
Birmingham Braves	8	12	8
Liverpool Trojans	8	12	8
Humberside Warriors	4	16	12

*In 1992, the National League played as an outlaw organization outside of the British Baseball Federation. Teams in its league were not eligible for the national title.

†In 1994, the National League played as an outlaw organization outside of the British Baseball Federation. Teams in its league were not eligible for the national title.

National Premier League (South)

Team	Wins	Losses	GB
Essex Arrows	13	7	-
Crawley Comets	13	7	-
Hounslow Rangers	13	7	-
Bedford Chicksands Indians	11	9	2
Brighton Buccaneers	8	12	5
Bristol Black Sox	2	18	11

NATIONAL CHAMPIONS: Humberside Mets.

1994 League Leaders

Batting Average

Lee Mayfield (Rangers)	.521
Andy Maltby (Mets)	.520
Ray Brownlie (Ryls/Mets)	.509

Wins

Steve Sewell (Hornets)	7–1
Don Knight (Rangers)	7–1
M. Stephenson (Mets)	6–0

Home Runs

Ray Brownlie (Ryls/Mets)	6
Four players tied	3

Earned Run Average

Gavin Marshall (Royals)	2.53
Don Knight (Rangers)	2.55
Paul Raybould (Arrows)	2.75

Runs Batted In

Ray Brownlie (Ryls/Mets)	32
Lee Mayfield (Rangers)	24
Steve Sewell (Hornets)	23

Strikeouts

D. Butler (Warriors)	103
Martin Sawyer (Black Sox)	94
Martin Godsall (Trojans)	91

National League (regular season records)

Team	Wins	Losses	%	GB
London Warriors	12	4	.750	-
Essex Eagles	11	5	.688	1
Waltham Forest Angels	11	5	.688	1
Enfield Spartans	10	6	.625	2
Tonbridge Bobcats	4	12	.250	8

LEAGUE CHAMPION: Enfield Spartans

1995 British Baseball Federation (II).

National Premier League (North)

Team	Wins	Losses	GB
Humberside Mets	19	5	-
Menwith Hill Pirates	18	6	5
Nottingham Hornets	12	12	11
Birmingham Braves	11	13	12
Liverpool Trojans	9	15	14
Humberside Warriors	8	16	15
Leeds City Royals	3	21	20

National Premier League (South)

Team	Wins	Losses	%	GB
London Warriors	19	5	.792	-
Enfield Spartans	16	8	.667	3

Team	Wins	Losses	%	GB
Brighton Buccaneers	14	10	.583	5
Hounslow Rangers	14	10	.583	5
Essex Arrows	11	13	.458	8
Hemel Red Sox	5	19	.208	14
Bristol Black Sox	1	23	.042	18

NATIONAL CHAMPIONS: Menwith Hill Pirates. RUNNERS UP: London Warriors. SCORES: 3–2, 7–6 (best of three).

1995 League Leaders

Batting Average			*Wins*	
Lee Mayfield (Rangers)	.565		Cody Cain (Lndn Warriors)	10–0
Sean Ozolins (Red Sox)	.547		Gavin Marshall (Mets)	9–1
Brian Thurston (Mets)	.537		Don Knight (Rangers)	9–4

Home Runs			*Earned Run Average*	
Jerry Foreman (Pirates)	7		Cody Cain (Lndn Warriors)	0.77
Jay Stichberry (Pirates)	6		Matt Arrildt (Pirates)	1.51
Two players tied	5		Alan Smith (Lndn Warriors)	2.05

Runs Batted In			*Strikeouts*	
Cody Cain (Lndn Warriors)	38		Don Knight (Rangers)	119
Ray Brownlie (Mets)	30		Cody Cain (Lndn Warriors)	106
Brian Thurston (Mets)	29		Martin Godsall (Trojans)	77

1996   British Baseball Federation (II).

National Premier League (North)

Team	Wins	Losses	GB
Menwith Hill Pirates	16	2	-
Birmingham Bandits	15	3	1
Hull Mets	10	8	6
Nottingham Stealers	10	8	6
Leeds City Royals	7	11	9
Hull Warriors	4	14	12
Liverpool Trojans	1	17	15

National Premier League (South)

Team	Wins	Losses	%	GB
London Warriors	19	2	.905	-
Enfield Spartans	12	9	.571	7
Brighton Buccaneers	12	9	.571	7
Hounslow Rangers	11	10	.524	8
Cambridge Monarchs	11	10	.524	8
London Wolves	8	13	.381	11
Essex Arrows	8	13	.381	11
Hemel Red Sox	3	18	.158	16

NATIONAL CHAMPIONS: Menwith Hill Pirates. RUNNERS UP: London Warriors. SCORES: 14–9, 11–23, 18–12 (best of three).

1997   British Baseball Federation (II).

Coors Extra Gold Baseball League—
National Premier League (North)

Team	Wins	Losses	GB
Kingston Cobras	24	3	-
Menwith Hill Patriots	23	5	1½
Birmingham Bandits	21	7	3½
Nottingham Stealers	16	12	8½
Hessle Warriors	9	19	15½
Lancashire Tigercats	9	19	15½
Leeds Luddites	8	20	16½
Liverpool Trojans	1	26	23

BBF National Premier League (South)

Team	Wins	Losses	%	GB
London Warriors	18	6	.750	-
Enfield Spartans	15	9	.625	3
Hounslow Blues	13	11	.542	5
Brighton Buccaneers	12	12	.500	6
Essex Arrows	2	22	.083	16

NATIONAL CHAMPIONS: London Warriors. RUNNERS UP: Kingston Cobras. SCORES: 11–5, 31–12 (best of three).

1997 League Leaders

Batting Average

Alan Bloomfield (Ldn Warriors)	.486
Craig Perry (Ldn Warriors)	.429
Iain Lanario (Spartans)	.413

Home Runs

Alan Bloomfield (Ldn Warriors)	13
R. Barry (Spartans)	8
Two players tied	6

Runs Batted In

Alan Bloomfield (Ldn Warriors)	46
T. Penwarden (Stealers)	31
H. Atwood (Warriors)	30

Earned Run Average

Don Knight (Blues)	2.71
Matt Atkinson (Cobras)	2.78
Martin Godsall (Bandits)	3.10

Strikeouts

Don Knight (Blues)	91
Iain Lanario (Spartans)	71
R. Alger (Tigercats)	63

1998   British Baseball Federation (II).

National Premier League (North)

Team	Wins	Losses	GB
Menwith Hill Patriots	19	1	-
Hessle Warriors	13	7	6
Kingston Cobras	11	9	8
Leeds Luddites	9	11	10
Lancashire Tigercats	6	14	13
Barnsley Strikers	2	18	17

National Premier League (South)

Team	Wins	Losses	%	GB
London Warriors	20	1	.952	-
Brighton Buccaneers	15	6	.714	5
Enfield Spartans	13	8	.619	7
Hounslow Blues	11	10	.524	9
Kitsons Cambridge Monarchs	10	11	.476	10
Birmingham Bandits	6	15	.288	14
Bracknell Blazers	6	15	.288	14
Essex Arrows	3	18	.143	17

NATIONAL CHAMPIONS: Menwith Hill Pirates. RUNNERS UP: London Warriors. SCORES: 13–5, 17–15 (best of three).

1999   British Baseball Federation (II).

Premier Division (North)

Team	Wins	Losses	GB
Menwith Hill Patriots	13	0	-
Kingston Cobras	10	4	3½
Preston Jazz	6	10	8
Hessle Warriors	4	11	10½
Leeds Luddites	2	11	11

Premier Division (South, Group A)

Team	Wins	Losses	%	GB
Enfield Spartans	19	5	.792	-
Windsor Bears	10	14	.417	9
Essex Arrows	9	15	.375	10
Croydon Pirates	8	16	.333	11
Hounslow Blues	4	18	.182	14

Premier Division (South, Group B)

Team	Wins	Losses	%	GB
London Warriors	24	4	.857	-
Brighton Buccaneers	20	6	.769	3
Bracknell Blazers	8	15	.348	13½
Cambridge Monarchs	9	18	.333	14½

NATIONAL CHAMPIONS: Brighton Buccaneers. RUNNERS UP: Windsor Bears. SCORE: 16–4.

1999 League Leaders (South)

Batting Average

Simon Pole (Warriors)	.564
Adam Roberts (Blues)	.553
Chris Dalton (Spartans)	.500

Home Runs

A. Phillips (Spartans)	8
D. Desaunois (Spartans)	8
Two tied with	6

Runs Batted In

D. Desaunois (Spartans)	44

Alan Bloomfield (Warriors)	39
Simon Pole (Warriors)	38

Wins

Kevin Coldiron (Warriors)	9
Mark Mills (Buccaneers)	7
Alan Smith (Warriors)	7

Earned Run Average

J. Uhrman (Arrows)	2.91
Mark Mills (Buccaneers)	4.02
Alan Smith (Warriors)	4.42

Strikeouts		T. Camacho (Bears)	72
J. Uhrman (Arrows)	82	Andy Gilbert (Monarchs)	66

2000 British Baseball Federation (II).

Premier Division (North)

Team	Wins	Losses	GB
Menwith Hill Patriots	27	3	-
Preston Jazz	25	5	2
Liverpool Trojans	14	16	13
Manchester	13	17	14
Hessle	11	19	16
Edinburgh Diamond Devils	0	30	27

Premier Division (South, Group A)

Team	Wins	Losses	%	GB
London Warriors	23	1	.958	-
Cambridge Monarchs	9	13	.409	13
Windsor Bears	8	12	.400	13
Essex Arrows	5	19	.208	18

Premier Division (South, Group B)

Team	Wins	Losses	%	GB
Brighton Buccaneers	14	1	.933	-
Croydon Pirates	8	12	.400	8½
Enfield Spartans	6	10	.375	8½
Bracknell Blazers	2	7	.250	9

NATIONAL CHAMPIONS: London Warriors. RUNNERS UP: Brighton Buccaneers. SCORE: 11–7.

2001 British Baseball Federation (II).

Rawlings National League

Team	Wins	Losses	%	GB
London Warriors	19	6	.760	-
Windsor Bears	18	7	.720	1
Brighton Buccaneers	18	7	.720	1
Bracknell/Richmond Wildfire	10	15	.400	9
Cambridge Monarchs	9	16	.360	10
Croydon Pirates	1	24	.042	18

NATIONAL CHAMPIONS: Brighton Buccaneers. RUNNERS UP: Windsor Bears. SCORE: 8–5.

2001 League Leaders

Batting Average		*Runs Batted In*	
Matt Gilbert (Monarchs)	.434	Craig Perry (Warriors)	33
Simon Pole (Warriors)	.409	S. Adam (Bears)	25
Grant Berman (Bears)	.400	Simon Pole (Warriors)	25

Home Runs		*Earned Run Average*	
Rene Herlitzius (Buccaneers)	4	Simon Pole (Warriors)	1.48
Oscar Lopez (Buccaneers)	3	N. Bashaw (Bears)	1.97
Seven tied with	2	Nick Carter (Buccaneers)	2.00

<table>
<tr><td>Strikeouts</td><td></td><td>Luke Russell (Wildfire)</td><td>69</td></tr>
<tr><td>Matt Gilbert (Monarchs)</td><td>118</td><td>Larry House (Bears)</td><td>57</td></tr>
</table>

2002 British Baseball Federation (II)

Rawlings National League

Team	Wins	Losses	%	GB
London Warriors	22	3	.880	-
Brighton Buccaneers	16	8	.667	5½
Bracknell Blazers	15	10	.600	7
Windsor Bears	12	12	.500	9½
Croydon Pirates	9	16	.360	13
Preston Stingers	0	25	.000	22

NATIONAL CHAMPIONS: Brighton Buccaneers. RUNNERS UP: Windsor Bears. SCORE: 5–1.

2002 League Leaders

Batting Average

Simon Pole (Warriors)	.473
Ryan Trask (Blazers)	.471
Rob Rance (Blazers)	.458

Wins

Matt Scales (Warriors)	7
Simon Pole (Warriors)	5
Two tied with	4

Home Runs

Simon Pole (Warriors)	4
Roddi Liebenberg (Pirates)	3
Several tied with	2

Earned Run Average

Simon Pole (Warriors)	0.69
Iain Lanario (Warriors)	1.00
Matt Scales (Warriors)	1.93

Runs Batted In

Josh Chetwynd (Blazers)	21
Mike Stewart (Pirates)	19
Matt Scales (Warriors)	19

Strikeouts

Matt Scales (Warriors)	66
Tom Gillespie (Blazers)	59
Simon Pole (Warriors)	39

2003 British Baseball Federation (II)

Rawlings National League

Team	Wins	Losses	%	GB
Windsor Bears	17	8	.800	-
Brighton Buccaneers	15	10	.600	2
Bracknell Blazers	15	10	.600	2
London Warriors	11	14	.440	6
Croydon Pirates	11	14	.440	6
Menwith Hill Patriots	6	19	.240	22

NATIONAL CHAMPIONS: Windsor Bears. RUNNERS UP: Brighton Buccaneers. SCORE: 9–4

2003 League Leaders

Batting Average (min 50 PA)

Ricardo Larrazabal (Blazers)	.500
Jon Miller (Blazers)	.462
Alex Malihoudis (Buccaneers)	.432

Home Runs

Simon Pole (Warriors)	6
Jon Miller (Blazers)	6
Ryan Trask (Blazers)	5

Runs Batted In		Earned Run Average (Min. 25 IP)	
Jon Miller (Blazers)	28	Dean Stoka (Bears)	1.13
Ryan Trask (Blazers)	23	Michael Close (Buccaneers)	2.21
Simon Pole (Warriors)	21	Simon Pole (Warriors)	2.57

Wins		Strikeouts	
Dean Stoka (Warriors)	8	Dean Stoka (Bears)	77
Nick Carter (Buccaneers)	7	Simon Pole (Warriors)	60
Simon Pole (Warriors)	6	Two Tied with	51

2004 British Baseball Federation (II).

National League (South)

Team	Wins	Losses	%	GB
Windsor Bears	23	7	.767	-
London Warriors	17	13	.567	6
Brighton Buccaneers	14	16	.467	9
Croydon Pirates	14	16	.467	9
Bracknell Blazers	13	16	.448	9½
Richmond Flames	8	21	.276	19½

2004 League Leaders (South)

Batting Average (min 60 PA)		Wins	
Dennis Grubb (Bears)	.478	Ian Bates (Pirates)	10
Jason Holowaty (Blazers)	.411	Ryan Koback (Bears)	9
Dean Stoka (Bears)	.409	Two tied with	6

Home Runs		Earned Run Average (Min. 30 IP)	
Dennis Grubb (Bears)	9	Aeden McQueary-Ennis (Flames)	2.40
Chris Lange (Bears)	7	Ryan Koback (Bears)	2.46
Two tied with	6	Dean Stoka (Bears)	2.92

Runs Batted In		Strikeouts	
Dennis Grubb (Bears)	43	Ryan Koback (Bears)	91
Jeff McDonald (Pirates)	34	Ian Bates (Pirates)	69
Cody Cain (Warriors)	31	Dean Stoka (Bears)	68

National League (North)

Team	Wins	Losses	%	GB
Liverpool Trojans	18	4	.818	-
Menwith Hill Patriots	15	7	.682	3
The Stars Baseball Club (Glasgow)	13	7	.650	4
Edinburgh Diamond Devils	10	12	.455	8
Hull Baseball Club	8	14	.364	10
Manchester Eagles	0	20	.000	17

NATIONAL CHAMPIONS: Croydon Pirates. RUNNERS UP: Windsor Bears. SCORE: 12–10

2005 British Baseball Federation (II).

National League—South

Team	Wins	Losses	%	GB
London Warriors	20	8	.714	-

Team	Wins	Losses	%	GB
Croydon Pirates	19	10	.655	1½
Brighton Buccaneers	17	10	.630	2½
Bracknell Blazers	12	18	.400	9
Richmond Flames	4	26	.322	17

2005 League Leaders (South)

Batting Average (min 60 PA)

Simon Pole (Warriors)	.571
Roddi Liebenberg (Blazers)	.482
Alex Malihoudis (Buccaneers)	.427

Wins

Ian Bates (Pirates)	8
Simon Pole (Warriors)	7
Alex Keprta	6

Home Runs

Simon Pole (Warriors)	8
Roddi Liebenberg (Blazers)	7
Ian Bates (Pirates)	7

Earned Run Average (Min. 30 IP)

Simon Pole (Warriors)	2.53
Matt Maitland (Blazers)	2.98
Nick Porter (Blazers)	3.48

Runs Batted In

Simon Pole (Warriors)	42
Roddie Liebenberg (Blazers)	30
Two tied with	25

Strikeouts

Alex Keprta (Warriors)	86
Byron Cotter (Pirates)	55
Ian Bates (Pirates)	50

National League—North

Team	Wins	Losses	%	GB
Liverpool Trojans	24	1	.960	-
Edinburgh Diamond Devils	17	11	.607	8½
Hull Hammerheads	15	10	.600	9
Menwith Hill Patriots	14	11	.560	10
Manchester Eagles	8	20	.286	17½
The Stars Baseball Club	0	25	.000	24

NATIONAL CHAMPIONS: Croydon Pirates. RUNNERS-UP: Brighton Buccaneers. SCORE: 11–4, 10–9 (best of three).

Appendix 7:
Great Britain National Team in Europe

Along with Great Britain's triumph in 1938 against the United States, giving Britain the first world championship title, the country has also consistently competed in the European baseball championships, which pits the national teams of Europe's baseball-playing countries against each other. Great Britain has appeared in the continent's top-tier "Champion Pool" nine times (including a silver medal performance in 1967) and in the second-tier "Qualification Pool" six times (through 2005). In 1988 and 1996, Great Britain won the "Qualification Pool" tournament, earning promotion to the "Champion" level. Here is a rundown of British performances.

1967—(Champion Pool) 2nd place out of five teams in Belgium (Record: 3-1)
1971—(Champion Pool) 7th place out of nine teams in Italy (Record: 1-3)
1984—(Qualification Pool) 3rd place out of four teams in Britain (Record: 1-2)
1986—(Qualification Pool) 3rd place out of five teams in France (Record: 2-2)
1988—(Qualification Pool) 1st place out of four teams in Britain (Record: 3-0)
1989—(Champion Pool) 7th place out of eight teams in France (Record: 3-5)
1991—(Champion Pool) 8th place out of eight teams in Italy (Record: 0-8)
1992—(Qualification Pool) 3rd place out of 10 teams in Germany (Record: 4-2)
1994—(Qualification Pool) 7th place out of 13 teams in Slovenia (Record: 5-1)
1996—(Qualification Pool) 1st place out of 10 teams in Britain (Record: 6-0)
1997—(Champion Pool) 9th place out of 12 teams in France (Record: 2-5)
1999—(Champion Pool) 9th place out of 12 teams in Italy (Record: 3-4)
2001—(Champion Pool) 10th place out of 12 teams in Germany (Record: 3-4)
2003—(Champion Pool) 9th place out of 12 teams in Holland (Record: 3-4)
2005—(Champion Pool) 7th place out of 12 teams in Czech Republic (Record: 4-4)

Appendix 8:
British Clubs in Europe

The European Baseball Confederation (CEB) holds a number of pan–European tournaments to decide various European club champions. These "cups" are the European Cup (Europe's top club championship), the Cupwinners Cup and the CEB Cup. Each event has two pools—the top-tier "Champion Pool" and the second-tier "Qualification Pool." Although Great Britain does not have a distinguished history in these events, British clubs have performed admirably in recent years. In 2003, the Windsor Bears won a Cupwinners Cup qualification competition and in the following two years the Bears and the Croydon Pirates have both placed respectively in the Champion Pool. Here is a look at the British clubs that have competed in these events, the location of the tournament and how they placed (as available through 2005).

1965—Stretford Saints (European Cup—Champion Pool)
1966—Hull Aces (European Cup—Champion Pool)
1968—Hull Aces (European Cup—Champion Pool)
1969—Hull Aces (European Cup—Champion Pool)
1988—Nottingham Southglade Hornets (European Cup—Qualification Pool) in Belgium (4th place out of seven)
1989—Enfield Spartans (European Cup—Qualification Pool) in England (4th out of eight)
1990—Enfield Spartans (European Cup—Qualification Pool) in France (2nd out of nine)
1992—Humberside Mets (Cupwinners Cup—Qualification Pool) in England (2nd out of nine)
1992—Nottingham Southglade Hornets (European Cup—Qualification Pool) in San Marino (6th out of 12)
1993—Leeds City Royals (Cupwinners Cup—Champion Pool) in Spain (8th out of eight)

1994—Crawley Comets (Cupwinners Cup—Qualification Pool) in Germany (6th out of six)

1995—Birmingham Braves (CEB Cup—Qualification Pool) in Belgium (4th out of five)

1996—Enfield Spartans (CEB Cup—Qualification Pool) in Austria (4th out of five)

1997—Birmingham Bandits (European Cup—Qualification Pool) in Hungary (4th out of seven)

1997—Hounslow Rangers (Cupwinners Cup—Qualification Pool) in France (2nd out of four)

1998—London Warriors (European Cup—Qualification Pool) in Germany (3rd out of six)

1998—Kingston Cobras (Cupwinners Cup—Qualification Pool) in Germany (2nd out of five)

1999—Hessle Warriors (European Cup—Qualification Pool) in Belgium (7th out of seven)

1999—Menwith Hill Patriots (Cupwinners Cup—Qualification Pool) in Belgium (5th out of six)

2000—Brighton Buccaneers (European Cup—Qualification Pool) in Belgium (2nd out of seven)

2003—Windsor Bears (Cupwinners Cup—Qualification Pool) in Belgium (1st out of six)

2003—Edinburgh Diamond Devils (CEB Cup—Qualification Pool) in Belgium (7th out of seven)

2004—Windsor Bears (Cupwinners Cup—Champion Pool) in Holland (5th out of seven)

2004—Edinburgh Diamond Devils (European Cup—Qualification Pool) in France (7th out of seven)

2004—Richmond Flames (CEB Cup—Qualification Pool) in Austria (7th out of eight)

2005—Croydon Pirates (Cupwinners Cup—Champion Pool) in Belgium (4th out of eight)

2005—Greater Berkshire 1938 (European Cup—Qualification Pool) in Sweden (4th out of eight)

2005—Edinburgh Diamond Devils (CEB Cup—Qualification Pool) in Lithuania (5th out of five)

Source: CEB

Appendix 9:
Major League Teams
Playing in the
United Kingdom and Ireland

Big league squads have come to Great Britain, Northern Ireland, and Ireland a number of times to present the game of baseball to the British and Emerald Isles. These tours and exhibitions have included some of the game's greatest players.

1874

Boston Red Stockings v. Philadelphia Athletics
14 games (head-to-head)
  Locations: London, Kensington, Crystal Palace, Richmond, Sheffield, Dublin, Liverpool, and Manchester
  Players included: Hall of Famers A.G. Spalding, Adrian "Cap" Anson, and Harry and George Wright

1889

Chicago White Stockings v. All-Americans
11 games
  Locations: London, Bristol, Birmingham, Manchester, Liverpool, Glasgow, Dublin and Belfast
  Players included: Hall of Famers Adrian "Cap" Anson, John Montgomery Ward and Ned Hanlon

1914

New York Giants v. Chicago White Sox
One game
  Location: London (Stamford Bridge, Chelsea FC)
  Players included: Hall of Famers Tris Speaker, Sam Crawford, and Urban "Red" Faber and Olympic hero Jim Thorpe

1924

New York Giants v. Chicago White Sox
   Locations: London, Liverpool, Birmingham, Dublin
   Players included: Hall of Famers Frank Frisch, Sam Rice, Travis Jackson and Ted Lyons

1989

Major League Alumni All-Stars (v. Great Britain National Team)
One game
   Location: Liverpool (Old Trafford cricket ground)
   Players included: Hall-of-Famers Bob Feller, Willie Stargell and Billy Williams

1993

Boston Red Sox v. New York Mets (Minor League players)
One game
   Location: London (The Oval cricket ground)
   Players included: Future Major Leaguers Quilvio Veras and Alan Zinter

Notes

1. The term "Speedway" throughout this book refers to a motorcycle or dirt track speedway.

2. The Cesarevitch is a huge event in British greyhound racing. Entrants for the final event (that was held at West Ham) were the winning dogs from a number of preliminary events held over the season.

3. Over the last decade as the "embourgeoisment" of live sports support has become endemic in Britain with the massive rise in the financial cost of attending or even watching (by way of pay-to-view television) popular sport. This seems to have brought a new audience to live sport, many of whom are more spectators than fans, being locked into "the immediate" and likely to change allegiance for the sake of being associated with success than was the case in the past. Once, if you lived in Exeter, or within the environs of that city of England's extreme southwest, you would support the Exeter City Football Club although they were invariably ensconced in the lower reaches in terms of status within their field of endeavor. For the last ten years or more, almost every weekend, convoys of buses roar out of the county of Devon heading north, their passengers clad in the red shirts of Manchester United, while their home club teeters on the edge of financial extinction for want of support. However, next season many of the same buses will be making for London and be full of people wearing the blue of the Chelsea football club. This is very similar to the "bandwagon" culture that is prevalent in American sports. When the Boston Red Sox won the World Series in 2004, fans far from New England began swearing their allegiance to the long-suffering team.

4. The Royal Docks dominated the shores of the Thames in East London containerization. The "Royals" comprised of three docks—the Royal Albert Dock, the Royal Victoria Dock and the King George V Dock. Collectively, these formed the largest enclosed docks in the world, with a water area of nearly 250 acres (1 km^2) and an overall estate of 1,100 acres (4 km^2)—equivalent in size to the whole central London from Tower Bridge to Hyde Park.

The Royals were built between 1880 and 1921 on riverside marshes. They were constructed to provide berths for large vessels that could not be accommodated farther upriver. They were a great commercial success, becoming London's principal docks during the first half of the 20th century. They chiefly involved in the import and unloading of food into the ranks of massive granaries and refrigerated warehouses that lined the quayside. The docks had collective span of over 12 miles (19 km) of quaysides, handling hundreds of cargo and passenger vessels.

The Royals suffered major damage from Nazi bombing in the Second World War, but recovered only to face a steady decline from the early 1960s onward. Containerization obliged the industry to move downstream to Tilbury in the county of Essex. Still, the Royals lasted longer than any of the other London docks. The finally closed to commercial traffic in 1981, which resulted in high levels of unemployment and social deprivation in the districts of North Woolwich and Silvertown.

5. A local nickname for the Isle of Dogs.

6. Rounders is a game played around bases in much the same manner as baseball, but is subject to a far more simplistic set of rules and less demanding techniques. It is generally associated with young children and was often used as something of a counterpart for cricket in the physical education of girls.

7. Financially, the trip was not a money maker for the American tourists. Adrian "Cap" Anson, a Hall of Fame player, wrote in his biography, "A Ball Player's Career," that players on Wright's Boston club had to suffer a pay cut to offset Wright's losses on travel expenses home. Anson quipped that the players had left for England "Argonauts" but "brought back but little of the golden fleece."

8. McWhirter would later, alongside his twin brother, Ross (who was "executed" by the IRA in 1975), edit the *Guinness Book of Records* and became involved in right-wing nationalist politics.

9. According to longtime British baseball writer and organizer William Morgan, two men, Nelson Cooke and British native James McWeeny, played a role in baseball's 19th century development in Britain. In the early 20th century, McWeeney, a journalist who covered soccer, continued his baseball missionary work, persuading some of the London area's most famous soccer teams—Tottenham Hotspur, Woolwich

Arsenal and Fulham, among others—to get involved with the sport. It seems newspapermen in general were taken by baseball as there was also a team called the "Non Descripts" that was composed of journalists.

10. The Midlands is probably the British equivalent of the United States' Midwest. It might be thought of as the area surrounding Britain's second city, Birmingham.

11. This was probably referring to soccer players although men from the Rugby code may also have been involved.

12. The Football Association Cup is the oldest soccer competition in the sport's history. It is a knock-out tournament that has included the most humble amateur and semi-professional teams (the record number of accepted entries for the FA Cup is 661 teams in 2004) as well as the giants of the professional game. At the start of the twentieth century (and for many decades after), the FA Cup Final was the most important and prestigious soccer game in the world and still commands great respect, being second only to English Premiership in terms of status as a competition, having an estimated television audience of around 400 million around the world.

13. It was destroyed by fire in 1936.

14. Relegation is the process by which teams finishing at the bottom of their league were demoted to a lower level. For example, currently the two teams finishing at the foot of the Premiership are relegated to the Championship, while the winners and runners up from the Championship are given automatic places in the Premiership.

15. One of the biggest greyhound racing championships in the British calendar.

16. Football Pools at the time involved gambling (by way of filling in a pre-printed coupon) on soccer teams achieving a drawn (tied) game. Selections were usually made from the 60 or so top flight games taking place in

Britain on any given Saturday. Dividends," a proportion of the "pool" of all the money wagered, were given for correctly predicting, say, 8 draws from a selection of 12. A "punter" could "invest" one or many "lines" (one marked a cross against the games one thought would end in a draw this exercise made a line of "x"s down the coupon) for as little as a penny a line. If there were few "correct lines" (probably because there had been a very limited number of drawn games) the payment could be substantial; if there were a high proportion of drawn games it was likely that many would have realized their predictions but the dividend would be low. At the height of the popularity of the "Pools," there were several large companies in the business, and their coupons could be the doorway to huge fortunes for the lucky winner.

17. It appears that West Ham United did not create a baseball side, unlike their London rivals Tottenham Hotspur and Arsenal. This may have been because the West Ham pitch was a relatively small area, but equally the fact that the playing surface was notoriously poor may also have been a factor in West Ham United's failure to emulate its competitors in terms of the adoption of baseball.

18. Bill Roberts referred to Wood as "Louis Wood."

19. Moores' National Baseball Association often referred to the rules their teams played by as "Canadian Rules," but these rules were essentially the same as the American code.

20. British colloquialism for "quite a sum of money."

21. The geographical center of the city of Salford and now the site of Salford City Reds rugby league side at The Willows.

22. The inaugural teams in the Yorkshire League were: Greenfield Giants, Hull Baseball Club, Wakefield Cubs, Bradford City Sox, Sheffield Dons, Leeds Oaks, Scarborough Seagull and Dewsbury Royals. The 1936 London

Major League Teams were: White City, West Ham, Hackney Royals, Harringay, Romford Wasps and Catford Saints. The Streatham and Mitcham Giants was also a founding member but folded weeks into the first season.

23. Kelly was the first manager of Everton (1939–48), and while he placed the club on a firm financial footing he did not have any great acumen for the game of soccer and led the great Liverpool club to the verge of relegation before reverting to his former role of secretary of the club. He also played a role in British baseball following the war, according to Morgan.

24. Commander of the British Empire medal awarded by the monarch.

25. There is a story that the shirts were stitched together out of scraps, the arms being blue and the rest of the shirt a claret red, but this seems to be a tale forged by wishes for West Ham not to be seen as plagiarists of any sort.

26. "Ham" is actually old English for "island" or "settlement" related to a small holding. West Ham was, in premodern times, a marshland district, situated on the "flats" of the Thames.

27. British baseball historian William Morgan, when interviewed in August 2005, was "quite sure" that Wood was Canadian, but it is uncertain whether he was from Canada or the USA.

28. Australian cricketers were known for integrating baseball techniques into their cricket play.

29. One key way in which players in all the British pro leagues were recruited was through advertisements in Canadian newspapers. William Morgan recounts talking to "Red" Holmes, a player from the Canadian prairie lands, who competed in the Yorkshire league. According to Holmes, he found out about the league through an ad in the paper.

30. The listed (preserved by law) stand and pavilion at Craven Cottage (home of Fulham Football Club) in west London probably being the best known.

31. British slang for gamblers.

32. Café-like provision, serving light refreshments (milk, shakes, sodas, etc.).

33. According to Wanda L. Rutledge, former administrative director for the United States Baseball Federation, Mann helped to form an informal group representing the worldwide community of American baseball. His contacts showed that 36 nations throughout the world had some form of organized baseball and as such plans were laid to develop the first international federation to include England, Canada, Hawaii, Cuba and the United States. In 1939 the Federacion International de Beisbol Aficionado (FIBA) was inaugurated in Cuba. It was this organization was gave rise to the formation of amateur World Baseball Championships.

34. The home ground of the Sheffield Dons. The presence of baseball in the steel city of Sheffield is still remembered. In 2005 Jon Carter, a native of Sheffield, recollected: "The good old Sheffield Dons were introduced to Owlerton ... in 1936 by my late father. The pitcher was a Canadian called Len Randall who stayed with Hope and Anchor brewery until he retired."

35. "Tyke" is an epithet for a person from Yorkshire, much in the same way as "cockney" denotes a person hailing from east London ("north of the River, east of the Tower, within the sound of the bell at Bow" to be precise).

36. There are no records of the proposed game between the two sides, but Sheffield's Sports Special ("Green 'Un") from Saturday, 1 August 1936, discussed the West Ham trip in detail; "Mention of West Ham reminds me that they are at Owlerton [the Sheffield Dons' home field] on Tuesday afternoon. Here's a chance for Sheffield people to see some baseball 'stars' in action."

37. To be called a "Jessie" in the north was an accusation of not only being effeminate, but probably at least naive and probably "virginal."

38. In 1932 a handful of Americans had petitioned to include baseball in the first Los Angeles Games, but primarily because the lateness of their request their efforts failed, according to Wanda L. Rutledge, former administrative director for the United States Baseball Federation.

39. Mann had advertised heavily for players to tryout for the Olympic team. One ad even included Babe Ruth, who was billed as the "commander in chief of the Olympic Baseball Committee," encouraging "the American Boy to represent His Country in its national Game." The advertisement said that "[e]very non-professional baseball player in the United State is eligible." Still, it seems that Mann had in mind the players he wanted to include from the start. Fourteen came from the Baltimore trials, while the other seven seem to have been hand-picked by Mann and his staff.

40. For example, those who supported the idea of a boycott included the future moderator (1943–44) of the General Assembly of the Presbyterian Church in the U.S.A., Henry Sloane Coffin; Al Smith, governor of New York; American Catholic radio priest Charles E. Coughlin; Brooklyn-born Heywood Broun, newspaper columnist, author, and one of the founders of the American Newspaper Guild; theologian and son of a German-American pastor of an Evangelical and Reformed church in Wright City, Missouri, Reinhold Niebuhr; American Socialist Party presidential candidate Norman Thomas; American editor and author—born in Wiesbaden, Germany—Oswald Garrison Villard; lawyer and judge Francis Beverley Biddle, who would become the United States solicitor general and, in 1941, attorney general of the United, although he is most famous for being the primary American judge during the Nuremberg war crime trials after World War II; onetime sports journalist Westbrook Pegler—he had been sympathetic to Franklin D. Roosevelt but in the 1930s

he became a controversial newspaper columnist with the *Chicago Daily News* and *The Washington Post* who openly expressed right-wing views; Paul Gallico, who first achieved notability as sports editor of the *New York Daily News* and later became a successful author of popular short stories and novels, many of which were adapted for motion pictures. He is perhaps best remembered for the story *The Snow Goose,* and for the motion picture based on his novel *The Poseidon Adventure.*

41. The Montreal Royals were not affiliated with any major league teams from 1928 to 1936. They were a farm team of the Pittsburgh Pirates in 1937 and 1938, then of the Brooklyn Dodgers.

42. The Provincial League went in and out of organized baseball, with stints in 1940 and 1950–55. There was a Provincial League up until 1970.

43. In 1942, Gladu attended spring training in Cooperstown, New York, home of the baseball Hall of Fame. http://www.baseball1.com/twiles/dirt23.html

44. A competition made up of the four top sides in the league. Frank "Shag" Shaughnessy, who served as International League president from 1936 up to 1960, introduced his playoff system to the league in 1933. Shaughnessy saw the need to maintain interest for more than one or two clubs to the end of each season and his playoff format allowed the top four teams to contest the Governor's Cup (which was so called as it was sponsored by the governors of New York, New Jersey, and Maryland, as well as the lieutenant-governors of the Canadian provinces of Quebec and Ontario).

45. This was a competition that pitted the winners of the International League winners of Governors' Cup against the other top minor leagues (not including the Pacific Coast League, which was isolated on the West Coast). In 1945 the Junior World Series was won by the Louisville Colonels

(Cincinnati) who defeated the Newark Bears 4–2.

46. Gladu played with black players at least as far back as 1935, with Lachine, who had a battery of Chick Bowden (catcher) and Charlie Calvert (pitcher), two local black players. Bowden played for the Forrest Freres, so they might have played together even before that.

47. Some sources claim that Fred Martin (St. Louis Cardinals 1946, 1949, 1950) was also part of this group, but according to Christian Trudeau this was another F. Martin.

48. Fred Martin played with Sherbrooke in 1949.

49. His Provincial League stats: 1948: .368-11-78; 1949: .305-19-81.

50. As the Provincial League teams became more strictly farm clubs of major league teams, the Laurentian League welcomed players who were too old or had less major league potential, which included many of the players who ruled in the old Provincial League.

51. In 1937 the Hackney Royals, continuing their existence under amateur status, joined the London Senior Amateur League and continued to play for an undetermined time. The location(s) of their home games is uncertain. The fact that the Royals continued to play might raise some questions about the team's affiliation with the Greyhound Racing Association. Although the Royals played in Hackney Wick Stadium in 1936, which was a GRA venue, it is unlikely that the GRA would have continued to run an amateur team, while not offering or insisting on them using GRA facilities (in the shape of a home venue). It seems likely that either the GRA severed its links with the Royals or the association's involvement with the club was more tenuous than those of L.D. Wood in West Ham.

52. A baseball hitter is depicted on the badge, but he looks far more like a cricket batter. The cap he wears is not really distinctive of anything akin to

baseball, but has some resemblance to the protective headgear worn in gridiron football, or rugby at the time. It seems that the organizers of the league tried to give authentic baseball, but had difficulty creating a badge that appeared genuine, at least the company that made the badge—Spencer & Co.—appeared to have had a problem of this sort.

53. It is unclear whether Wilson was Mormon as he would ultimately leave the team to play for the non-sectarian Hull squad. His inclusion would, therefore, bring into question whether the Saints maintained their purely amateur status in 1937.

54. The league set relatively strict rules about transfers and "poaching" players. As this was the first year in London in which there was no professional league, the remaining players from the pro league who did not move north must have been in high demand. Clearly, the East London Baseball League was aware and worried about this situation. To that end, the league did not allow players who had played in three games in the other top amateur league. There were also stringent rules relating to poaching. In the league handbook it threatened, "Any Club guilty of inducing or attempting to induce a registered player or players of another League Club to join them shall be dealt with by the Committee."

55. Rugby Union was a strictly amateur code; the league game was a professional sport, without scrums or line-outs. League, with its 13 a-side encounters (Union teams consist of 15 players on the field) has always provided a swifter-moving, more dramatic and aggressive spectacle than the more gentle—relative to League anyway—Union code. However, there is an old saying in soccer that goes "Rugby" in general "is a man's game ... a mad man's game."

56. As Wanda L. Rutledge was to relate, England, together with the USA, Japan, China, the Philippines, Germany, Hawaii (not then a state in the American union), Mexico and Cuba, had signed up to play in the 1940 Olympic Games that had been scheduled to take place in Tokyo.

57. A factory worker in wartime could expect to earn about £4 per week. This was considered relatively well paid. Four shillings was 5 percent of this total, so the comparable price of the book today would be relatively expensive. But all books were luxury items in Britain prior to (and particularly during) and immediately after the war, before modern mass production.

58. Harrington had been the commander in chief of the Allied armies occupying Turkey after the First World War and he was in total control of Istanbul for a time. He played a part in removal of the authority of the Khilafah.

59. All English international cricketers.

Bibliography

Books

Bedingfield, G. (1999). *Images of Sports: Baseball in World War II Europe.* Charleston, South Carolina: Arcadia Publishing (an imprint of Tempus Publishing).

Belton, B. (1997). *Bubbles, Hammers and Dreams.* Derby: Breedon Books.

_____. (1999). *Days of Iron.* Derby: Breedon Books.

_____. (2003). *Founded on Iron.* Gloucestershire: Tempus.

_____. (1998). *The First and Last Englishmen.* Derby: Breedon Books.

_____. (2005). *The Men of 64.* Gloucestershire: Tempus.

_____. (2007). *War Hammers.* Gloucestershire: Tempus.

Bjarkman, P. (2005). *Diamonds Around the Globe: The Encyclopedia of International Baseball.* Westport, CT, and London: Greenwood Press.

Blakeman, M. (2000). *Nunhead Football Club: 1888–1949.* Middlesex: Yore Publications.

Blows, K., and T Hogg. (2000). *West Ham: The Essential History.* Swindon: Headline.

Brown, W. (1996). *Baseball's Fabulous Royals.* Montreal: Robert Davies Publishing.

Butler, B. (1987). *The Football League 1888–1988: The Official Illustrated History.* London: Queen Ann Press.

Clegg, B. (1993). *The Man who Made Littlewoods: The Story of John Moores.* Liverpool: J & C Moores, Ltd.

Cheshire, S. *Chelsea Football Club Chronicle: 1905–6 to 1910–11.* London: Chelsea Football Club.

Cook, C., and J. Stevenson. (1988). *Modern British History.* London: Longman.

Crane, N. (1891). *Baseball: The All-England Series.* London: Bell.

Elfers, J. E. (2003). *The Tour to End All Tours: The Story of Major League Baseball's 1913–1914 World Tour.* Lincoln: University of Nebraska Press.

Evans, B. (1994). *Romford, Collier Row & Gidea Park.* Chichester, West Sussex: Phillimore.

Fabian, A. H., and G. Green, eds. (1961). *Associated Football.* London: Caxton.

Finn, R.L. (1972). *The Official History of Tottenham Hotspur FC 1882–1972.* London: Robert Hale.

Fishman, W.J. (2001). *East End 1888.* London: Hanbury.

Gibson, A., and W. Pickford. (1905). *Association Football and the Men Who Have Made It.* Oxford: Oxford University Press.

Green, G. (1953). *The History of the Football Association.* London: Naldrett Press.

Groves, R. (1947). *Chelsea.* London: Famous Football Clubs.

_____. (1948). *West Ham United.* London: Famous Football Clubs.

Harding, J. (1991). *For the Good of the Game: The Official History of the Professional Footballers' Association.* London: Robson.

Harrison, P. (1989). *Southern League Football: The First Fifty Years.* Gravesend: Harrison.

Harvey, C., ed. (1959). *Encyclopedia of Sport* London: Sampson Low, Marston.

Hawthorn, F. H., and R. Price. (2001). *The Souless Stadium: A Memoir of London's White City.* Upminster, Essex: 3-2 Books.

Hayes, D. (1996). *The Deepdale Story: An A to Z of Preston North End.* Chorley: Sport in Word.

Hogg, T., and T. McDonald. (1995). *West Ham United Who's Who.* London: Independent UK Sports Publications.

Hutchenson, J. (1982). *The Football Industry.* Glasgow: R. Drew.

Inglis, S. (2005). *Engineering Archie: Archibald Leitch—Football Ground Designer.* Swindon: English Heritage.

_____. (1987). *The Football Grounds of Great Britain.* London: Willow.

_____. (1988). *League Football and the Men who Made It.* London: HarperCollinsWillow.

Irving, D. (1968). *The West Ham United Football Book.* London: Stanley Paul.

_____. (1969). *The West Ham United Football Book No.2.* London: Stanley Paul.

Jacobson, L. (1990). *Herman Goldberg: Baseball Olympian and Jewish American in Baseball History 3,* Levine, P. (ed.) London: Meckler Publishing.

Johnston, F. (ed.) (1934). *The Football Encyclopedia.* London: Associated Sporting Press.

Joyce, N. (2004). *Football League Players' Records 1888 to 1939.* Nottingham: Soccer Data.

Kaufman, N., and A. Ravenhill. (1990). *Leyton Orient: A Complete Record 1881–1990.* Derby: Breedon Books.

Kerrigan, C. (1997). *Gatling Gun George Hilsdon.* London: Football Lives.

Knowles, R.G., and Morton, R. (1896). *Baseball.* Manchester and New York: George Routledge & Sons, Ltd.

Korr, C. (1986). *West Ham United.* London: Duckworth.

Levine, P. (1985). *A.G. Spalding and the Rise of Baseball.* New York and Oxford: Oxford University Press.

_____. (1992). *Ellis Island to Ebbets Field: Sport and the American Jewish Experience.* New York and Oxford: Oxford University Press.

Lovesey, P. (1970). *The Official Centenary History of the Amateur Athletic Association.* London: Guinness Superlatives.

Marriott, J. (1991). *The Culture of Labourism—The East End Between the Wars.* Edinburgh: Marriott.

Mason, T. (1980). *Association Football and English Society 1863–1915.* Brighton: Harvester Press.

McDougall, D. (ed.) (1936). *Fifty Years a Borough 1886–1936.* West Ham: Curwen Press.

Mearns, A. (1883). *The Bitter Cry of Outcast London: An Inquiry into the Condition of the Abject Poor.* Leicester: Leicester University Press.

Mills, M. (1999). *The Early East London Gas Industry and Its Waste Products.* London: M. Wright.

Moynihan, J. (1982). *The Chelsea Story.* London: Arthur Baker.

_____. (1984). *The West Ham Story.* London: Arthur Baker.

Northcutt, J., and R. Shoesmith. (1993). *West Ham United: A Complete Record.* Derby: Breedon Books.

_____. (1994). *West Ham United: An Illustrated History*. Derby: Breedon Books.

Oliver, G. (1995). *World Soccer (2nd ed)*. Bath: Guinness.

Richler, M. (2002). *Dispatches from the Sporting Life*. Toronto: Vintage.

Shaoul, M., and T. Williamson. (2000). *Forever England—A History of the National Side*. Gloucestershire: Tempus.

Shearon, J. (1994). *Canada's Baseball Legends*. Ontario: Malin Head Press, Kanata.

Turner, D., and A. White. (1987). *Fulham: A Complete Record 1879–1987*. Derby: Breedon Books.

_____. (1998). *Fulham Facts and Figures 1879–1998*. Hants: Northdown.

Wall, F. (1935). *Fifty Years of Football*. London: Cassel.

Walvin, J. (1975). *The People's Game: A Social History of British Football*. Newton Abbot: A. Lane.

Ward, A. (1999). *West Ham United 1895–1999*. London: Octopus.

White, A., and B. Lilliman. (2005). *The Football Grounds of London*. Gloucestershire: Tempus.

Whitehead, E. (1939). *Baseball for British Youth*. London: Link House.

Wigglesworth, N. (1996). *The Evolution of English Sport*. London: Frank Cass.

Willmore, G. (1996). *The Hawthorns Encyclopedia: An A–Z of West Bromwich Albion FC*. Edinburgh and London: Mainstream.

Winston, G.R. (ed.) (1997). *The East End Then and Now*. Essex: After the Battle.

Wolter, T. (2002). *POW Baseball in World War II: The National Pastime Behind Barbed Wire*. Jefferson NC: McFarland.

Wood, L.D. *Baseball for Boys & Beginners*. Liverpool: Issued by the National Baseball Association, printed by J. & C. Moores.

Journals

Bloyce, D. "Major League Baseball in England: 125 Years of Effort and Still Not at First Base." Paper presented at the North American Society for Sociology of Sport Conference; Indianapolis, Indiana (Nov. 6–9, 2002).

Chetwynd, J. "Do You Remember When ... Great Britain were the first baseball world champions?" in *Observer Sport Monthly*. Issue No. 30, August 2002.

Dickens, C. "Londoners over the border" in *Household Words*, a weekly journal. Issue No. 390, 12 September, 1857.

Kerrigan, C. "Upton Park F.C. 1866–1887: Gentlemen footballers in West Ham Park," in *Rising East: The Journal of East London Studies*. London: Lawrence and Wishart (1999).

Gottlieb, M. "The American Controversy Over the Olympic Games," in *American Jewish Historical Quarterly*. LXI (March 1972), pp. 181–213.

Levine, P. "My Father and I, We Didn't Get Our Medals': Marty Glickman's American Jewish Odyssey" in *American Jewish History*. LXXVIII (March 1989), pp. 399–424.

Morgan, W. "96 and Counting: British baseball history" in *First Base Magazine* (Autumn 1986).

Richardson, B. "It may have been the last title, but it was hardly the best" in *The Boston Globe* (22 October 2004).

Ross, M. "Babe Ruth Makes Waves at Arsenal" in *The SABR UK Examiner* (11 July 1999).

Rutledge, W.L. (administrative director for the United States Baseball Federation in 1983). "Baseball's 80-Year Road to Los Angeles: A Dream Come True" in *The 1984 Olympic Baseball Program*; pp. 34–35, 38–39.

Shapiro, E.S. "The World Labor Athletic Carnival of 1936: An American Anti-

Nazi Protest" in *American Jewish History*. LXXIV (March 1985), pp. 255–273.

Smyth, I. "The Story of Baseball in the North of England." *Leeds Polytechnic Faculty of Cultural and Education Studies* (1992), pp. 1–52.

Travaglini, M.E. "Olympic Baseball 1936: Was es das?" *The National Pastime*, a publication of the Society for American Baseball Research (Winter 1985), pp. 45–55.

Weekes, R. "Oval turns diamond for the day; New York produce tale of the unexpected to beat the Red Sox" in *The Independent*, London (4 October 1993).

Whitehead, R. "How football turned one of its finest into a pariah." *The Times*, London (25 August 2001).

Wilson, J. "Baseball in England, and Its Rivals" in *The Strand* (1898).

Athletic News
Atlanta Constitution
Anglo American Sports (UK)
Baseball Mercury (UK)
Baseball (in Britain) *Monthly*
Baseball News (UK)
Baseball Review (UK)
Baseball Times (UK)
Baseball (UK)
Brit-Ball (UK)
Canadian Baseball News
County Express (Stretford area)
Daily Mail (Hull)
Daily Mirror (London)
Daily News and Leader
Derby Evening Telegraph
Dewsbury Reporter
Double Play (UK) magazine
East End News
East Ham and Barking Free Press
East Ham Echo
East and West Ham Gazette
East London Advertiser
The Express (West Ham)
Evening (London) *News*
Evening News & Chronicle (Stretford area)
The Field
Financial Times
First Base (UK) magazine
Hornsey Journal
Lewisham Borough News

Liverpool Echo
Los Angeles Times
New York Times
Manchester Comet
Mike Ross' Transatlantic Baseball Times
Oldham Evening Chronicle
Outing Magazine, an Illustrated Monthly Recreational Magazine
Racing Post
The (Romford) Recorder
The Romford Times
The (Ashton-under-Lyne) Reporter
SABR UK Examiner
Scarborough Evening Post
Sheffield Telegraph
Soccer History
South Essex Mail (this would become the *West Ham Herald*)
Sports Special (Green 'Un) (Sheffield)
Sporting Chronicle
The Sportsman
Sports Times
Stratford Express
The (New York) Sun
The Independent
The Times
Touching Base (UK)
Transatlantic Baseball Bulletin (UK)
Transatlantic Baseball Review (UK)
Transatlantic Baseball News & Review (UK)
West Ham Guardian

Newspapers

Other

1889 Spalding's Official Base Ball Guide

1890 Spalding's Official Base Ball Guide
1907 Cassell's Book of Sports and Pastimes
1912 Spalding's Official Base Ball Guide
1935 Encyclopedia of Sports Games and Pastimes (published London at Fleetway House)
1939 Spalding's Official Base Ball Guide
One More Inning, A Baseball Time Machine for the Future (Journal) July 2004: Volume 8: Number 84 (article on the 1936 Olympic Team)
1984 Olympic Baseball Program (two articles): "History of Olympic Baseball" by Phil Elderkin of *The Christian Science Monitor* and "Former Baseball Olympians" by Loel Schrader of the *Long Beach Press-Telegram*
"Baseball in England" by Richard Morton, *The Badminton Magazine* (Date unclear—circa mid–1890s)
"Baseball in England, and Its Rivals" by James Wilson, *The Strand* magazine (Date unclear—circa mid–1890s)
2002 BaseballSoftballUK Media Guide
2002 Old Timers Baseball Club (London, England) Media Guide
http://www.baseballeurope.com
http://www.baseballlibrary.com
http://www.baseballsoftballuk.com
http://www.baseball-reference.com/
http://www.feldgrau.com/1936olymp.html
http://www.hockeydb.com/
http://www.hullkr.co.uk/the_club/about.php
http://www.ilbaseball.com/govtomlb.html
http://www.kzwp.com/lyons2/fullers.htm
http://www.livjm.ac.uk/history/
http://www.liverpooltrojansbaseball.co.uk/History%20Merseyside.htm
http://www.usabaseball.com/sports/m=oly=basebl/archive/usab-m-oly-history-early.html.

Index